IMAGES
of America

UKRAINIANS OF THE DELAWARE VALLEY

I0792646

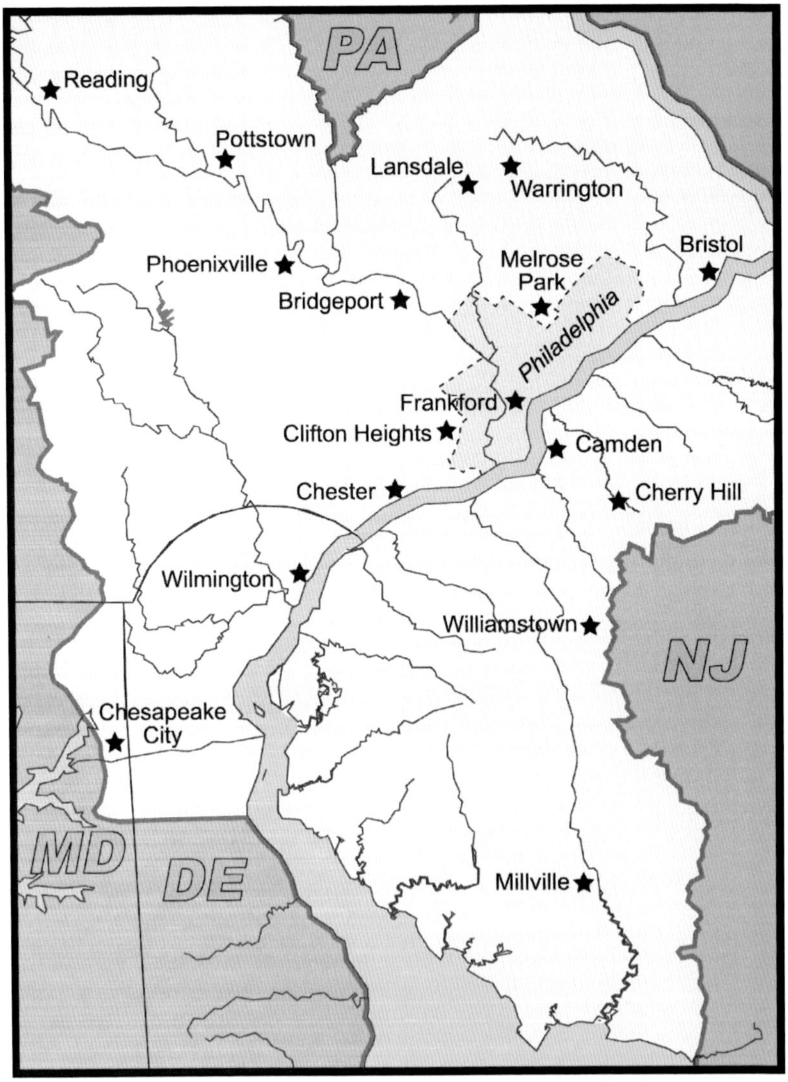

This map of the Delaware Valley, as designed by Oleh Antonyuk, depicts major Ukrainian settlements with a star. Settlements with smaller Ukrainian populations include Brookhaven, Coatesville, Jenkintown, Parkside, Skippack, and Wallingford in Pennsylvania; Marlton, Pitman, and Vineland in New Jersey; and scattered farms in Cecil County, Maryland, and south of Wilmington, Delaware. The settlement in Philadelphia was covered by Arcadia in the author's previous book, *Ukrainians of Greater Philadelphia*.

On the cover: The dream of Bishop Soter (Ortynsky) of the Order of St. Basil the Great (OSBM), the first Ruthenian Ukrainian bishop in the United States, was to establish a much-needed orphanage for children whose parents died. His other ambitions included housing for the Sisters of St. Basil the Great who would dedicate themselves to the care of the orphans and a seminary to train future priests. In his search for such a location he came upon Chesapeake City, Maryland. It was ideal. It could be reached by road or by water down the Delaware River and into the Chesapeake and Delaware Canal. He dedicated the cornerstone for the Sisters of St. Basil the Great monastery in Chesapeake City, Maryland, on July 12, 1912. The OSBM is for both men and women. (Courtesy of Treasury of Faith Archieparchial Museum, Philadelphia.)

IMAGES
of America

UKRAINIANS OF THE DELAWARE VALLEY

Alexander Lushnycky, Ph.D.

ARCADIA
PUBLISHING

ISBN 978-0-7385-6526-2

Published by Arcadia Publishing
Charleston, South Carolina

Printed in the United States of America

Library of Congress Control Number: 2008940073

For all general information, please contact Arcadia Publishing:
Telephone 843-853-2070
Fax 843-853-0044
E-mail sales@arcadiapublishing.com
For customer service and orders:
Toll-Free 1-888-313-2665

Visit us on the Internet at www.arcadiapublishing.com

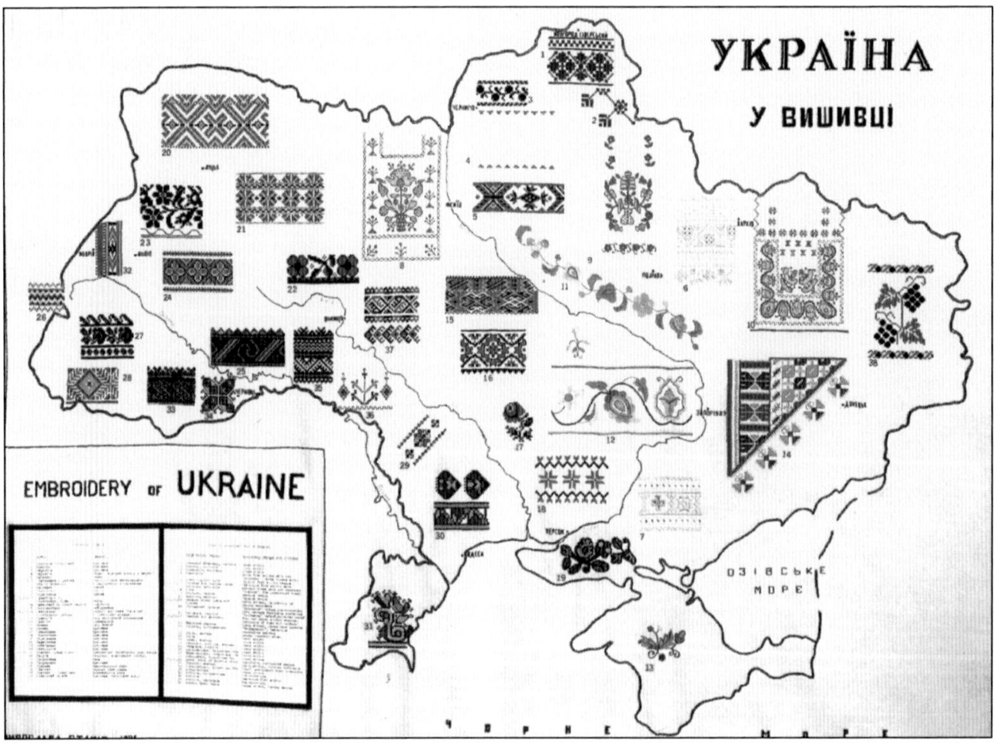

Over the years, immigrants came from these regions of Ukraine bringing with them their most cherished possession: their culture—embroidery being one of its most distinctive manifestations. It is from them, through us, that this book is dedicated to you—a testimonial for future generations.

Contents

Acknowledgments

Foremost I want to thank the following institutions for their assistance: Providence Association of Ukrainian Catholics for the newspaper photograph files of *America*; Sisters of St. Basil the Great Archives; Ukrainian Archival Library at Stamford; Treasury of Faith Archieparchial Museum; Ukrainian Museum in New York City; and Ukrainian Educational and Cultural Center.

Pastors of Ukrainian Baptist, Catholic, and Orthodox Churches deserve special recognition, as they were indispensable for the completion of this book: Revs. Ihor Bloshchynsky, Wasyl Bunik, John Ciurpita, Roman Dubitsky, Stephen Hutnick, Mykola Iwanov, Vasiliy Kravchuk, Volodymyr Klanichka, Pavlo Labinsky, Gregory Maslak, Ronald Popivchak, Andrij Rabiy, Ihor Royik, Petro Semenych, and Deacon Theophil Staruch.

Other individuals who assisted in the collection of rare photographs and materials were Vera Andryczyk, William Bijansky, Eryna Cvikula-Korchynska, Roman Dubenko, Edward Falcone, Jessica Hall, Taras Halushka, Marie Hanusey, Orysia Hewka, Rose Holub, Lesya Horodysky, Luba Kalyta, Maria Kaminska, Patricia Keevill, Albert Kipa, Petro Kluk, Alexander Kobasa, Michael Kowalchuk, Joan and Paul Kravchak, Bohdan Kulchyckyj, Irene Kulick, Lydia Kyj, Maria Lazar, Helen Lesagonicz, Orest Lesiuk, Lesia Leskiw, Roksolana Luciw, Anna Maksymowych, Myra Matus, Ulana Mazurkevich, Stephen Meckes, Anthony and Maria Murowany, Mark Murowany, Olha Nahayewska, Wasil Ostapyk, Maria Panczak, Alexander Pastuczek, Mary Pastuczek, Borys Pawliuk, Lillian Pecko, Christine Pluta, Anatol Prasicky, Ulana Prociuk, Barbara Rivera, Michael Romach, Nicholas Rudnytzky, Wasyl Salak, Patricia Saunders, Chrystia Senyk, Halia Shabatura-Gottschalk, Anna Slotwinski, Ihor Smolij, Alexander Solowij, Myron Soltys, Elizabeth Souchak, Myroslava Stachiv, Helen Stachniw, Aristida Staruch, Anna Steciw, Judy Steciw, Halyna Utrysko, and Russell Zguta.

Special gratitude is given to Bishop Robert (Moskal), Christine Kulchckyj, Richard Luyster, Askold Skalsky, and to my family (Mary, my wife, and our God-given children Ulita and Andrej). Sincere appreciation is given to my editor Erin Vosgien for her guidance in this project and to my proofreader Amanda Freeman.

INTRODUCTION

The church is a gift given to us by our parents and grandparents. It is a gift based on love; their love of God, for their Faith, and for their traditions. Because of this love, God has caused our people to succeed and to prosper in their endeavors.

—Nancy Tysowsky, Wilmington

Delaware Valley is a geographical and geocultural term denoting the land on both sides of the Delaware River, from the "rapids" several miles south of Trenton, New Jersey, to where it empties into Delaware Bay and into the Atlantic.

Historically it includes parts of three states: Delaware at its mouth, Pennsylvania on the west bank, and New Jersey on the east bank, with almost all the settlements lying on the western side, dating back to the 17th century and with Philadelphia as the main port. Over time, the radio stations, local maps, and television networks in the tristate area came to refer to this region as Delaware Valley when Philadelphia (see *Ukrainians of Greater Philadelphia*) expanded into the bordering suburbs.

Ukraine, located on the southeastern edge of the European continent, has a slightly larger landmass than France and holds the distinction of being the largest country in Europe. From its beginnings in the 9th century as the kingdom of Kievan Rus', Ukraine's 1,000-year history was marked by fluctuating borders and, because of its rich soil and mineral deposits, by subjugation by its more powerful neighbors, mainly Poland in the west and the Russian Empire in the east. Ukraine's 1918 independence was short lived, and the 1941 attempt was dissolved almost immediately. It was only with the disintegration of the Soviet Union in 1991 that Ukraine, after generations of repression, became a self-governing entity leaning toward democracy and the West.

Historically and economically, Ukraine, called the "bread basket" or "granary" of Europe, has for millennia been one of the most important agricultural regions of the world. Widely known for its rich black soil and mild continental climate, it produces a variety of grains that make the country self-sufficient and enable it to export its bountiful harvest to its neighbors. Because it is also rich in minerals, it serves as an easy target for envious neighbors, resulting in constant struggles against political, economic, social, and cultural oppression, and with emigration always imminent.

In recent history, two factors led Ukrainians to leave their native land: first, a dire need for laborers, miners, and factory workers as a result of the Industrial Revolution, especially in the post–Civil War period in the United States, and, second, the economic status of Ukrainian peasants in Western Ukraine, then a part of the Austro-Hungarian Empire. The peasantry was poor beyond belief, although living on very rich lands, and greatly overpopulated in the hilly areas and the Sub-Carpathian region of Western Ukraine. Large families were needed to work in the fields because the Industrial Revolution had yet to reach this corner of the world. Also the archaic system of virtual serfdom practiced by the nobility and the governing regime made sure that the peasants remained "in their place" by denying them education and any ability to improve themselves.

Agents of free enterprise and those seeking to escape from endless poverty began the largest mass emigration of Ukrainians to the United States in history, halted only by World War I. In time, three other phases of immigrants followed, but all were different in nature and purpose.

During the first phase of immigration, the Ukrainians arriving in the United States faced similar problems as did most newcomers, including no knowledge of English, the strange customs and mode of life in the New World, and exploitation by ruthless employers. But the Ukrainians were handicapped by still another problem, which was theirs exclusively: their identity was unrecognized. Laboring under ignorance that sprang more from confusion than lack of education, American customs officials identified the first two waves of Ukrainian immigrants as Poles, Magyars, or Russians, the very names that denoted for these newcomers the oppressors they were fleeing.

During the second phase of Ukrainian immigration to the United States, which occurred between the two world wars and which was severely restricted by the quota system, the "red scare," and isolationism, only up to 20,000 Ukrainians entered the United States. The majority consisted of educated people and professionals, who upon disembarking became leaders of Ukrainian community life in the large Ukrainian centers in the United States.

The third phase occurred in the years following World War II (1946–1958) and consisted of "Ukrainian Displaced Persons" (DPs), about 500,000 of whom received sponsors and were permitted to emigrate.

The fourth period, following Ukrainian independence in 1991, is still ongoing and is estimated to total nearly one million immigrants.

There were also four distinct periods in which Ukrainians settled in the Delaware Valley and formed separate unique ethnic centers.

The first phase of Ukrainian settlements occurred around 1900. These Ukrainians, then known as Ruthenians, disembarked at the ports along the Delaware River and acquired work, some returning to their homeland but the largest number remaining in Philadelphia and others settling in Chester, Frankford, and in Wilmington, Delaware. The exceptions were those who had no intention of returning and settled in the farmland areas around Chesapeake City, Maryland, and Williamstown, New Jersey. Ukrainian newspapers in Philadelphia and Jersey City, New Jersey, spread the news that good inexpensive farmland was available for a "Ukrainian Village." Another group settled in Clifton Heights, Pennsylvania, where a small community of Ukrainian entrepreneurs catered to vacationers from Philadelphia.

The second period, 1910 to 1925, saw Ukrainians who, for economic reasons, left the coal-mining areas of Pennsylvania and moved south to settle in Reading, Pottstown, Phoenixville, Bridgeport, and Lansdale, Pennsylvania. Around the same time, Ukrainians went south from the New York and Jersey City areas to settle on the New Jersey side of the Delaware River around Camden and the agricultural areas of Williamstown, Millville, and, later, Bristol, Pennsylvania.

The third period was that of the DPs from World War II (1946–1960), who settled in the above-mentioned locations and, because of Philadelphia's expansion into the suburbs, also established additional communities in Cherry Hill, New Jersey, and Melrose Park and Warrington in Pennsylvania.

After Ukraine's independence in 1991, numerous Ukrainians left their homeland for the United States in search of better economic conditions. They settled in large cities such as Philadelphia and in time expanded into the surrounding suburbs, the largest number of them reinvigorating the Ukrainian communities of Frankford, Melrose Park, Jenkintown, Warrington, and northeast Philadelphia.

Ukrainians in the United States are known for their resourcefulness, levelheadedness, stability, and strong work ethic, as well as their deeply held beliefs and observances of their Christian faith; all of these contribute to their unique Ukrainian culture. In this manner, they have lived their lives throughout their 120-year stay in the United States.

The following pages bear witness to their stay in the Delaware Valley.

One

Trailblazers

Every Ukrainian emigrant dreamed that if he married and had children, they would grow to be God fearing and well educated, possess a "Ukrainian heart" nurturing love for their native land, and by their exemplary life foster Ukrainian heritage here and in Ukraine.

—Rev. Vladimir Derzyruka, Chester

They came to Delaware Valley from all directions. Around 1890, Ukrainians arrived from the old country, not staying long unless they had kin or work in the area. Village ties were the most important element, both in bringing them to the United States and determining their place of settlement. Because of their nationality predicament, they referred to themselves according to their place of birth: Rusins from the Carpathian Mountains area, and Ruthenians who lived in Austria-Hungary. The first wave of immigrants took only bare necessities, a walking cane symbolizing a journeying man in one hand and a small package of essentials in the other. They left with tears in their eyes and a prayer of hope on their lips. Since they intended to return, these pioneers brought little of value with them except their Ukrainian culture and a deep spiritual commitment to their Eastern Catholic faith. Upon disembarking, it was their duty to seek people who spoke their language and observed their customs. Their priority was to have their own house of worship, building their churches not only for themselves but also for the people who would succeed them. The Eastern Christian Church was, and is, the backbone of Ukrainian culture in diaspora.

They settled in the Delaware Valley for varied reasons: to look for work during slowdowns or strikes in Pennsylvania's anthracite mining regions, and others who had worked in the mines sought different employment. They were the ones who settled in Phoenixville, Pottstown, and Bridgeport; others came to the booming towns of Chester and Trainer; and a large portion of Ukrainians settled in Wilmington. Ukrainians who were unable to adjust to the robust way of life in 20th-century New York City traveled south looking for work and seeking friends from their villages. However, learning that cheap land was available in New Jersey, they went back to their former profession, farming, and bought land around Vineland and Millville. As is true of many immigrants, Ukrainians eventually intended to return and many did, bringing their earnings with them to purchase homesteads in the old country, but the outbreak of World War I froze others in their places. Thanks to their adaptability, they remained in the Delaware Valley.

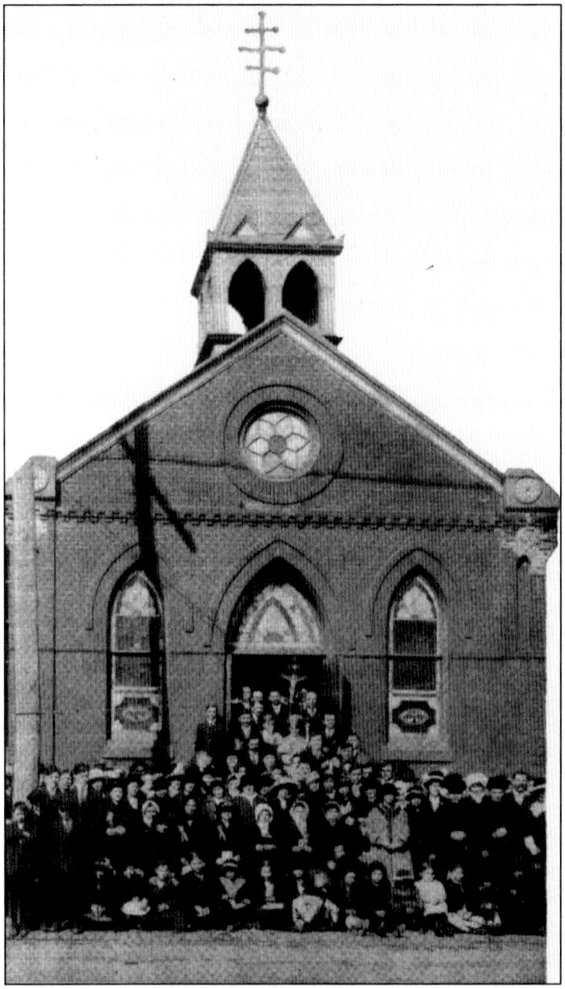

Ukrainians, known at the time as Ruthenians or Rusins, were Catholics of the Eastern Rite who, upon arrival in the Delaware Valley, ignored the Latin Rite hierarchy and began forming their individual communities with their church at the center, asking their church hierarchy for their own priests who understood their customs and their language. The Holy Ghost Byzantine Rite Catholic Church in southwestern Philadelphia became such a hub from 1893 to 1905. Although the goal of Holy Ghost Society, founded in 1886, was the continuation of Eastern Rite traditions, it was not until 1893 that Rev. John Hrabar built a small brick church. The later model in the above c. 1926 photograph served Slavic Eastern Rite Catholic immigrants until 1905, when distinct nationality traits divided the Ruthenian parish regional alliances: Carpatho-Rusins and Galician Rusins who eventually became known as Ukrainians. Galician Ukrainians founded St. Michael's Church, which served the community until the arrival in 1907 of Bishop Soter (Ortynsky). It is customary in the Eastern Christian Church for the bishop to select a saint's name and to drop his family name. For the Ukrainian Catholic bishops the last name is seldom used and only in parentheses. The Ukrainian Orthodox bishops are only known by their chosen first name. When the church was not signed over to his jurisdiction, the bishop purchased a church that became the center of Ukrainian life in Philadelphia. However, by this time Ukrainian communities in Wilmington and Chester made plans to build or purchase their own churches. To illustrate the ambiguities of identity, Holy Ghost remained Rusin, St. Michael's switched to Russian Orthodox, and the cathedral on Franklin Street became Ukrainian.

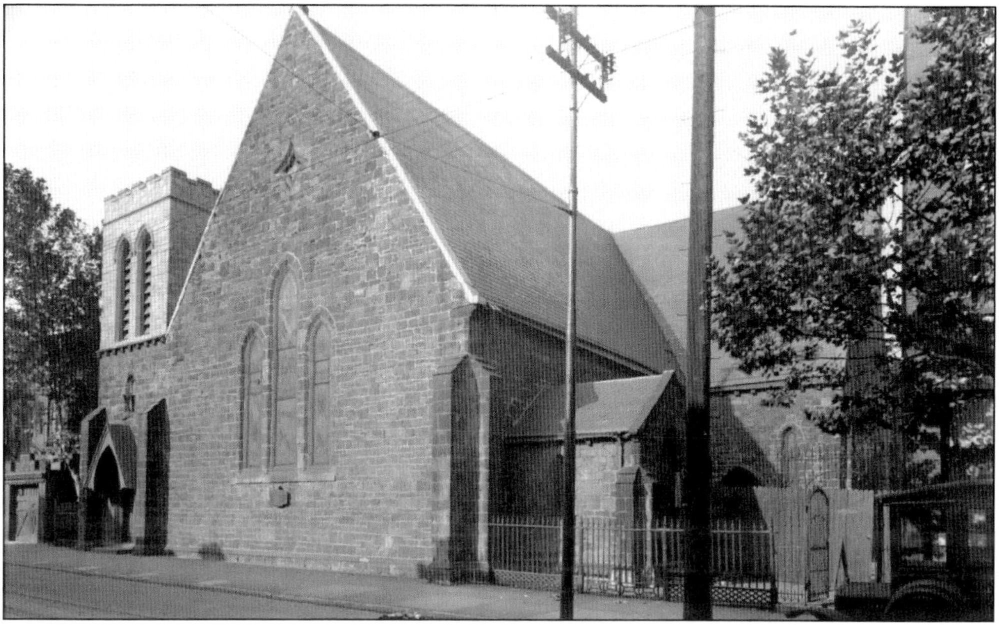

Before renovations were made, this was the edifice of the future Cathedral of the Immaculate Conception of the Blessed Virgin Mary Ukrainian Catholic Church (UCC) as purchased by Bishop Soter in 1908. Before they built their own churches in Delaware Valley, the cathedral served all Ukrainian immigrants who lived east, west, and north of Philadelphia. It was the "mother church" for newly established communities during his short pastorate.

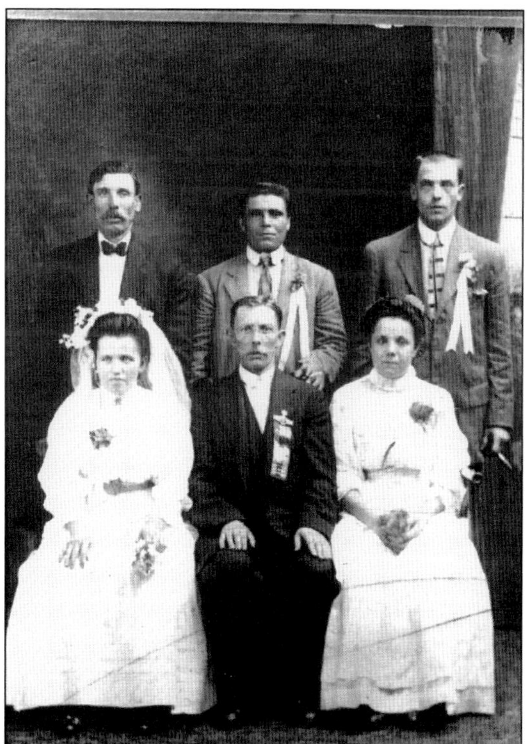

Before World War I, about 60 percent of the Ukrainians who came over to the Delaware Valley returned home. Some revisited the United States again and again, but most did not. However, their children did come. Such was the case with the Wozny family. Pictured is the bridal party of Michael Wozny and Maria Kowcz. They were married at the old cathedral in 1912. Wozny was one of the organizers of the Ruthenian Ukrainian Catholic Church in Wilmington and the first parish secretary. Both were born in Lacko, Dobromil, Ukraine, and returned to Ukraine prior to World War I never to return to the United States.

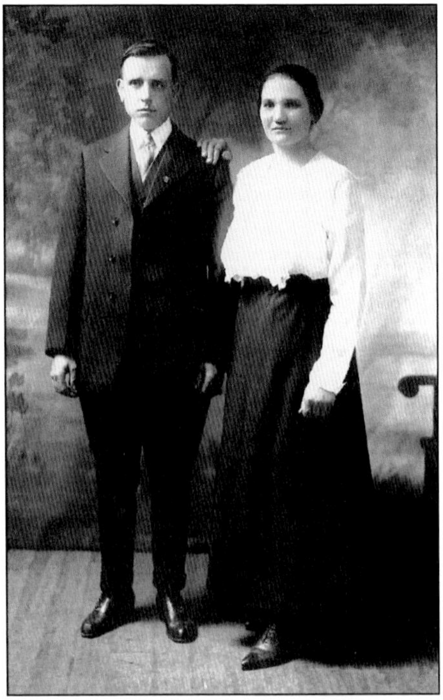

Forty percent of the Ukrainians who settled in the Delaware Valley prior to World War I did not return. In order to live in a Ukrainian environment they brought over their kin. This was the case of the Marushchak family. Catherine Tesowska and Theodore Marushchak, both born in Dobromil, Ukraine, were married at St. Basil's Greek Catholic Ruthenian Church in Wilmington on May 29, 1910. The Marushchak family (they had six children) became the pillars of St. Nicholas UCC in Wilmington, saving the church during the troubled years of 1928 to 1930 when only a dozen families chose to remain with the church. Their son Michael chronicled the history of the parish.

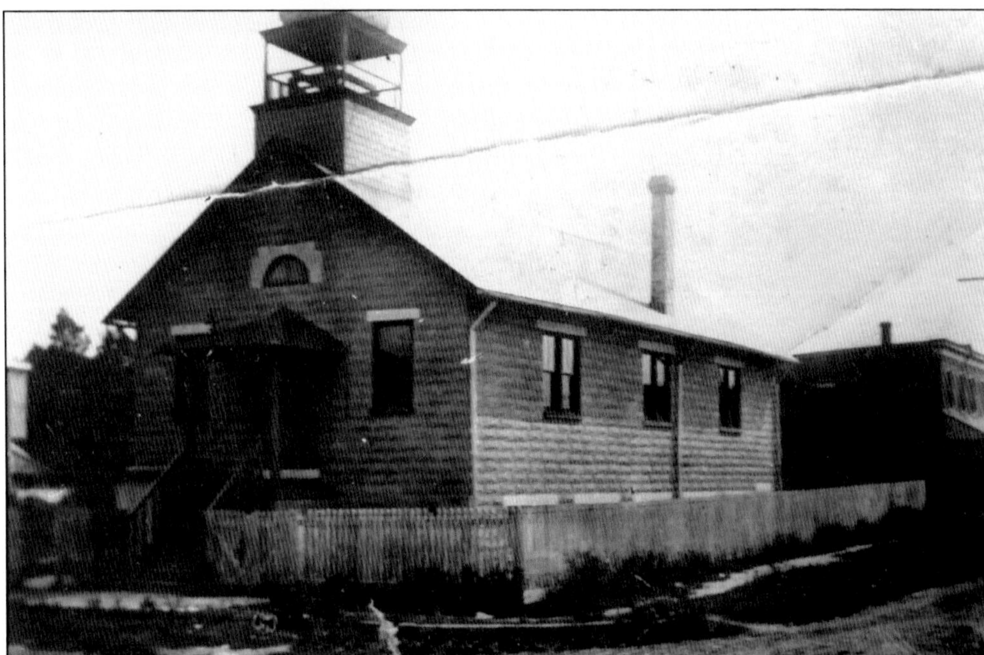

St. Michael's United Greek Catholic Ruthenian Church in Wilmington was organized in 1903. This church was converted from a stable owned by Semen Fedoriga and served the parishioners from 1905 to 1909. The location was vital; Wilmington was halfway, via the railroad, between Philadelphia and Baltimore, Maryland. The church was located near the railroad and factories where the parishioners worked. By 1910, St. Michael's United Greek Catholic Ruthenian Church became St. Basil's and was renamed in 1912 as St. Nicholas UCC.

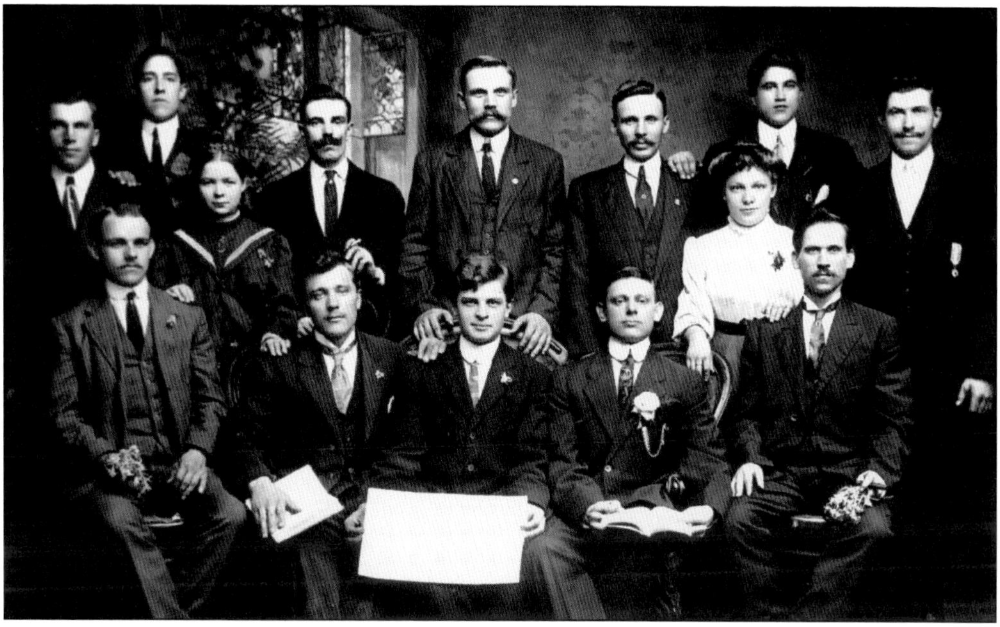

Prior to the outbreak of World War I amateur theaters flourished in Ukrainian communities. Their repertoire included comedies and dramas depicting life in the old country as well as life as they found it in Wilmington. The first Ukrainian Amateur Theatrical Group from 1911 is, from left to right, (first row) John Bukay, Petro Levitsky, Tyman Kolody, Theodore Shatynsky, and Basil Malinowsky; (second row) John Baran, Petro Jaremchuk, Eva Levitsky, Dmytro Cycyk, Stephen Figun, Michael Markevich, Anna Sywy, unidentified, and John Sywy.

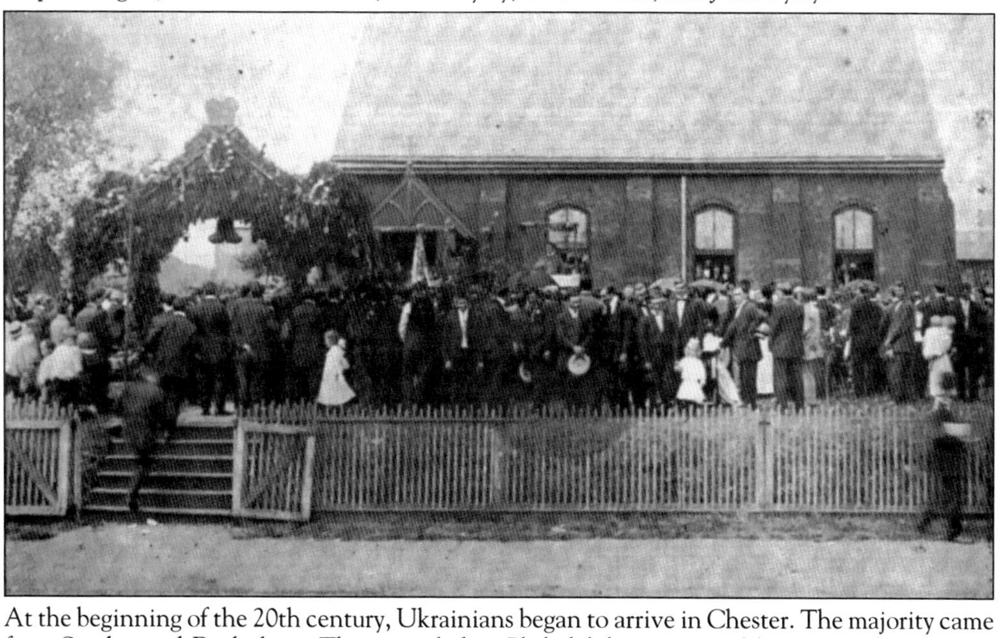

At the beginning of the 20th century, Ukrainians began to arrive in Chester. The majority came from Sambir and Drohobycz. They traveled to Philadelphia to attend liturgy, as they had no church of their own. Upon arrival of the bishop to Philadelphia, they decided to purchase their own church in Chester. Thus Holy Ghost UCC was organized in 1908 and blessed by Bishop Soter in 1910.

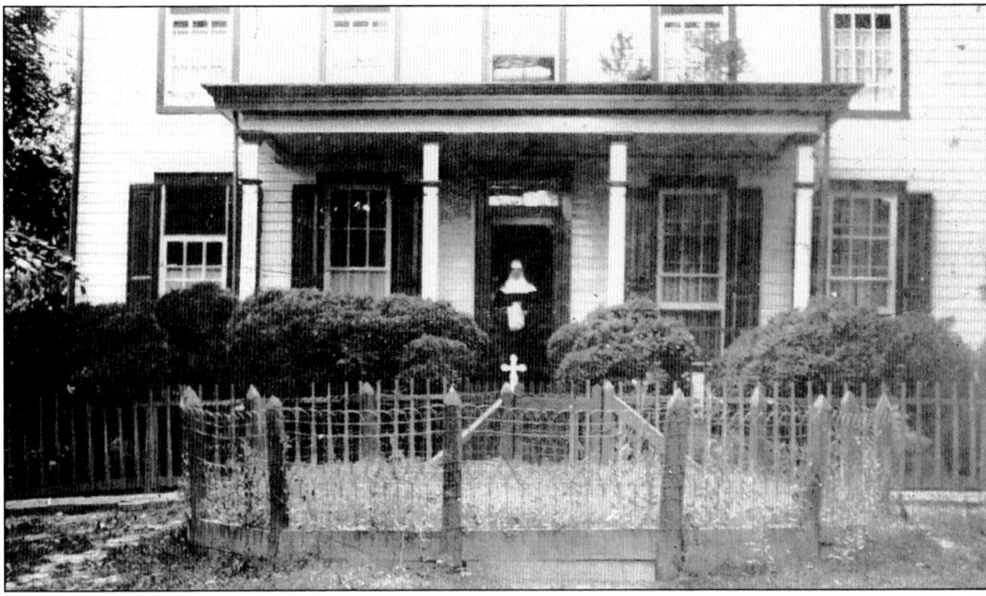

By 1911, realizing the needs of his flock, Bishop Soter invited the Sisters of St. Basil the Great to come. In 1913, they opened their Novitiate in Chesapeake City. Standing in the doorway of their first home is Sister Monica, OSBM.

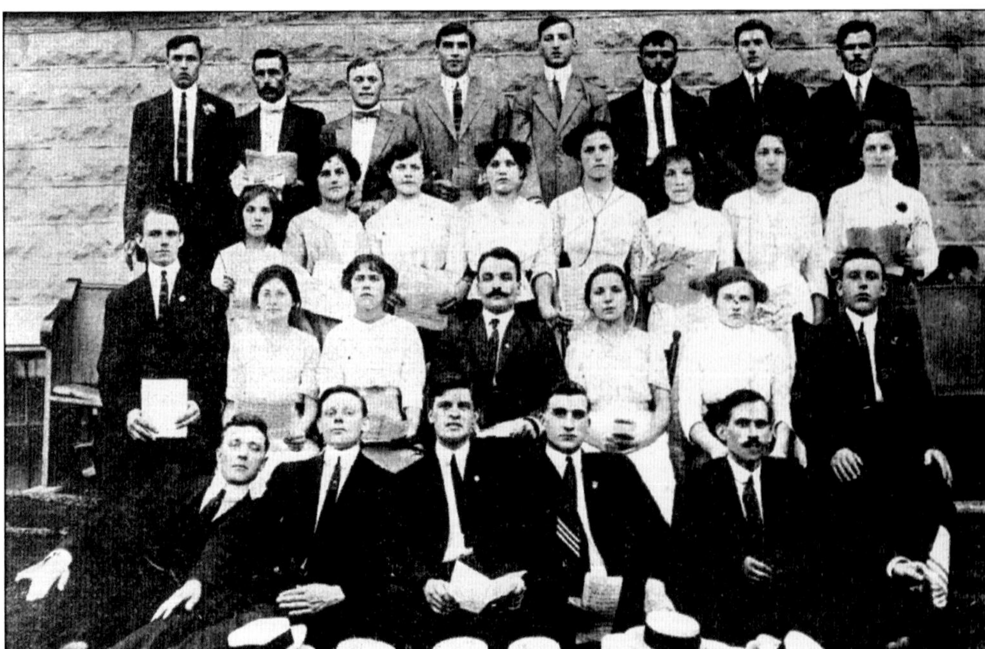

Congregations petitioned their home villages to send cantors to direct choirs for church and social activities. Thus John Bukata was recruited to St. Nicholas UCC in Wilmington. In 1912, the choir is photographed with Bukata (second row, center) in front of the old church.

Ukrainian entrepreneurs, in their establishments, served as pivotal sources of information and refuge for the incoming Ukrainians. The Pastuszek family has held that position for four generations in Chester. Michael Pastuszek and Mary Koring Pastuszek of Chester honeymooned in Atlantic City in 1912. Mary, a second-generation Ukrainian, was born in Chester. Her father became a policeman in Philadelphia. The Pastuszek family went on to become patrons of the Ukrainian Orthodox community in Chester, and their real estate business expanded into the outlying areas. Photographic cards were a popular way to let friends and relatives know where and how one was.

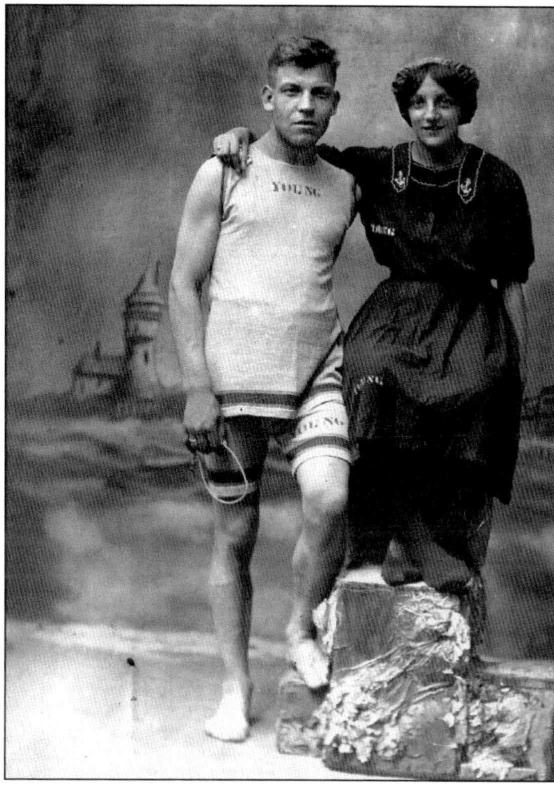

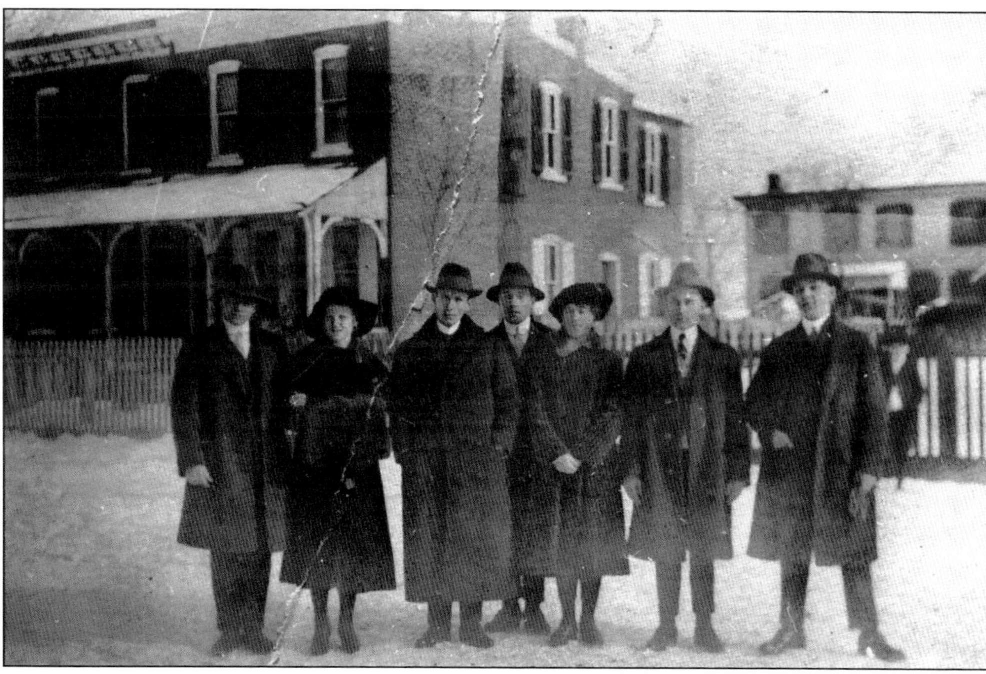

Members of St. Nicholas UCC, Wilmington, take a break from caroling in 1913 to preserve for future generations their elegant style. Caroling, the ancient tradition, took on a new meaning when it became not only time for friends and fun but also a church fund-raiser.

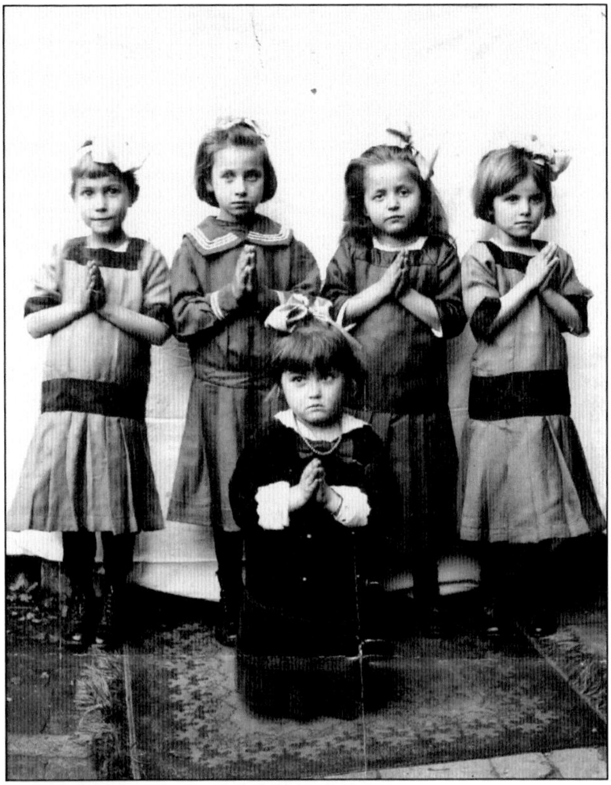

Throughout its 90-plus-year history in Chesapeake City, the Sisters of St. Basil the Great dedicated themselves to the care of orphans. To support their mission, here and in Philadelphia, for decades they operated a successful dairy and vegetable farm. They continued the care of the orphans, and in time, the novitiate was moved to the motherhouse in Fox Chase. Pictured is the original group of orphans at Chesapeake City during the summer of 1914.

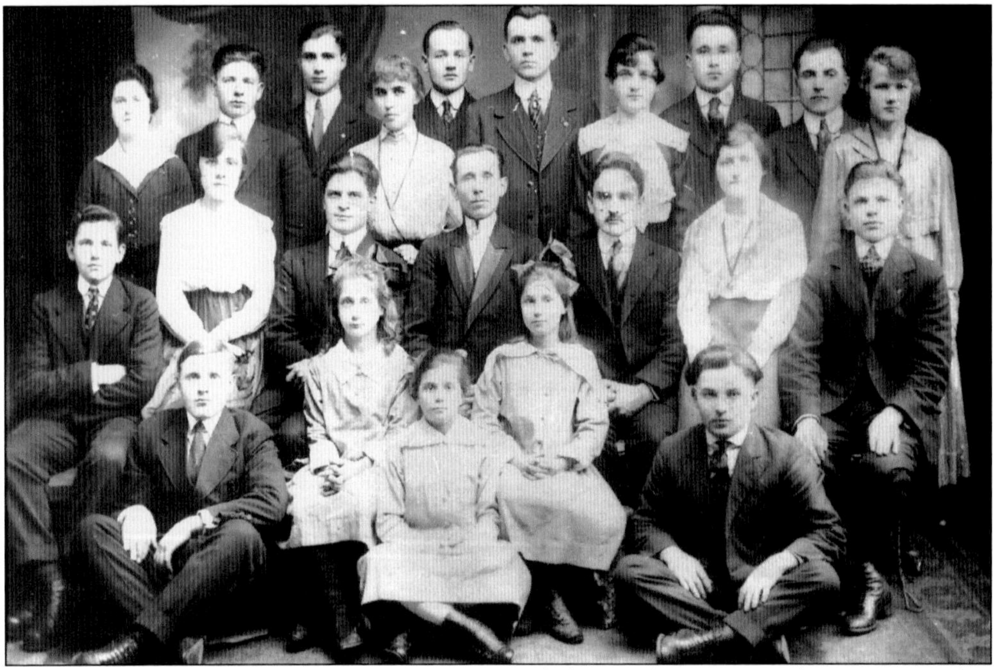

St. Nicholas UCC Choir in Wilmington was not only known for its singing during services, but also its staged performances. In 1914, Theodore Yaworsky (second row, third from left) directed the group in *Ukrainska Druzhinka*.

Two

SEARCHING FOR OPPORTUNITIES

Within these hallowed walls our children are taught a love of their own Rite and the language of their forefathers. It is in these elements that Ukrainian culture and tradition will be preserved and handed down through generations.

—Michael Kupchick, Chester

The war years had a devastating effect on Ukrainians here and in occupied Ukraine. In the old country, they were divided by the then existing empires: the Russians in the eastern part, the Austro-Hungarians in the western part, both inimical to Ukrainians during World War I. This brother-against-brother civil war mentality, even though begun in 1914, did not come to a conclusion in 1918 but continued marginally into 1922, ending after World War II when the Soviet Union enslaved all the Ukrainian lands.

Throughout these times, Ukrainians in the Delaware Valley who took active sides during World War I aggravated their already existing identity crisis. The ensuing conflicts separated newcomers and existing immigrants into two groups: the first, Ruthenians and Rusins and the second, Ukrainians. They became two distinct nationalities sharing the same culture. The United States government caused further complications with its newly inaugurated quota system based on nationality. Ukrainian institutions organized and founded prior to World War I became permanent fixtures for Ukrainians here, while Rusins established separate organizations and eventually referred to themselves as Byzantine Rite Rusins.

The foremost institution governing Ukrainian lives was the Eastern Catholic faith as reflected in its churches, but even the Catholic Church, then known as the Ruthenian Catholic Church, had to split in 1916 according to national ties. In 1924, two distinct dioceses were founded, both claiming to be somewhat Ukrainian, yet neither formally named as such. This abnormality created a social-spiritual vacuum soon filled by the Orthodox religions on one side and the spiritually bankrupt socialists/communists on the other, creating further strife.

In the last years of World War I and for some time thereafter, many Ukrainian political intellectuals immigrated to the United States, promoting and fueling the conflict. They took it upon themselves to redirect the Ukrainian population into their sphere of influence, creating a hostile environment in many of the Ukrainian communities in the Delaware Valley and even establishing their own political party affiliations in some.

Nevertheless, the cultural life of Ukrainian Americans in the Delaware Valley, although under stress, did not break, for it is in this particular and somewhat unorthodox environment that they found their true identity.

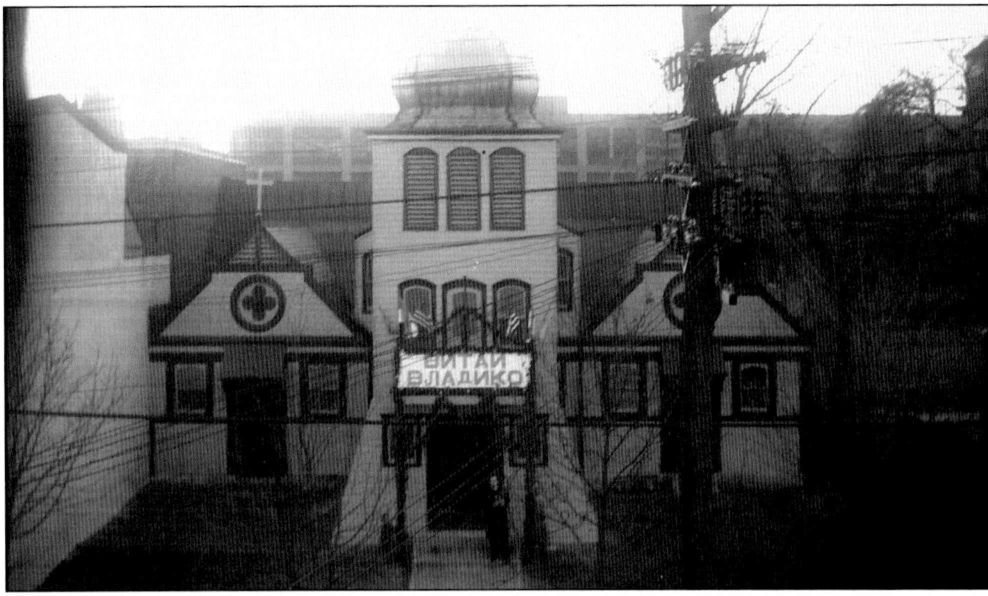

Frankford and Bridesburg sections of today's Philadelphia have a unique and separate Ukraine immigrant history. The settlers arrived in the 1890s from Brody and later Berezany regions. A church was purchased in 1916. St. Josaphat UCC's individuality lay in its unique construction and the naming of its bell as Soter Ortynsky. The community's isolation continued until the arrival of the refugees after World War II. This necessitated the building of a larger church and involvement in Ukrainian society in Philadelphia.

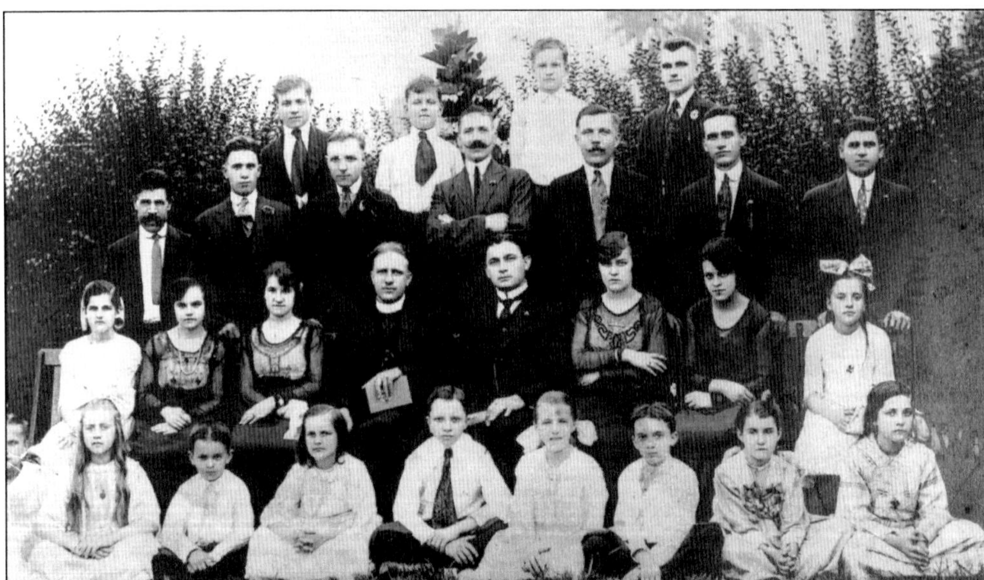

For centuries, the liturgy was sung in Church Slavonic. Children were urged to learn this liturgical language as they spoke Ukrainian or English at home. Second row, fourth from left, is Rev. Vladimir Derzyruka, and next to him is Yakim Rohach, the Holy Ghost UCC choir director in Chester in 1916.

Yakim and Catherine Rohach pose for their wedding portrait. He was born in Ukraine and arrived in 1907. For five years, he served as cantor in the UCC in Ansonia, New York. He visited the old country and one year later returned to Chester. There he was the head teacher, choir organizer, cantor, and civic leader of the Catholic community. He organized Providence Association of Ukrainian Catholics (Providence) Branch 105. Their large family was active in Ukrainian affairs in the Delaware Valley.

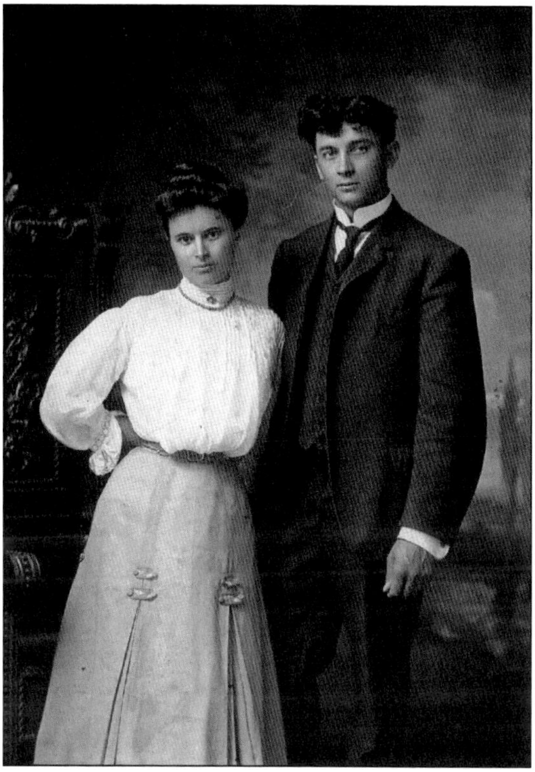

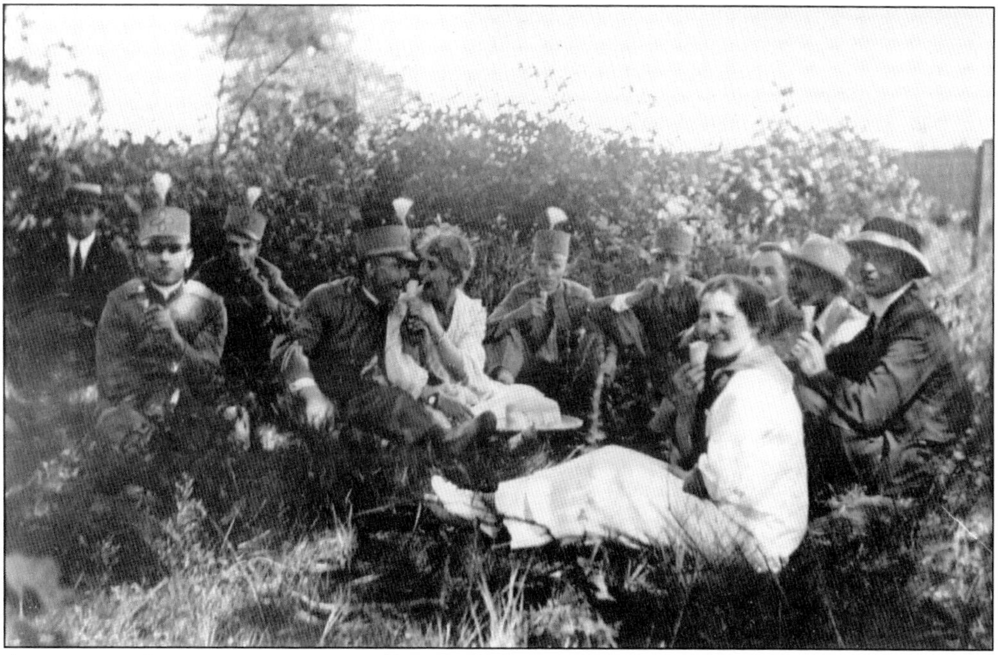

A man in uniform is most attractive. During this picnic in 1916 at Newport, Delaware, members of Sitch, in their uniforms, are enjoying a pleasant afternoon with their friends in the cool shade. Sitch promoted national consciousness by raising educational and cultural levels of Ukrainians. Their program included parades, concerts, and choreographed exercises.

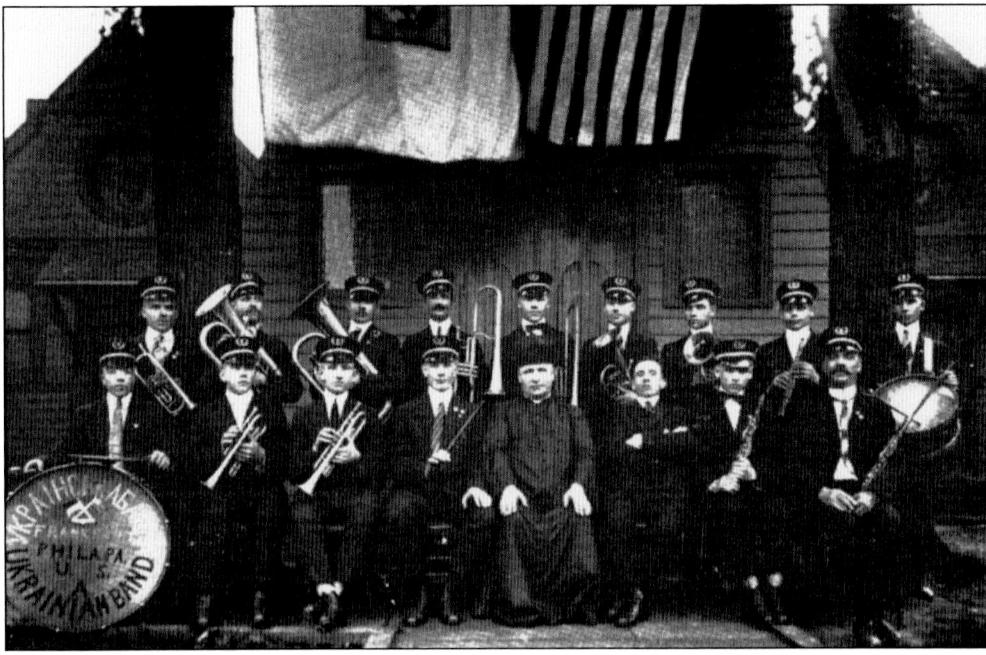

The oldest Ukrainian musical group in Delaware Valley was Mykola Lysenko Orchestra organized in 1913 in Frankford. The 1916 members are, from left to right, (first row) Emil Leskiw, Tymko Pohorily, Paul Bahlay, Michael Bahlay, conductor Rev. Vladimir Petriwsky, cantor Nicholas Demkiw, Stephen Slywka, and Nicholas Gudziak; (second row) Anthony Dynia, Daniel Gramiak, Joseph Raytca, Stephen Sloboda, Michael Bodnar, Paul Rega, Stephen Kolody, Basil Tantala, and John Fedoriw.

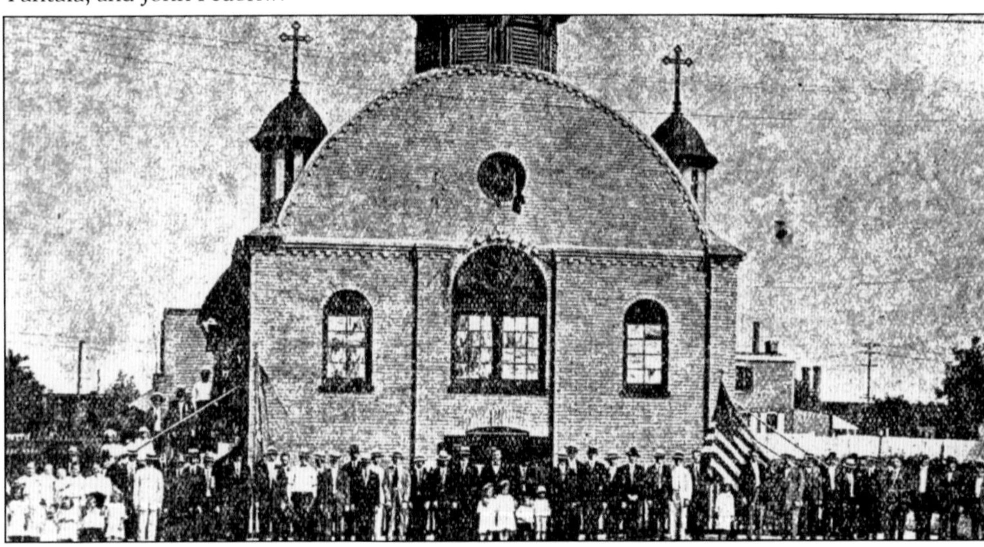

Because they could not afford to have the church built professionally, the parishioners of St. Nicholas UCC, Wilmington, took this task upon themselves in true pioneer spirit. South Heald Street, at this time, had sections of cobblestones, concrete, asphalt, and dirt. Over these various surfaces, they took their wheelbarrows and hauled the cinder blocks they purchased, from the plant near the Third Street Bridge, to build their house of worship. A new front was added in 1918.

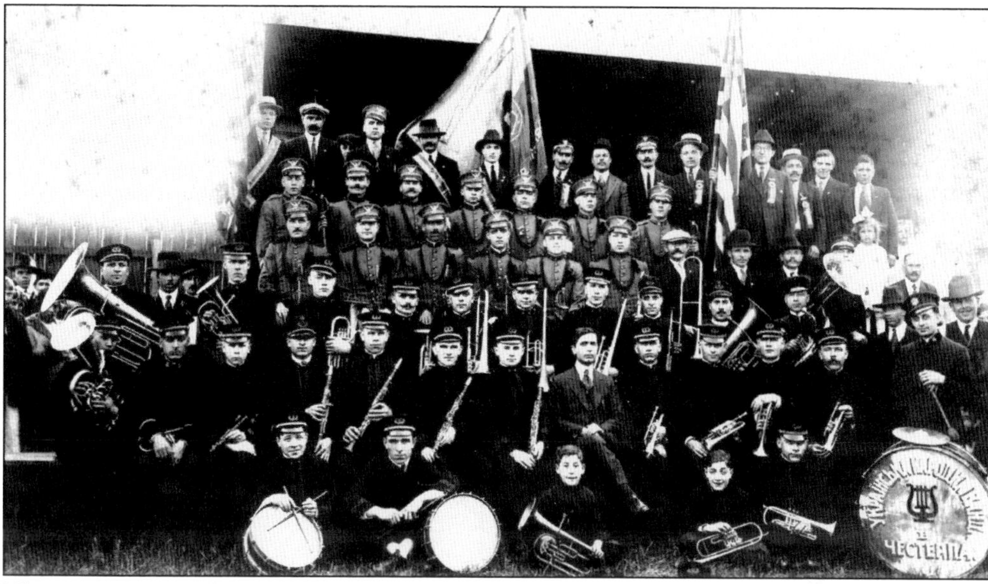

Ukrainian National Association (UNA) Branch 388 in Chester was organized under the banner of Zaporizka Sitch, in memory of the Cossacks who lived along the Dnipro River. At the Chester fairgrounds in 1916, they combined with Sitch council under the banner of Hetman Petro Sahajdachnyj, a Ukrainian hero, and became the Ukrainian National Band. Both groups wore their distinctive dress uniforms.

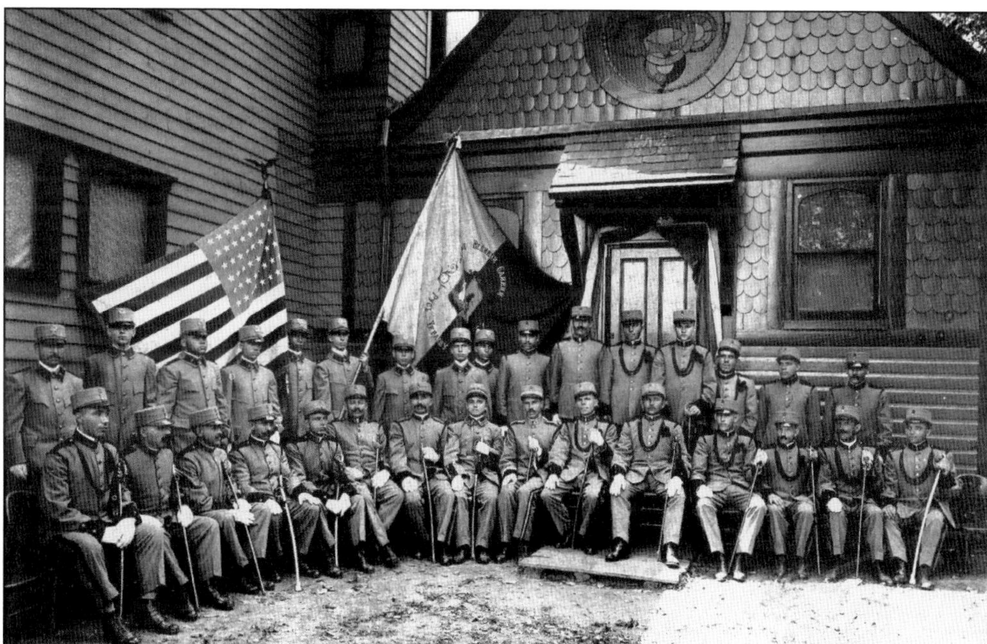

The Ukrainian community in Frankford supported Ukraine more strongly than those in other localities. During World War I, Galician Ukrainians in Austria formed a separate military legion, the Sitchovy Striltsi. Their brethren in Frankford established the Society of Ukrainian Sitchovy Striltsi in the United States in 1916 and posed in their new uniforms.

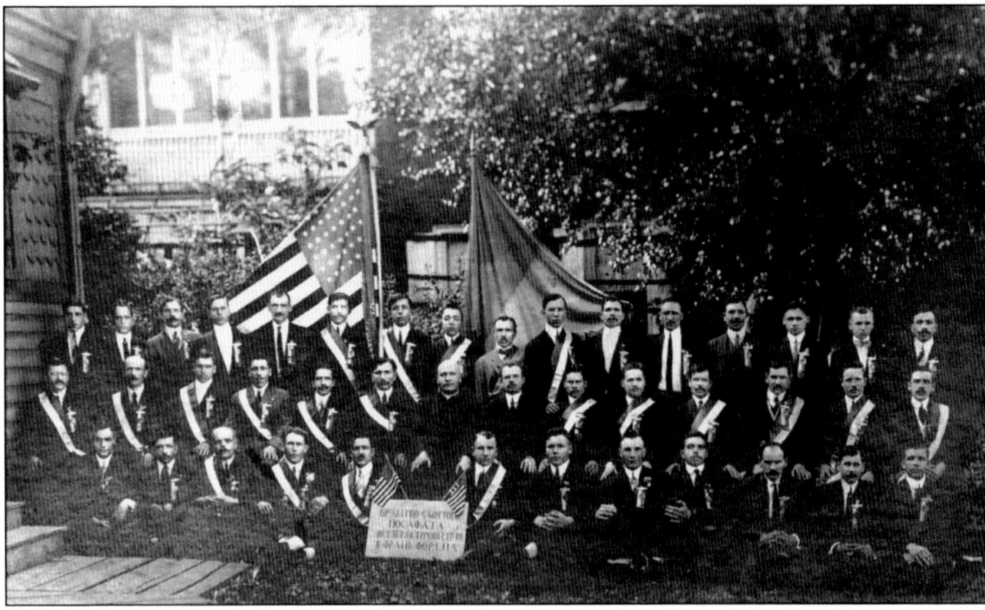

This distinguished group belongs to St. Josaphat's Branch 14 of Providence structured in 1914 as a male-only society. By 1915, women organized their own group, and by 1918, the two joined, forming the largest and most active Providence Branch for the next two decades in the Delaware Valley.

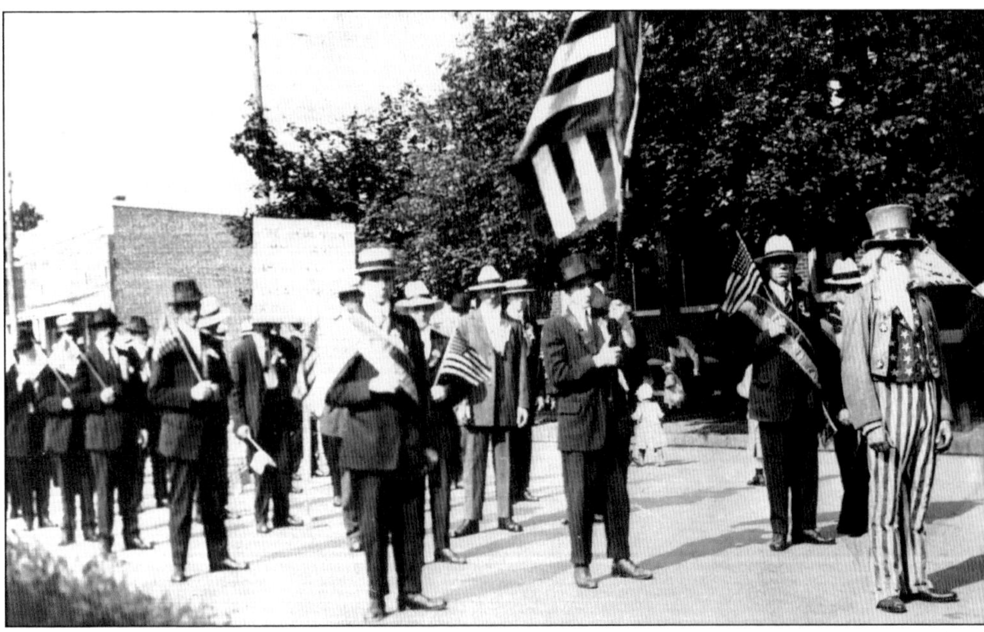

Ukrainian communities wholeheartedly supported the war effort. The liberty parade and bond rally in Wilmington in 1918 shows them as a unit patriotically marching in the parade. Uncle Sam is Theodore Yaworsky; behind him are, from left to right, (first row) Michael Bejon, Joseph Skochepis (carrying the large flag), and Wasyl Hirnyk; (second row) in the light suit is John Edynak.

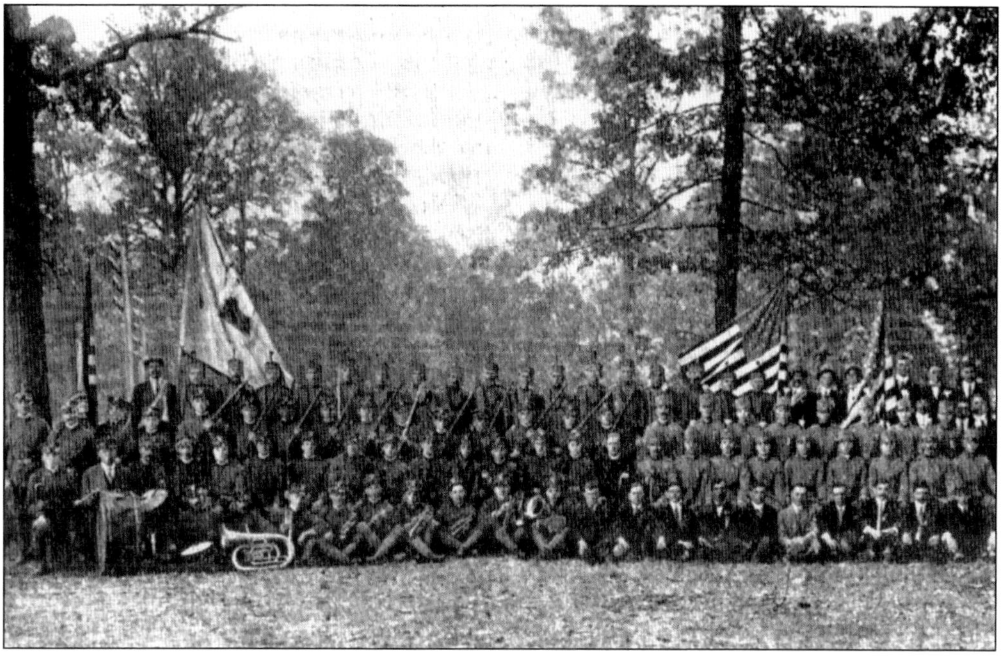

Music was the most important form of entertainment. It was not uncommon for two or more parishes to hold picnics with each parish showing off their band. In this 1916 photograph, the Sitch Band of Chester and Wilmington and the Wilmington Band performed drills and music for the enjoyment of their communities.

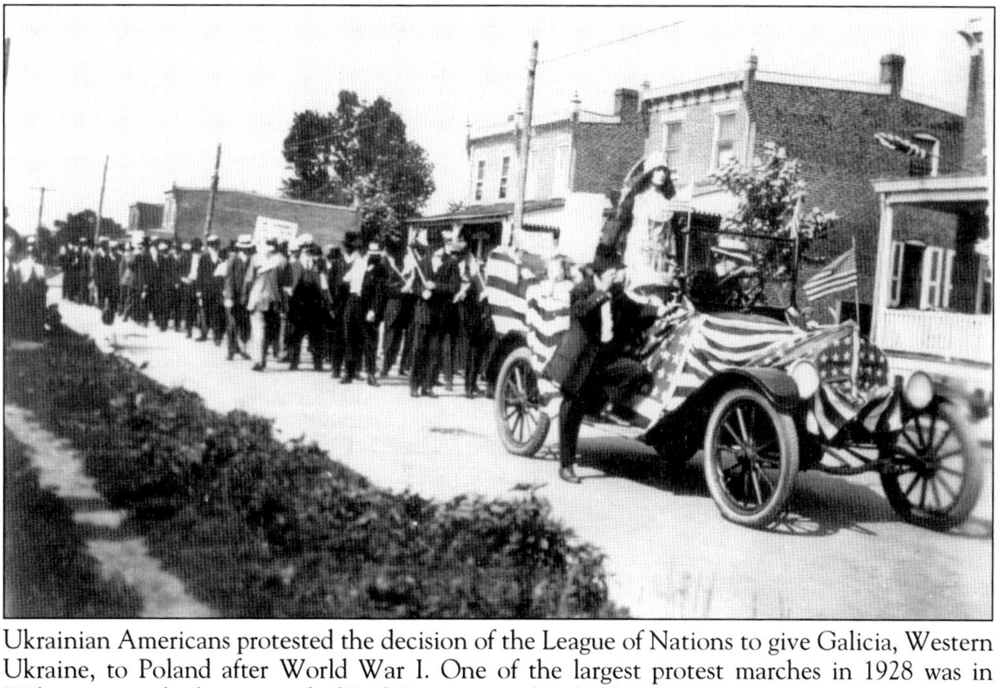

Ukrainian Americans protested the decision of the League of Nations to give Galicia, Western Ukraine, to Poland after World War I. One of the largest protest marches in 1928 was in Wilmington, which consisted of Red Cross nurses headed by Tatianna Kressa, Boy Scouts, and UNA led by the Sitch Band. In the photograph, Miss Liberty is riding in Theodore Shatynsky's band car.

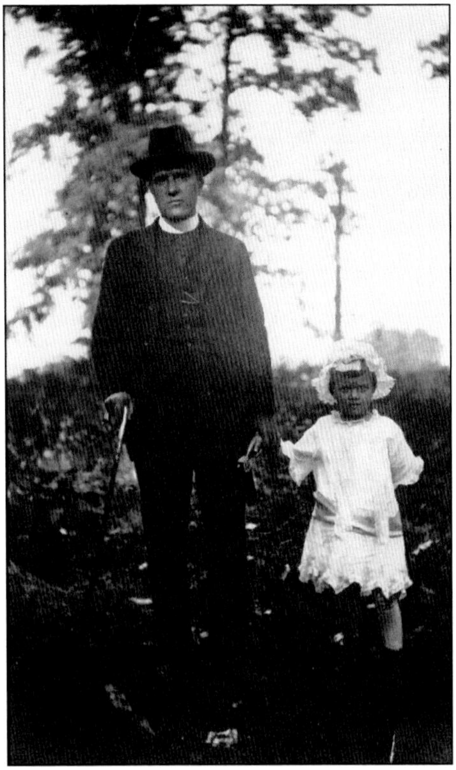

Rev. Vladimir Derzyruka, administrator of UCCs in Chester and Wilmington, was a prolific writer, poet, and novelist, editor of several Ukrainian newspapers and calendars, and translator of the works of Mark Twain. Throughout his life, he was active in Ukrainian communities. He is photographed with Lydia, one of his daughters.

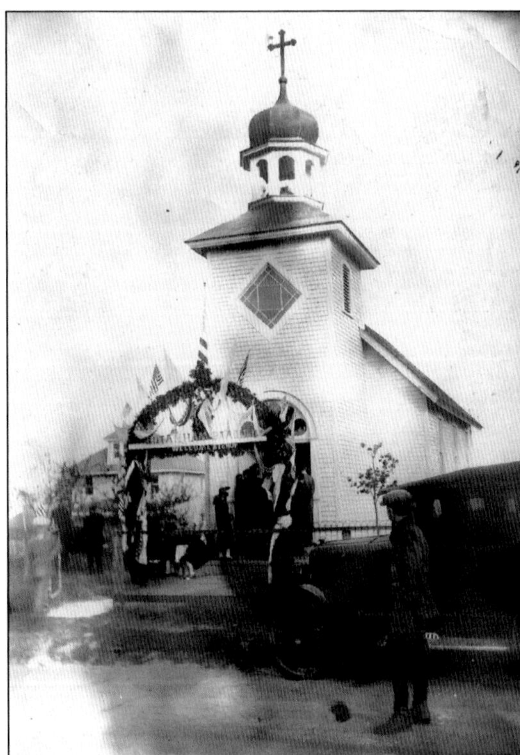

From 1910 through 1917, church services in Chesapeake City were held at the homes of the faithful. In 1917, Joseph Ortynsky, brother of Bishop Soter, offered one acre of forestland to cut trees for the lumber needed to build a church. The congregation worked under the supervision of the carpenters Alexander Krochak, John Hrabec, Michael Breza, and Alexander Hotra, and the project was completed in 1920. Thus the dream of St. Basil's UCC was realized.

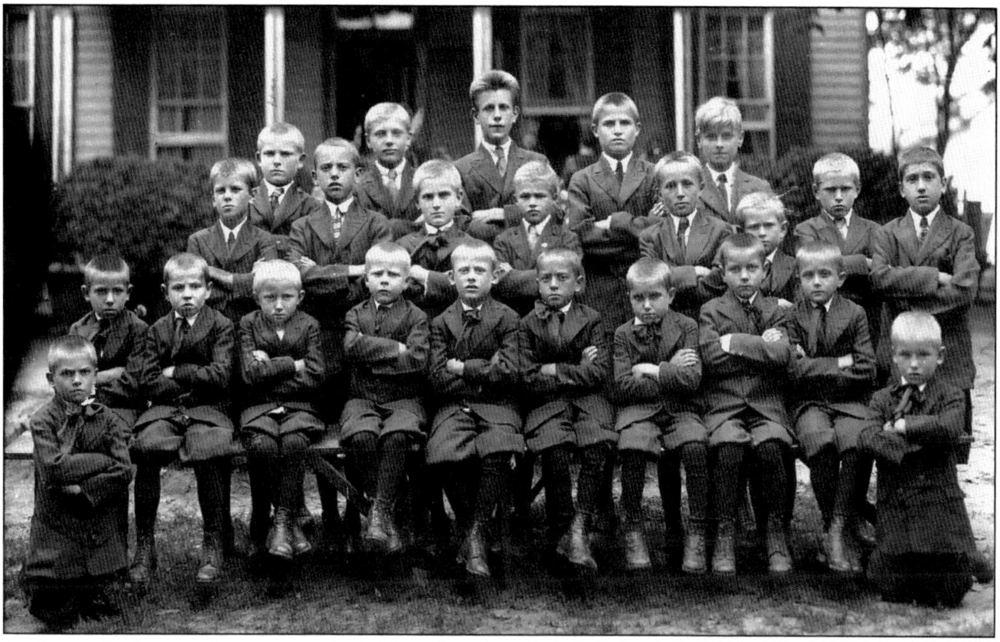

In the early days, only preschool children lived at the orphanage in Chesapeake City. Annually in the summer, the boys of St. Basil's Orphanage in Philadelphia spent vacation time helping the Sisters and learning the trade of farming. In the photograph are vacationing orphan boys at St. Basil's Orphanage in 1920.

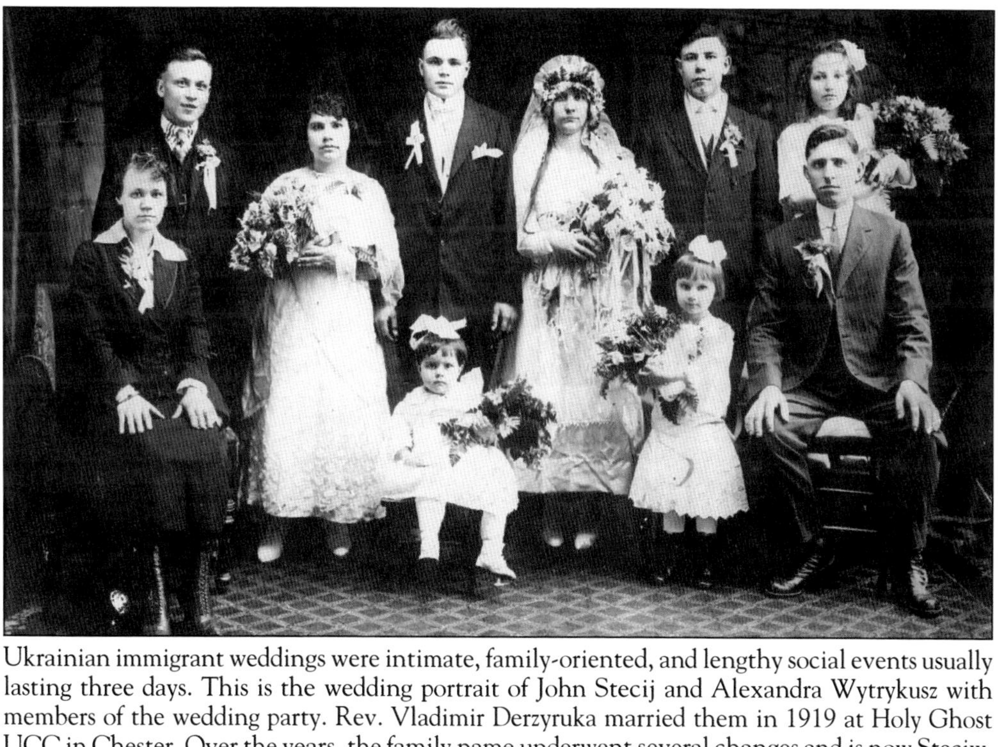

Ukrainian immigrant weddings were intimate, family-oriented, and lengthy social events usually lasting three days. This is the wedding portrait of John Stecij and Alexandra Wytrykusz with members of the wedding party. Rev. Vladimir Derzyruka married them in 1919 at Holy Ghost UCC in Chester. Over the years, the family name underwent several changes and is now Steciw, and Alexandra became Alice.

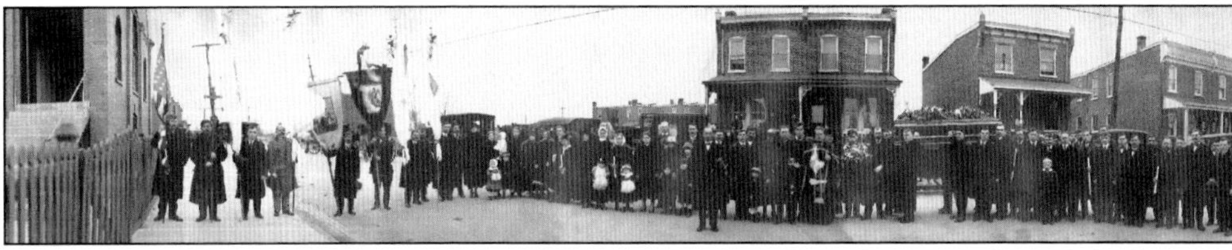

The final farewell was an elaborate social event. Wasyl Malhowski, a member of the UCC in Wilmington, died in 1919. Church organizations with insignias led the procession, followed by women, the casket, and men. Some of the mourners held candles. In this photograph, the church is on the left. Rev. Vladimir Derzyruka is in the center; the cantor (with the incense holder) is to his right, with the family and the choir around them. In front holding his hat is Stanley Yacyk, the undertaker. In the cemetery the body is laid to rest facing the east, awaiting the Second Coming because the Lord will be coming from where the sun rises. Since the Ukrainian parish in Wilmington did not have its own cemetery, as did some of the other parishes, they used the local cemetery.

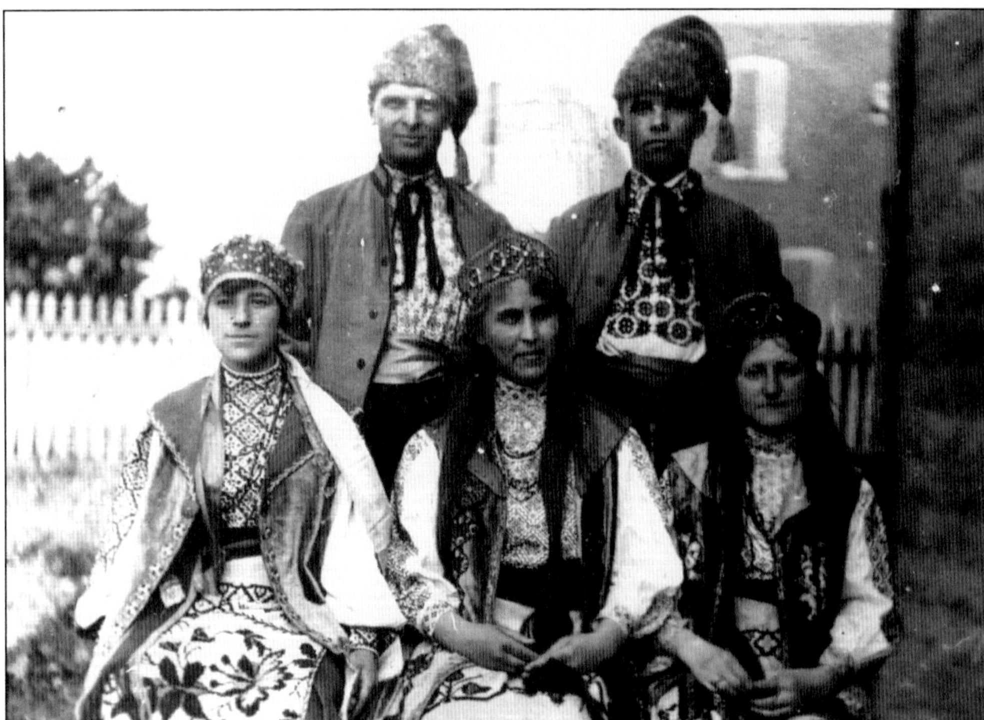

Various theatrical groups vied for the endorsement of the public as they retold Ukrainian culture onstage. This troupe from the early 1920s in Wilmington includes, from left to right, (first row) ? Boris, Tatianna Kressa, and Lucy Surma; (second row) Tyman Kolody and ? Machuda.

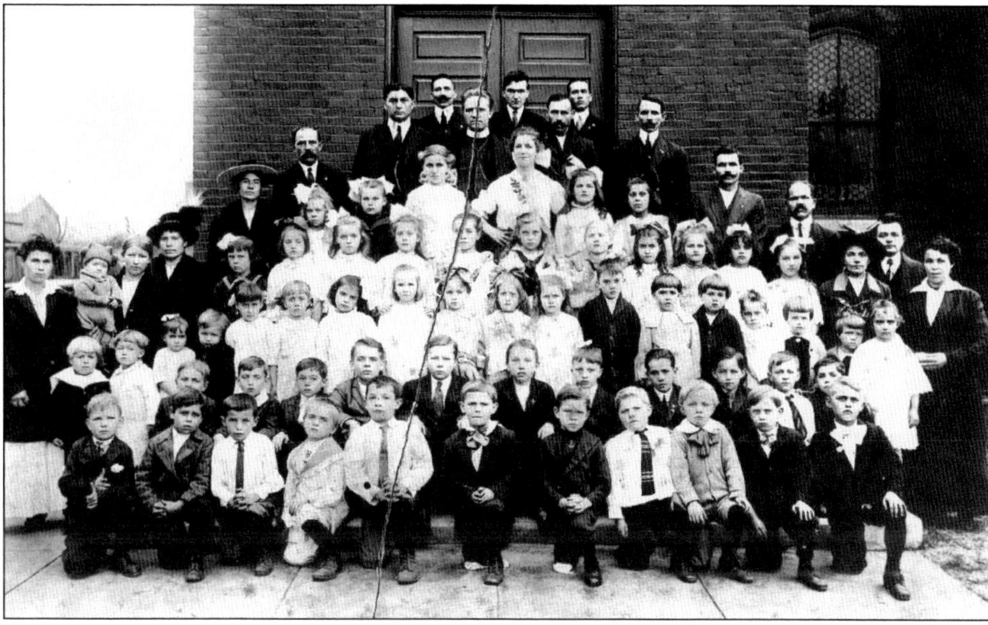

Schooling was very important to the pastors serving in the Delaware Valley. Regardless of the number of young ones, these missionaries took it upon themselves to form evening or Saturday or Sunday classes. Rev. Vladimir Derzeruka in 1918 is photographed in front of the church in Chester with the students and their parents at the completion of the school year.

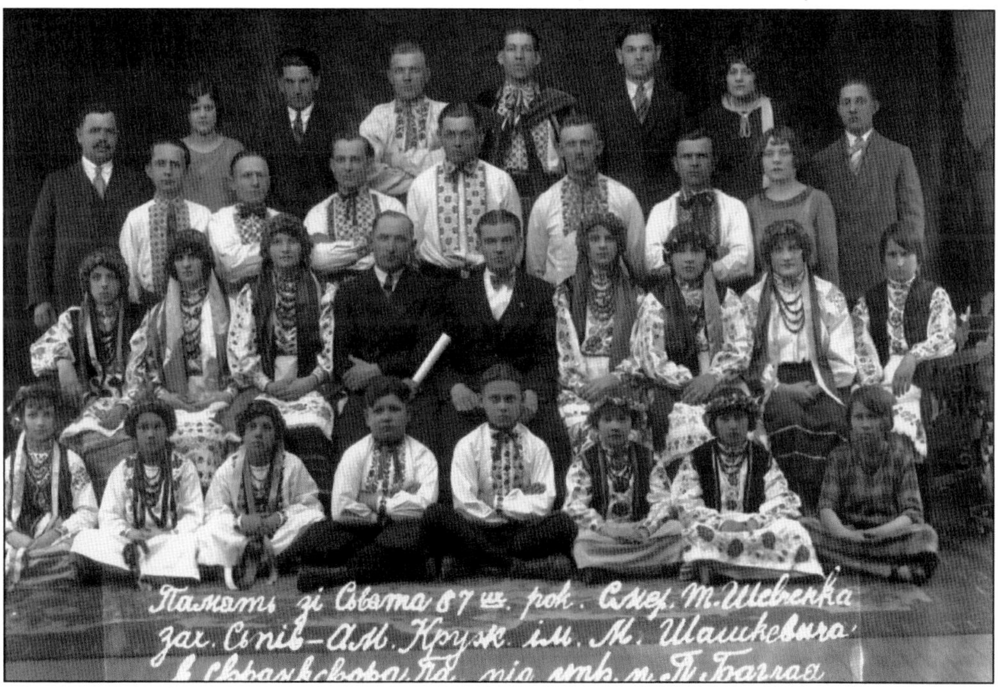

Rev. Markian Shashkewych Choir in Frankford in 1928 commemorated the 67th anniversary of the death of Taras Shevchenko, the great Ukrainian bard. Choir director Paul Bahlay, seated in the second row, is holding the musical score rolled up in his hand. All choirs performed at civic events.

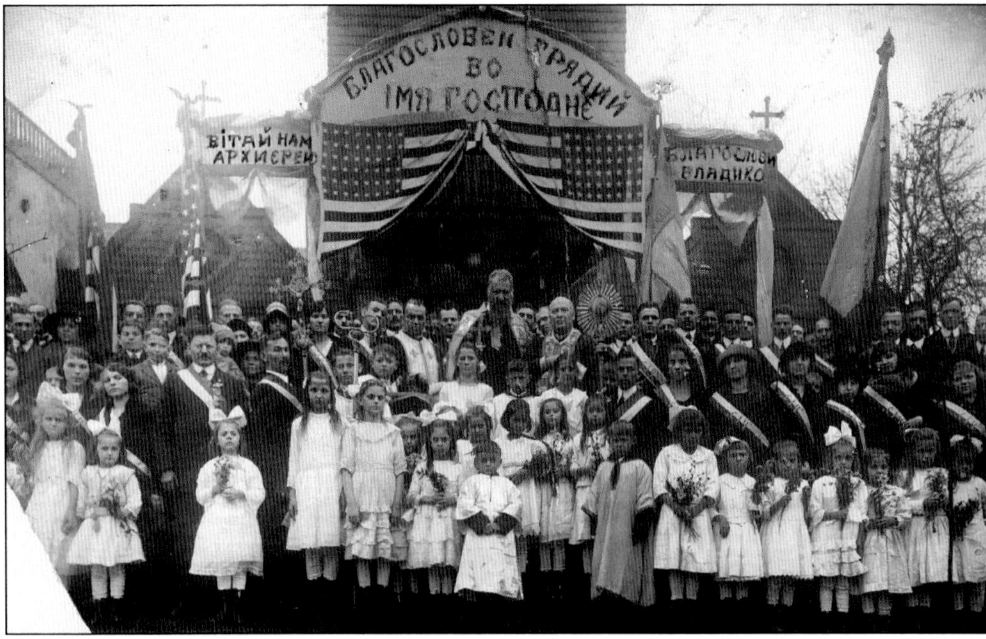

In 1921, the metropolitan of Lviv, Ukraine, arrived in the United States for pastoral visitations. One of his stops was at St. Josaphat's UCC in Frankford where this photograph was taken. The stately figure of Metropolitan Andrej Sheptytsky towers above the assembled.

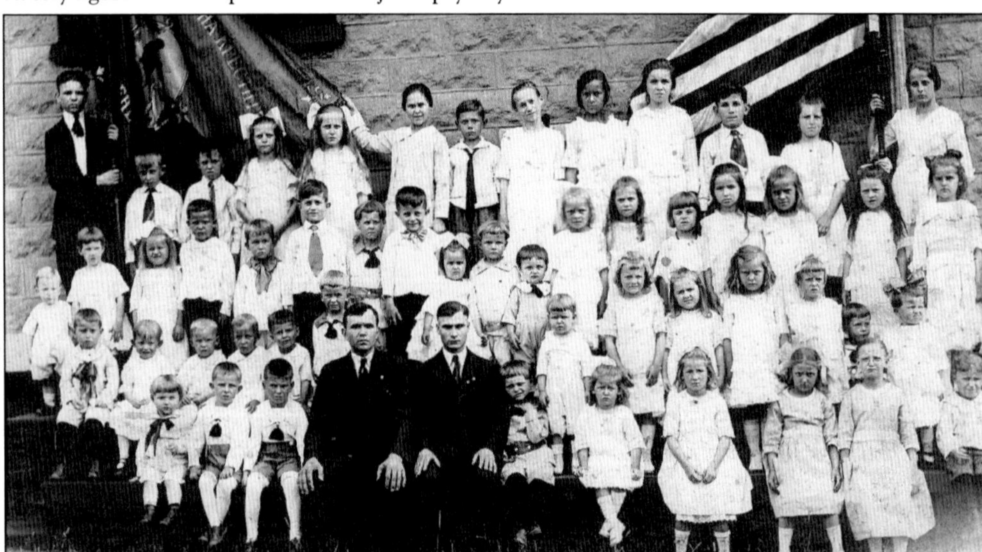

UNA Juvenile Branch 247, in Wilmington, from left to right, includes (first row) Anne Gula, Stephen Gula, John Gula, Michael Bejon, Harry Kosowsky, unidentified, Rose Belay, Mary Belay, and three unidentified; (second row) six unidentified, Michael Cycyk, Mary Zavkowsky, Ann Sass, Ann Bohonis, and three unidentified; (third row) five unidentified, Mitchell Kuchapski, five unidentified, Tilly Figun, Anna Zankowski, unidentified, Mary Kasowsky, Mary Figun, Kate Starobranski, and Mary Jaremchuk; (fourth row) Charles Kasowsky, two unidentified, Mary Hnatowski, Katherine Hnatowski, Caroline Trush, Mike Edynak, Mary Kaczmar, Katherine Figun, Catherine Kasowsky, John Kuchapski, Ann Belay, and Anna Kaczmar.

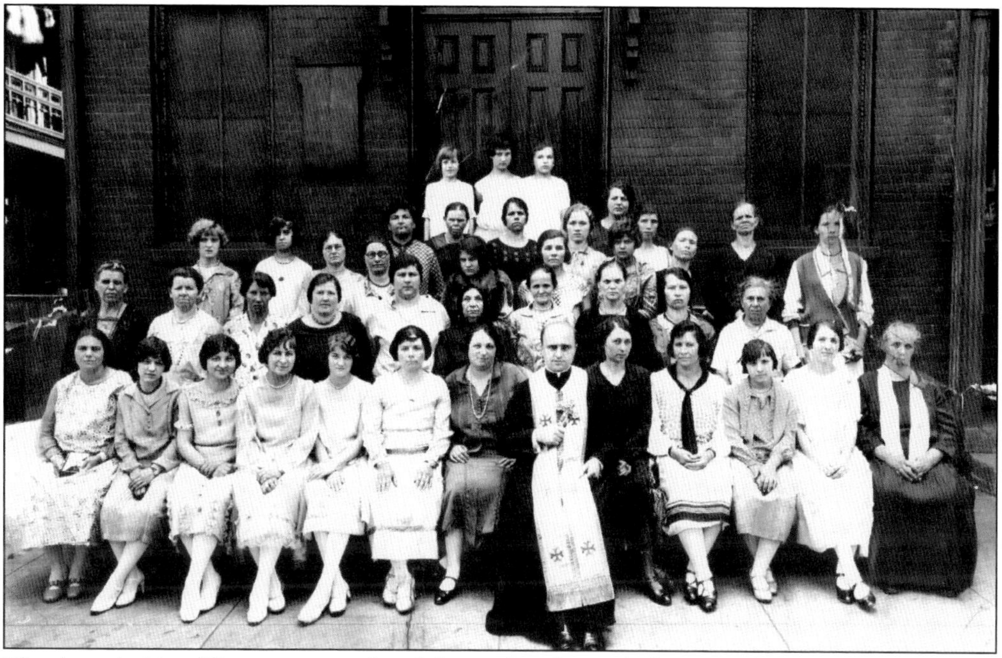

The Apostleship of Prayer is a sisterhood devoted to the goal of support through prayer and work for the church. Rev. Stephen Pobutsky poses with the 1926 members in front of Nativity of the Blessed Virgin Mary (BVM) UCC in Reading.

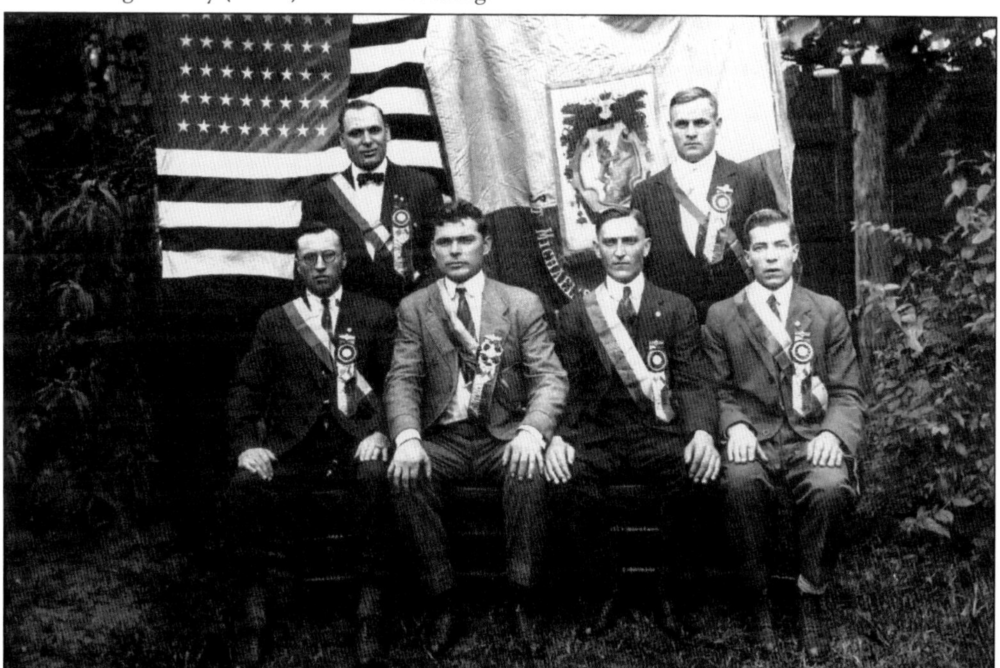

UCC in Camden was started in 1924 by Providence Branch under the patronage of St. Michael, which was organized in 1915. The founding members, seen here in 1925, are, from left to right, (first row) Onofrij Lazar, unidentified, Nicolas Lapiska, and Stephen Haday; (second row) Peter Plaskon and Anthony Chubik, church trustees.

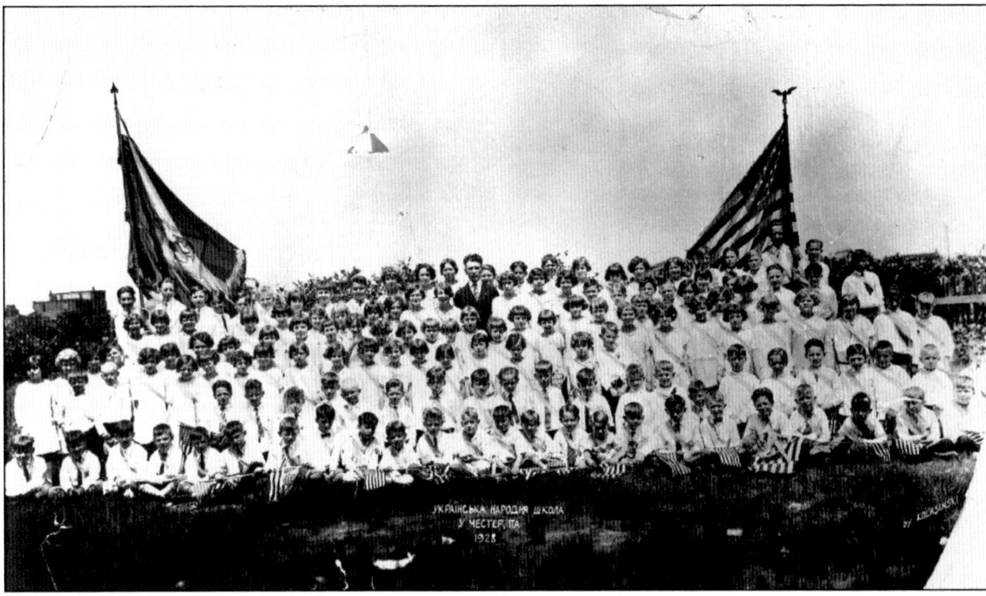

During the 1920s, there were two Ukrainian schools in Chester, one at the west end and the other at the east end. With the building of the Ukrainian American National Home (UANH) in 1927 the schools merged, becoming the Ukrainian National School. Principal Yakim Rohach is standing in the middle of the combined school in 1928.

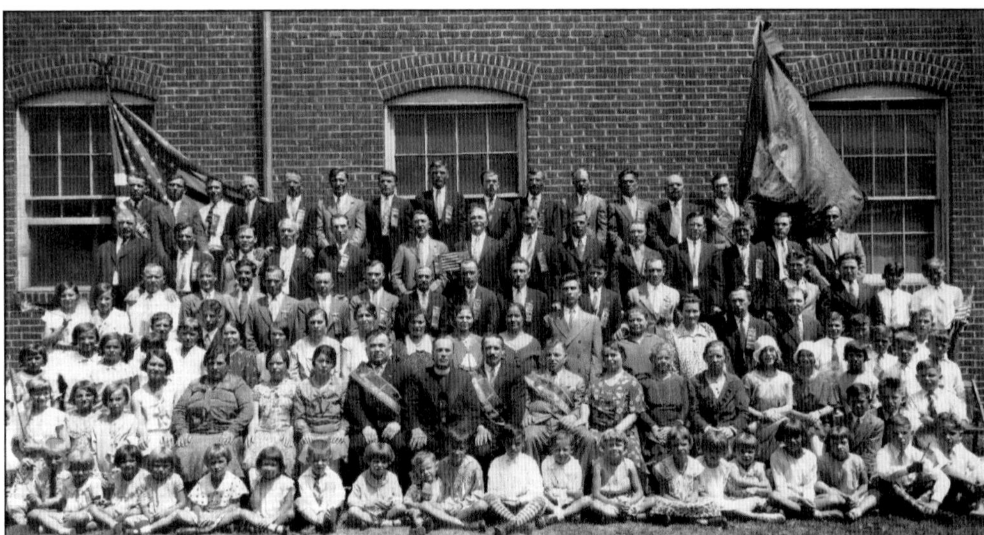

In 1928, UNA St. John the Baptist Branch 247, founded in 1909 in Wilmington, separated from St. Nicholas UCC and founded SS. Peter and Paul Ukrainian Orthodox Church (UOC). Its first liturgies were in the newly acquired Ukrainian National Home (UNH). The few remaining members of Branch 247 were issued another charter and became St. Vladimir Branch 173. The photograph was taken just before the breakup in front of UNH.

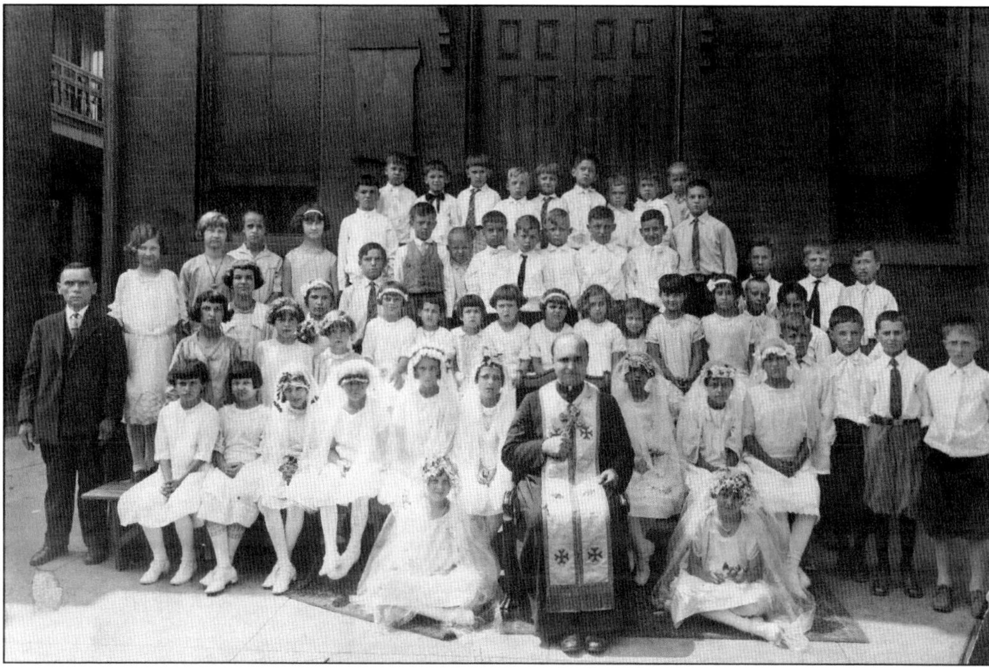

Rev. Stephen Pobutsky (center), Nativity BVM UCC, poses in Reading in 1923 with children of the parish. The girls who made their First Holy Communion wore headdresses. The boys were stylish in knickerbockers.

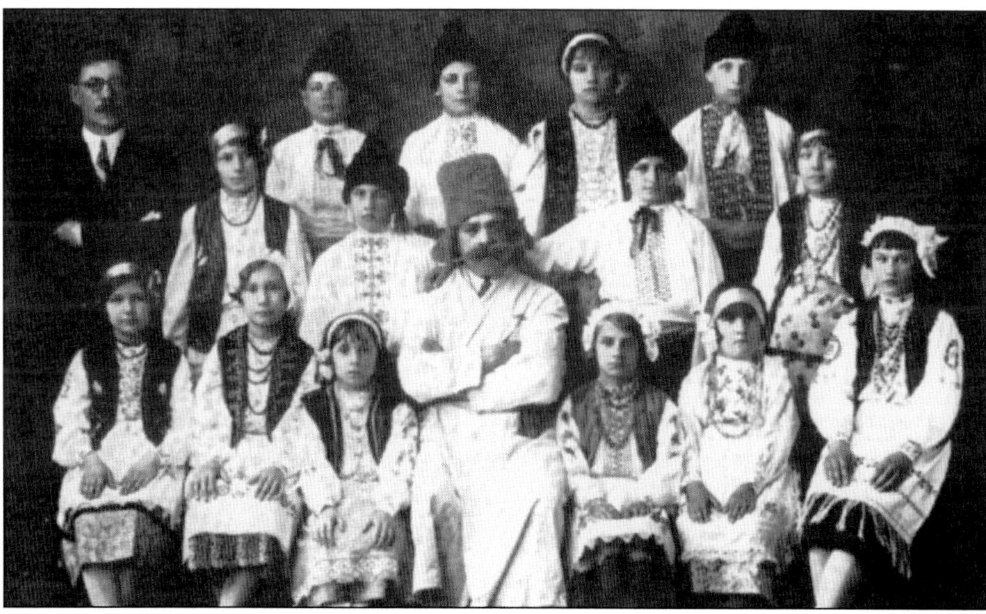

After choirs, minstrels were most popular. Members of the Ukrainian Minstrels of 1928 at SS. Peter and Paul UCC in Bridgeport are, from left to right, (first row) Anna Petrosk, Josephine Bukata, Mary Janoski, John Bukata, Caroline Glowa, Helen Serbeniuk, and Anna Demura; (second row) Helen Hutzuliak, Michael Bukata, John Bobby, and Anna Makowiak; (third row) director Peter Martyniuk, Michael Shemar, Frank Kataryniuk, Ann Perusiak, and John Ewanick.

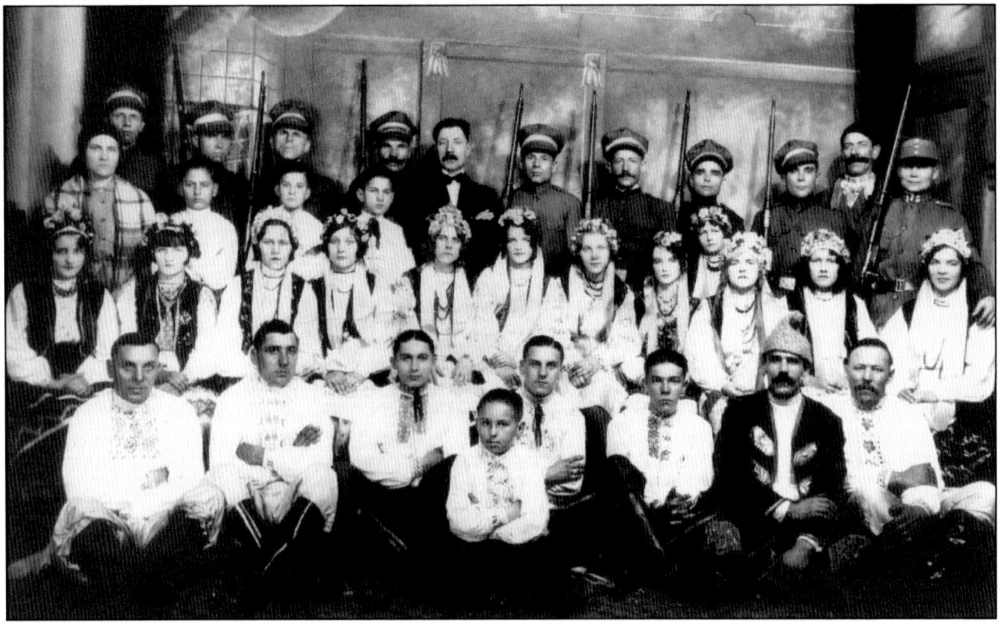

Members of the Ukrainian Dramatic Troup in Bridgeport in 1928 are, from left to right, (seated in front) Raymond Wowk; (first row) Ignatius Sabo, Hryhory Holobeny, Stanley Ovcharick, Joseph Sabo, John Mingo, Michael Kozak, and Prokip Wowk; (second row) Anna Stepanick, Olga Stepanick, Mary Holobeny, Mary Sarabun, Mary Bukata, Helen Stepanick, Michaylyna Sarabun, Josephine Stepanick, Suzanne Kuchna, Stella Martyniuk, and Mary Mingo; (third row) ? Bobby, ? Holobeny, Michael Bilyk, Hilary Bobby, and Anna Wowk; (fourth row) John Burry, Michael Wowk, Panko Betchyk, Wawro Kozak, Peter Martyniuk, ? Ovcharick, Samuel Kozak, Theodore Savitsky, George Holinda, ? Mocherniuk, and Joseph Bobby.

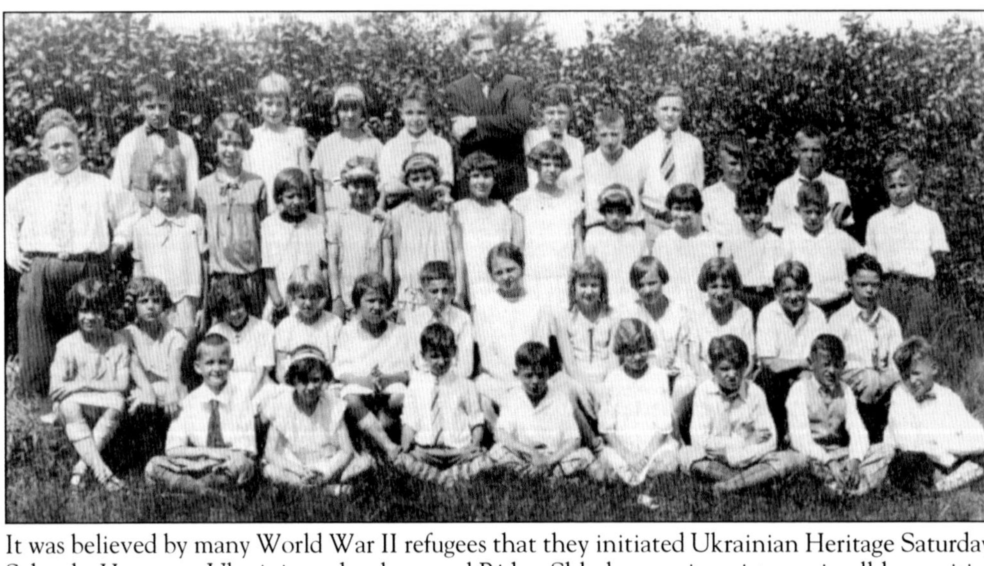

It was believed by many World War II refugees that they initiated Ukrainian Heritage Saturday Schools. However, Ukrainian schools named Ridna Shkola were in existence in all large cities with Ukrainian populations since 1919. Chester's UNA Branch 156 had organized the school earlier than this 1929 photograph.

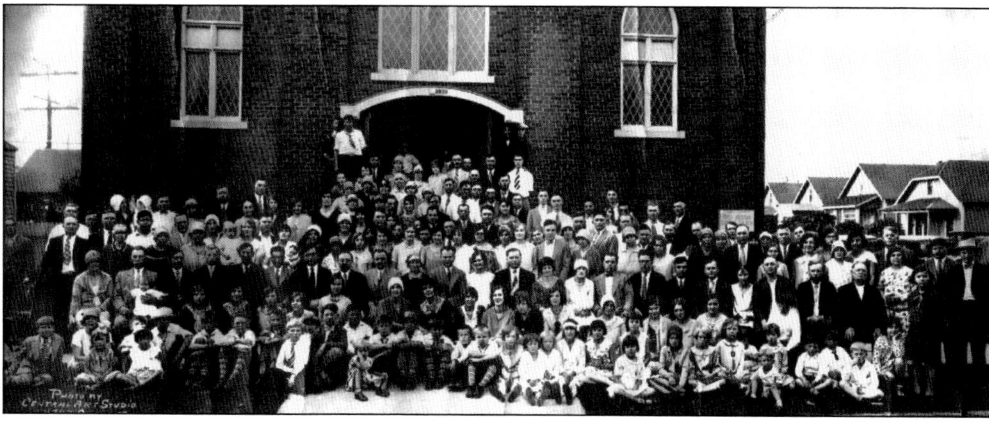

Since the 1890s, the Stundists, later called Baptists, were persecuted in Ukraine. Being pacifists by nature, they were mistrusted by people living in surrounding areas. Upon immigration, they attended American Baptist churches. Because of the language barrier, they formed their own groups in time. The Chester Ukrainian Baptists are shown in front of their House of Prayer in the 1930s.

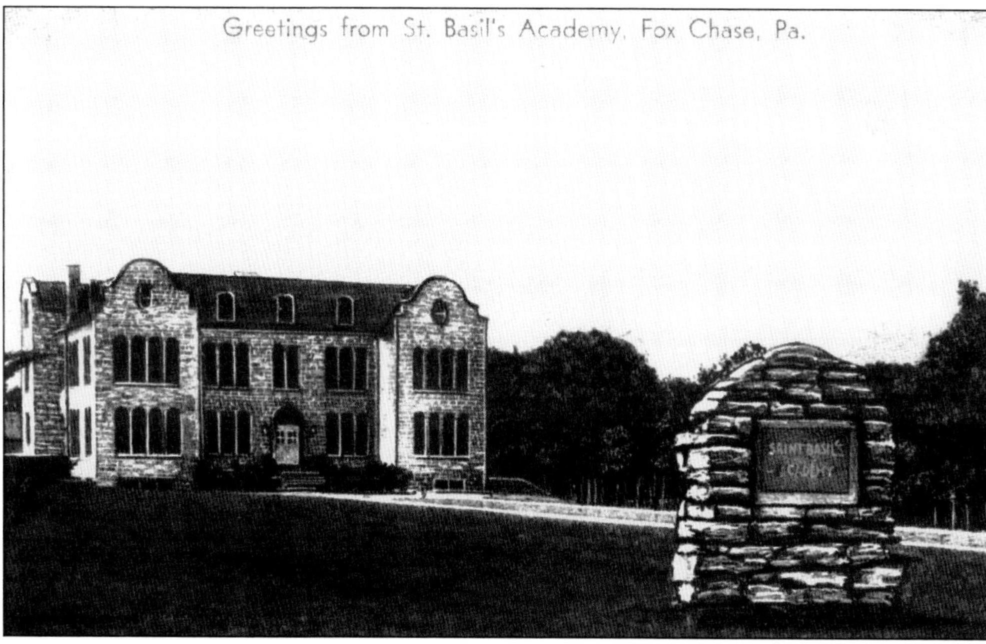

St. Basil's Academy in Fox Chase, as pictured in 1931, was the continuation of their elementary schools. It was a private high school for girls administered by the Sisters of St. Basil the Great. Later the academy was moved across the street, and this became the motherhouse.

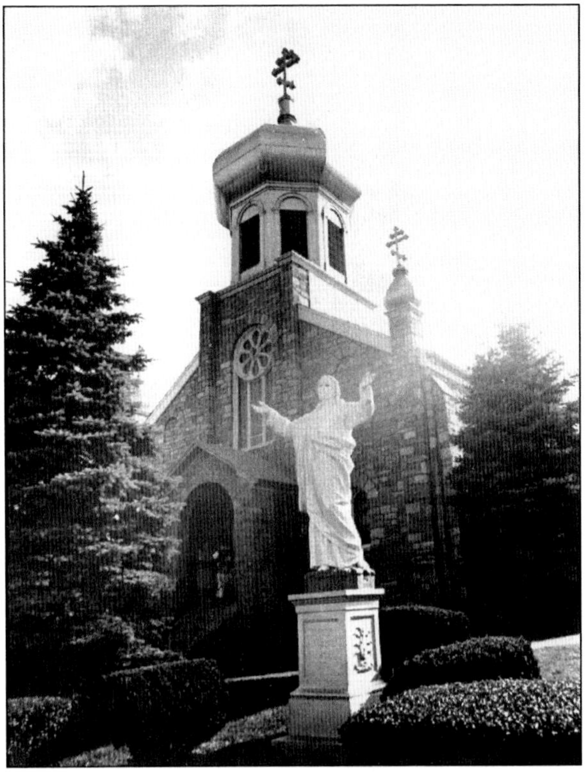

St. Monica's Hall on Bridgeport's Ford Street was the site of SS. Peter and Paul UCC in 1924. From 1924 to 1936, a former bonnet factory was the Ukrainian house of worship. The faithful were called to worship with a 700-pound bell. It continues to call the descendants of the pioneers to liturgy and prayer. In 1936, a new church was built, and the bell keeps ringing.

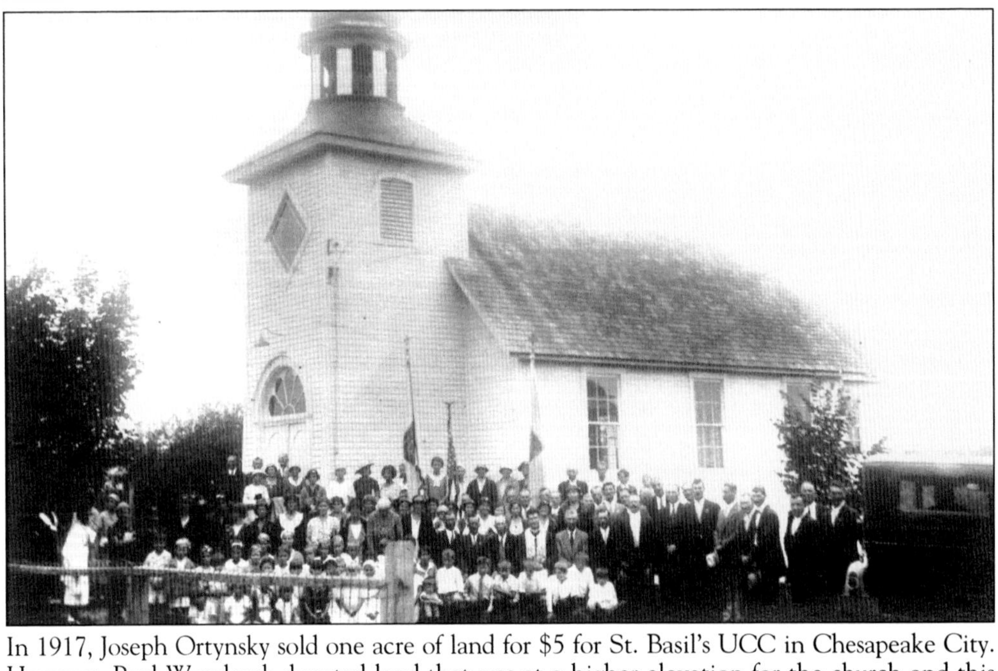

In 1917, Joseph Ortynsky sold one acre of land for $5 for St. Basil's UCC in Chesapeake City. However, Paul Wasylczuk donated land that was at a higher elevation for the church and this proved to be more suitable. Ortynsky's land was used for church picnics, dances, and other social events. With this income, a parish hall was built in 1931. By 1936, the Chesapeake and Delaware Canal widening project procured this land, and today it is part of the levees along the canal.

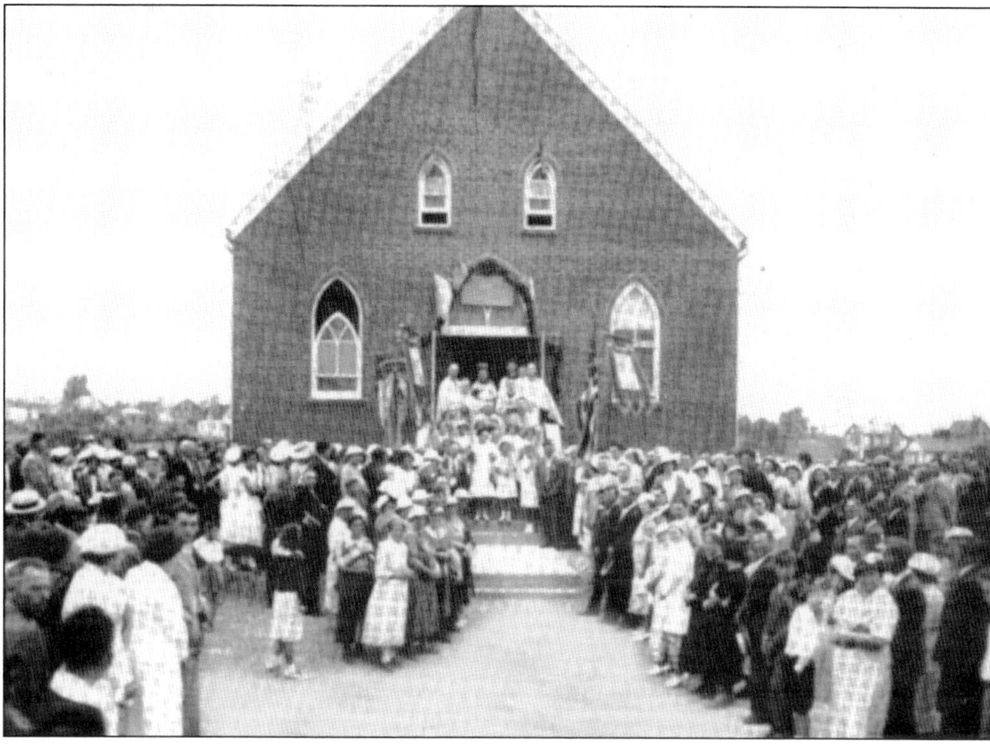

The first Ukrainians came to the Pottstown region before World War I. Some were immigrants from western Ukraine, and others came from the anthracite mining areas of Pennsylvania. In 1935, they built their own church. The photograph shows the pontifical blessing of St. Michael the Archangel UCC in 1937 by Bishop Constantine (Bohachevsky).

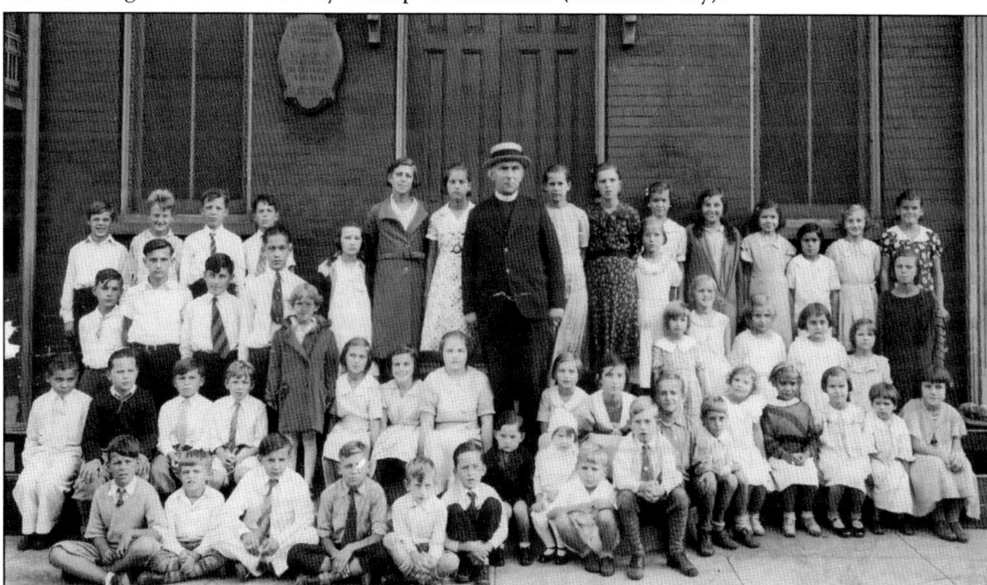

Nativity BVM UCC in Reading was organized in 1906. During his short term as pastor, Rev. Jacob DeBour (standing in center) started a school. The plaque on the building identifies it as Ukrainian and a Catholic church. The photograph is of the 1933–1935 classes.

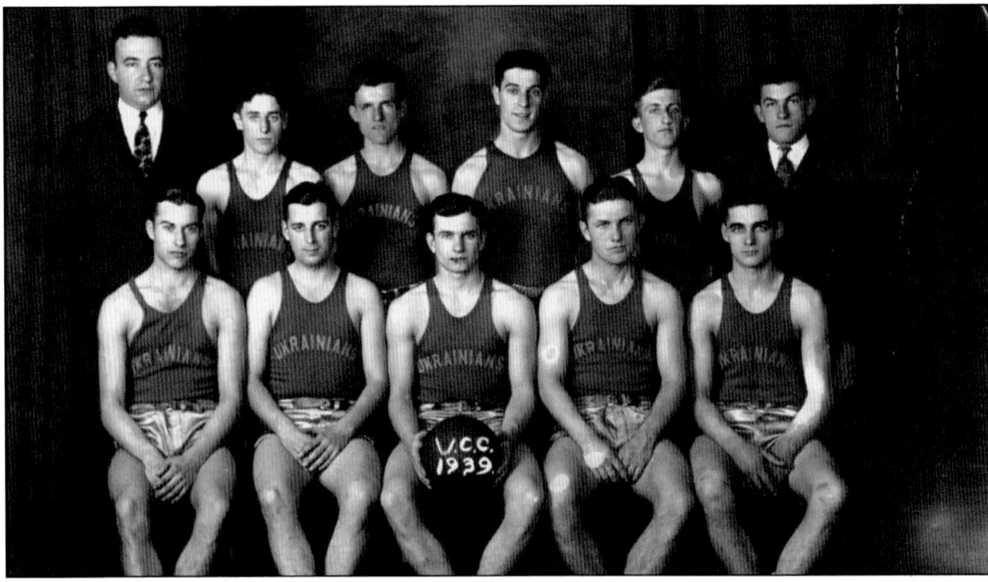

SS. Peter and Paul UOC was very active. At first, it was housed at UNH with other Ukrainian organizations in Wilmington. Among them were the choir Dnipro under the direction of Alexander Kolisnychenko, which also performed on radio; Ukrainian Citizens' Club; Sisterhood of St. Ann; Ukrainian National Aid Association (UNAA) Branch 151 Blessed Virgin Mary Sisterhood; UNAA Branch 152 Ivan Franko Brotherhood; Sunday school; and the Ukrainian basketball team seen above.

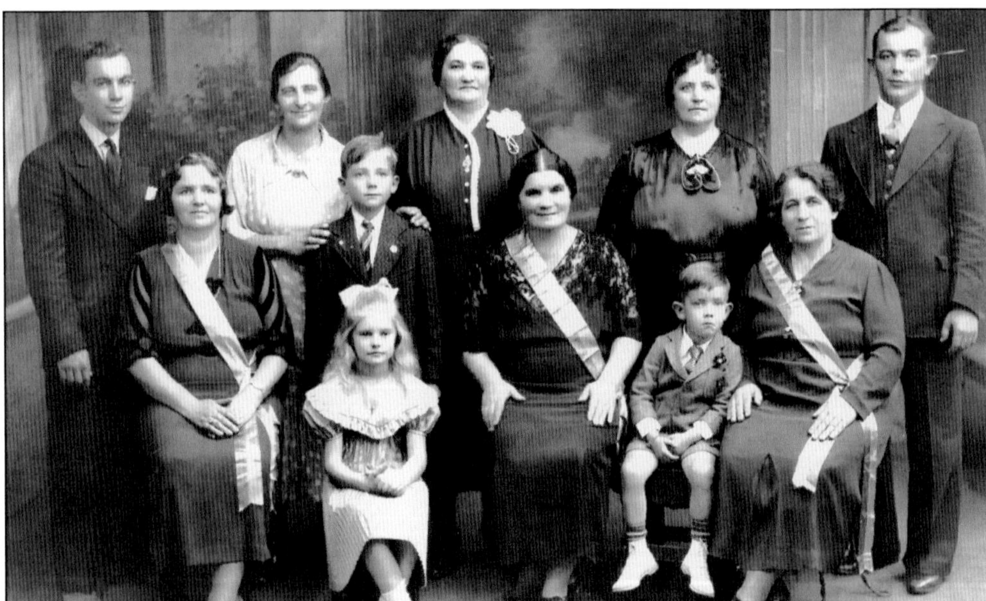

Organized as St. Olga's Sisterhood in Wilmington in 1924, they joined Providence Branch 167 as St. Olga's Society. They worked to help St. Nicholas UCC. Members in 1938 are, from left to right, (first row) Ludwyga Saletska, Doris Luczyszyn, Anna Baran, unknown, and Elizabeth Kuchapska; (second row) Walter Baran, Rosalia Cerkownuk, unidentified, Catherine Marushchak, Anna Luczyszyn, and Stephan Baran.

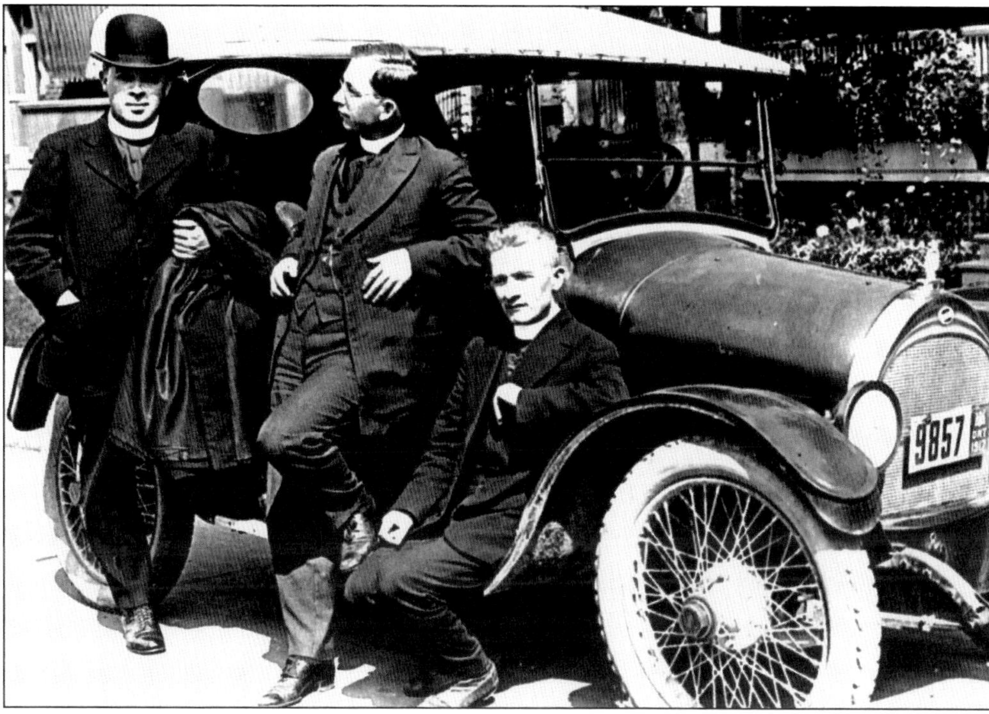

In the early days, the clergy who served Ukrainian immigrant communities could be described more accurately as missionaries rather than pastors of single churches. The priests seen in the photograph administered, at one time or another, the church communities in Wilmington and Chester. From left to right are Revs. Anthony Lotowycz, Joseph Boyarchuk, and Vladimir Derzyruka.

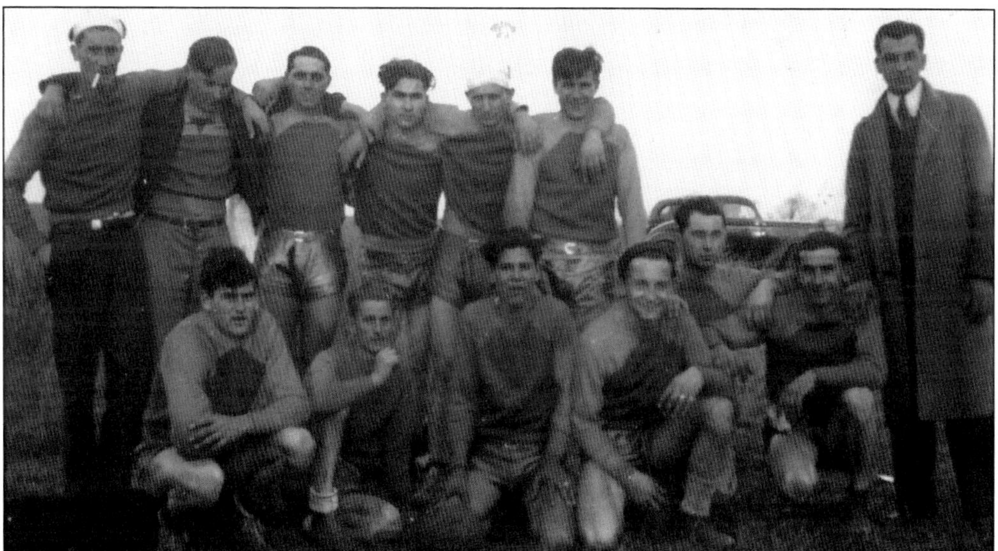

Soccer was the sport of Ukrainians in the United States, especially in the Chesapeake City area. Above is the 1939 St. Basil's UCC soccer team; from left to right are (first row) Michael Schagala, Peter Barahura, Edward Losten, Paul Arkatin, Roman Chicosky, Joseph Chicosky, and Michael Blendy; (second row) Samuel Ortinski, John Motowylak, Walter Loburk, John Luzetsky, Michael Hrabec, and Walter Chicosky.

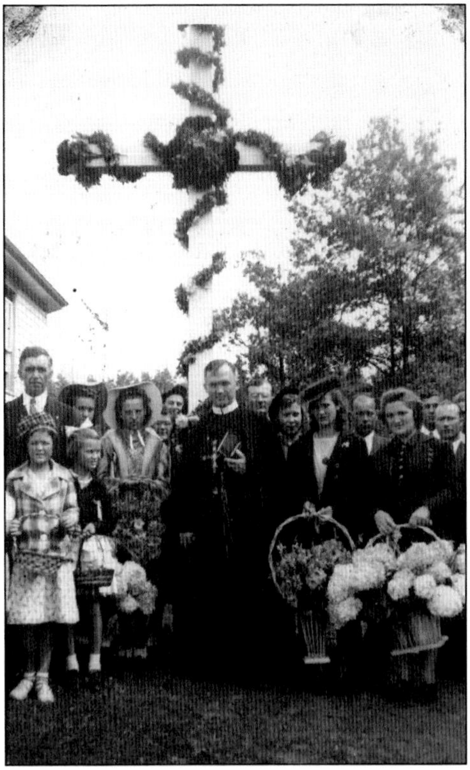

Annual missions were common before Easter. Most of the time missionaries of the Order of St. Basil the Great (OSBM) were called upon to conduct these three- or seven-day missions. Sometimes these missionary priests were able to stay longer in parishes that did not have residing priests performing pastoral duties. On Easter Sunday in 1940, at SS. Peter and Paul UCC in Williamstown, parishioners pose with Rev. Mykola Kohut, OSBM, beneath the decorated cross.

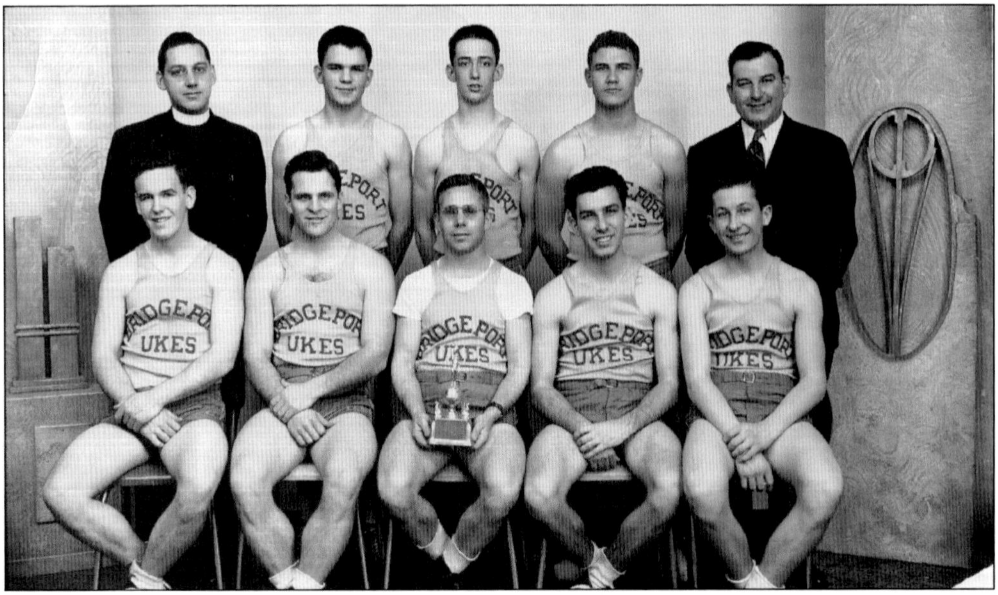

By the late 1930s, most Ukrainian communities formed basketball teams, especially if there was a UNH nearby. There was keen rivalry among the teams, and the winner of these playoffs was awarded a trophy. Bridgeport Ukes, the championship team of 1939, are, from left to right, (first row) Frank Brady, Harry Spangler, Andrew Ottaviano, George Homa Sr., and George Dudas; (second row) Rev. Basil Sheremeta (pastor of SS. Peter and Paul UCC and team sponsor), John Skemar, Eugene Yoder, Joseph Mardi, and coach Steven Homa.

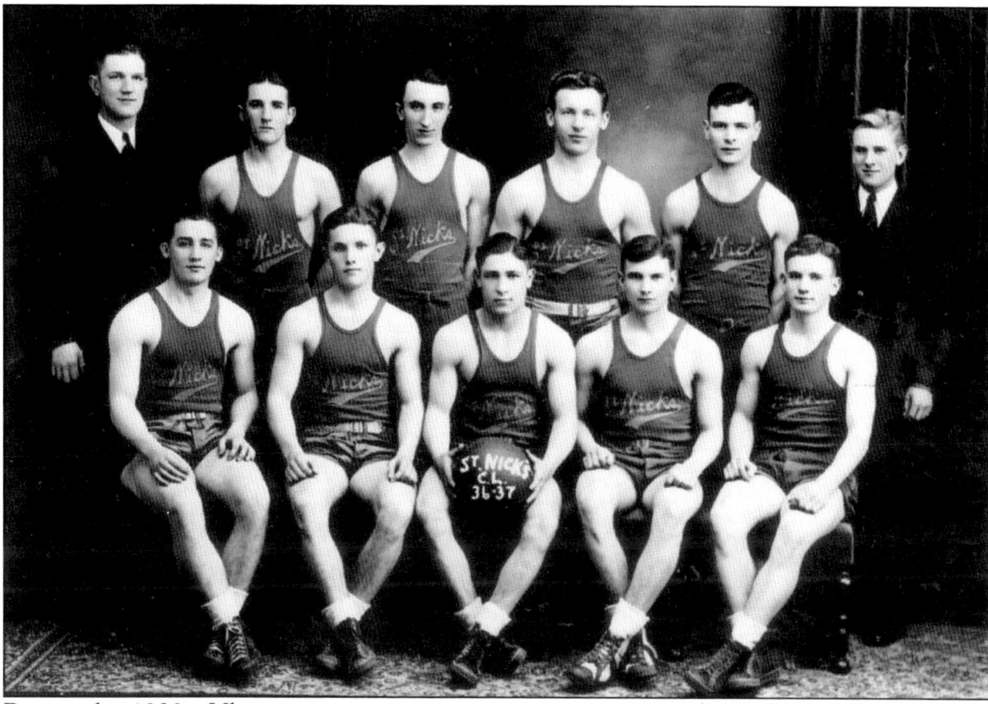

During the 1930s, Ukrainian community sports teams competed against each other as well as various ethnic opponents. This St. Nicholas UCC basketball team, pictured during the 1936–1937 season, brought home several championships to Wilmington.

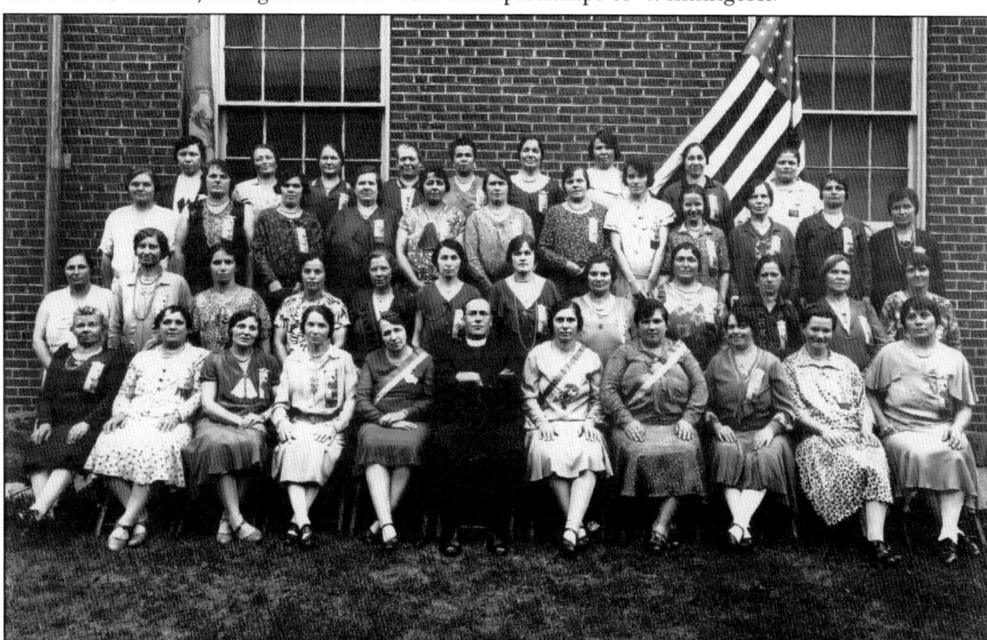

Sisterhood of Blessed Virgin Mary, UNAA Branch 151, mostly Orthodox fraternal organization, was active in Wilmington especially in humanitarian aid to fellow parishioners. The 1938 group was photographed in front of UNH.

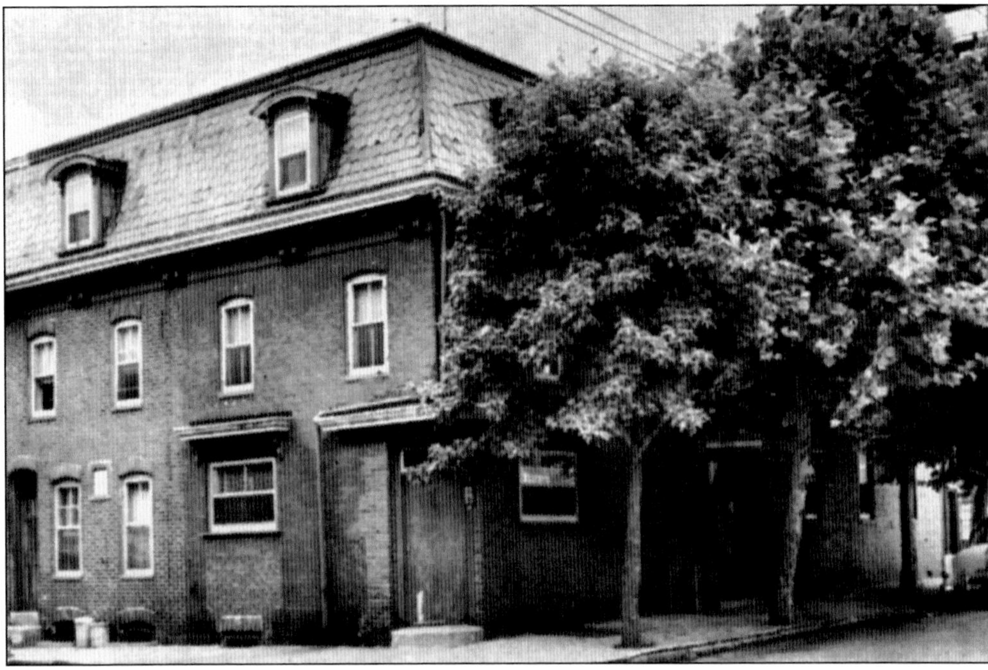

There were two UNA Homes in Chester. One was on the east end and the other on the west end. The East End Home (above), bought in 1938 by UNA Branch 156, was used for various social activities. It was also the headquarters of American Ukrainian League and Soyuz Ukrainok Chapter 15.

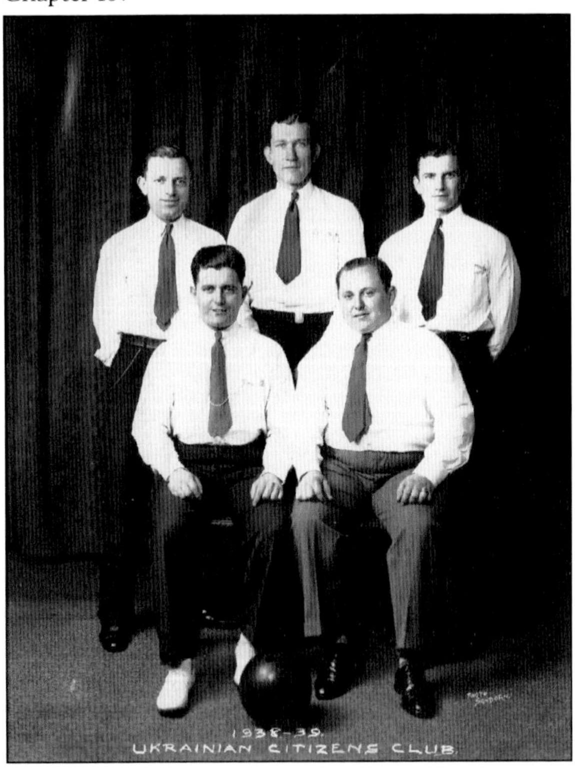

Ukrainian Citizens Club of Wilmington, affiliated with SS. Peter and Paul UOC, began behind the church in a house converted into a hall. Dances were held four times a year. Later they moved to the church hall, then to UNH. They competed in many sports. The 1938–1939 bowling team is pictured. They also had an excellent basketball team, and after World War II, they were one of the best baseball teams with members from Ukrainian Orthodox and Catholic churches.

A characteristic of Ukrainians is their love of singing. The Ukrainian Hillbillies of St. Basil's UCC performed at various social functions in and around Chesapeake City. The group in 1940 included Michael Blendy, Nicholas Waclawsky, John Luzetsky, Paul Arkatin, and John Motowylak. Their repertoire included, besides country-and-western music, Ukrainian folk songs.

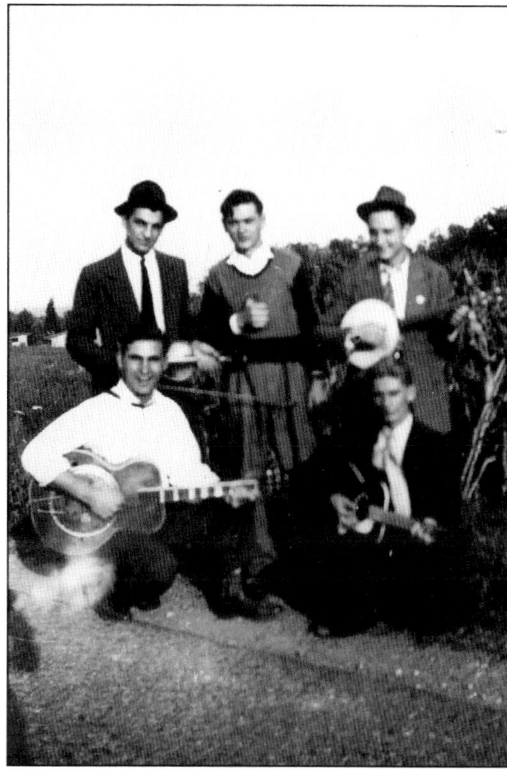

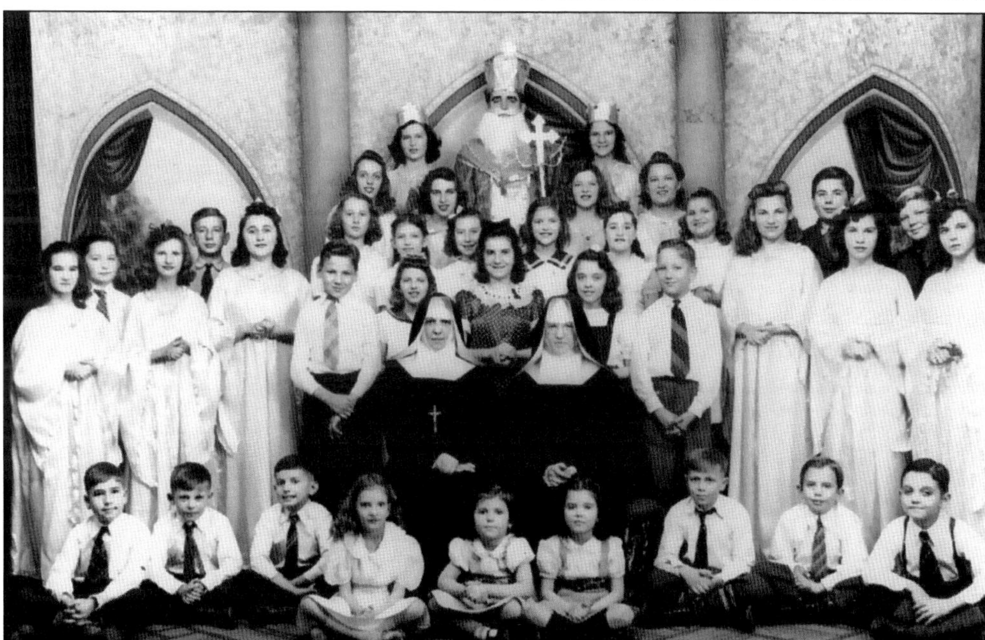

The feast of St. Nicholas is annually celebrated with a pageant that retells the story of his life. At the conclusion of the play, with angels as helpers, St. Nicholas distributes gifts to the deserving. Sisters Anisia and Oksana, who produced the 1941 show, are in the center. The Sisters of St. Basil the Great taught evening classes at Nativity UCC in Reading.

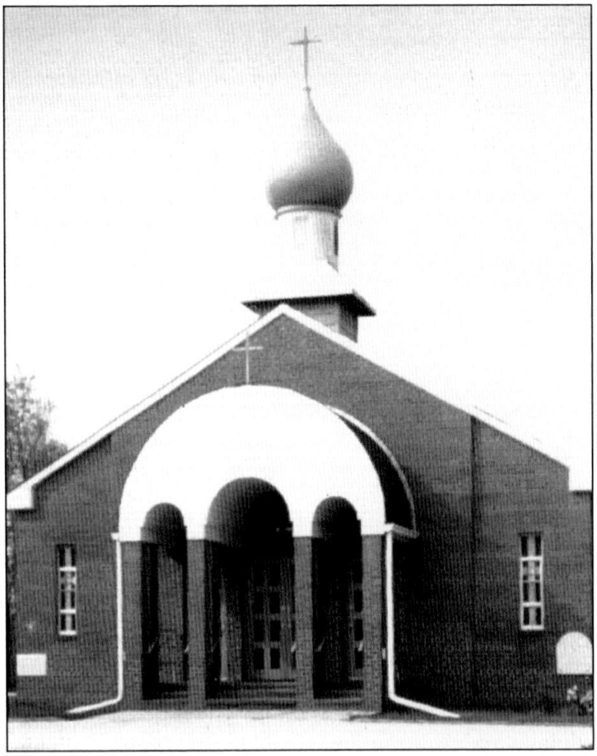

Ukrainians from northern New Jersey and New York who were unable to return to the old country because of World War I started the community of Williamstown in 1915. Unhappy with their previous work, they decided upon farming and chose the area around Cecil and Williamstown. There they founded SS. Peter and Paul UCC and various community societies. A new church was built in 1970.

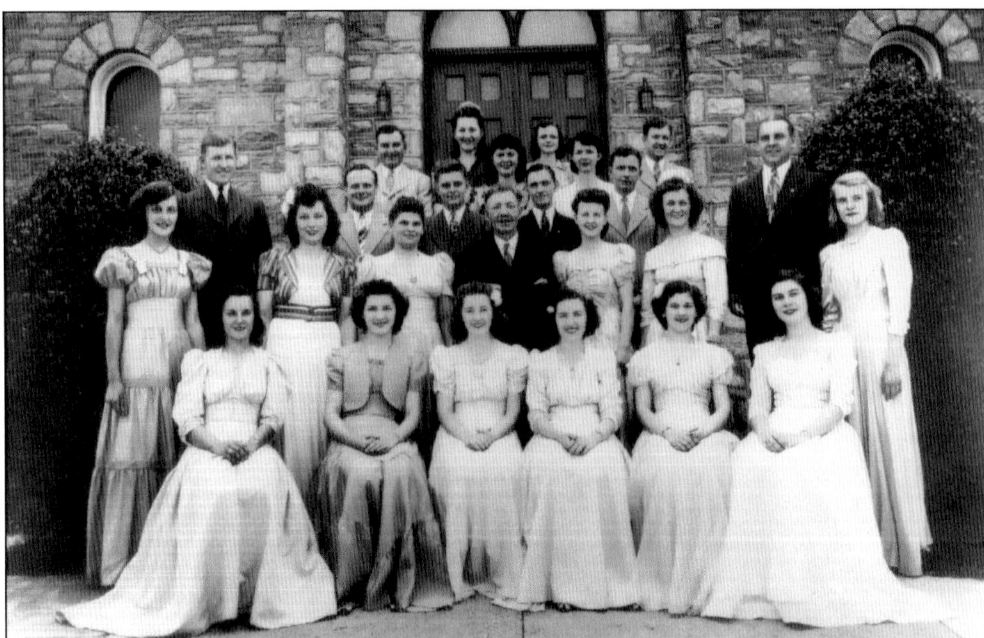

Peter Martyniuk (second row, center) poses with his "War Choir" at SS. Peter and Paul UCC in Bridgeport in the early 1940s. It was so named because so many choir members served in the U.S. armed forces during World War II.

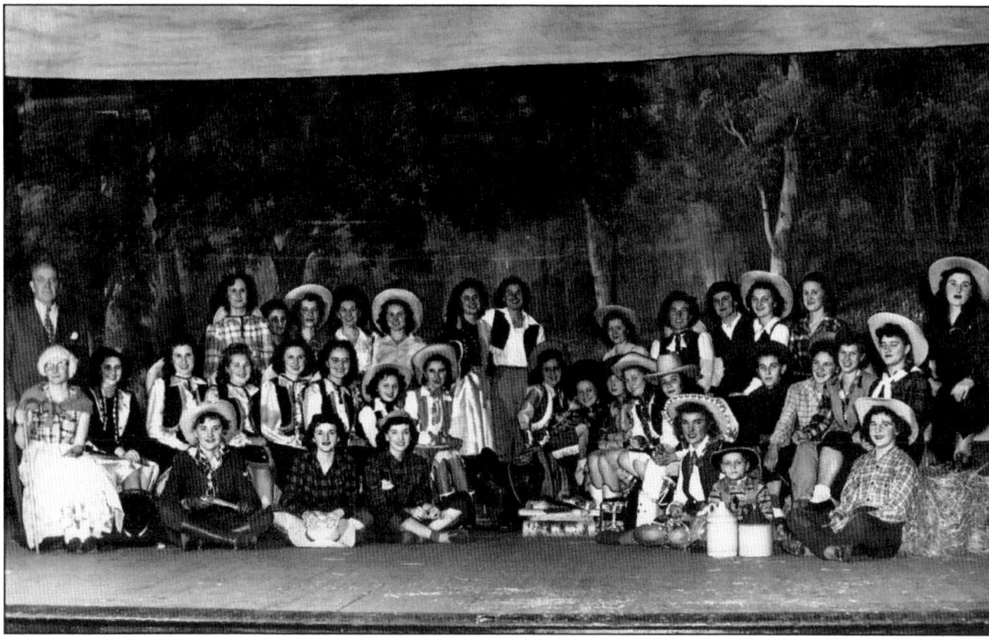

During World War II, women of the various Ukrainian organizations in Chester joined forces and became especially active. They staged plays and musicals to lift the wartime moral. In 1942, one of the annual productions that they staged was the *Last Roundup*.

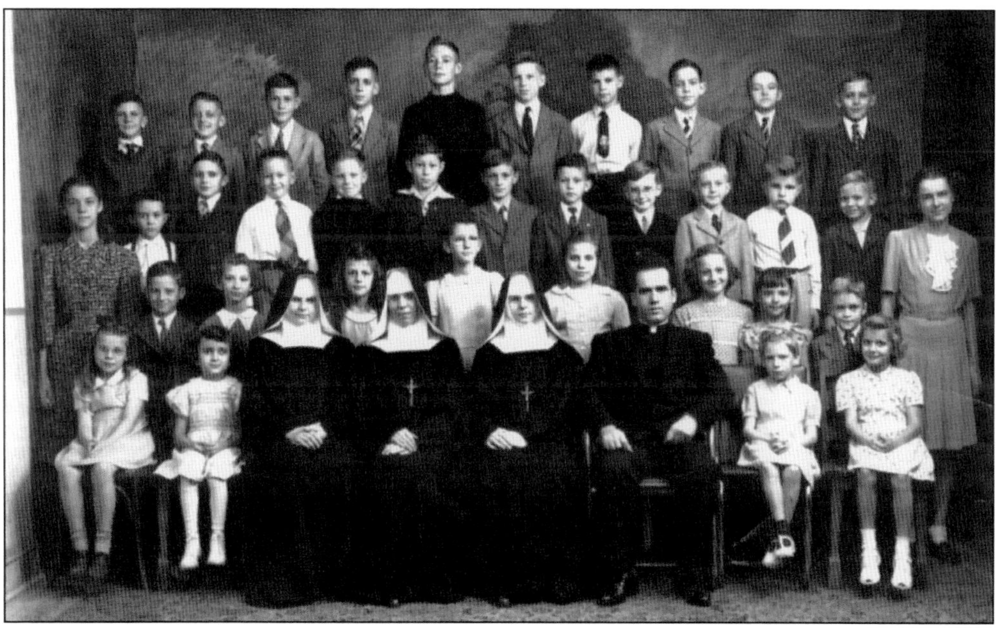

Ukrainian parochial schools began with the Sisters of St. Basil the Great. Lay teachers were added in specific areas. Gradually, as the number of vocations declined or the sisters saw the need for other work, the lay faculty increased. In the end, it was the lay personnel that not only administered the schools but also made up the faculty. In this 1942–1944 Chester's Holy Ghost Parochial School photograph, the adults are, from left to right, Sisters Dorothy, Dominica, and Neonilia, and Rev. Walter Bilynsky, the pastor.

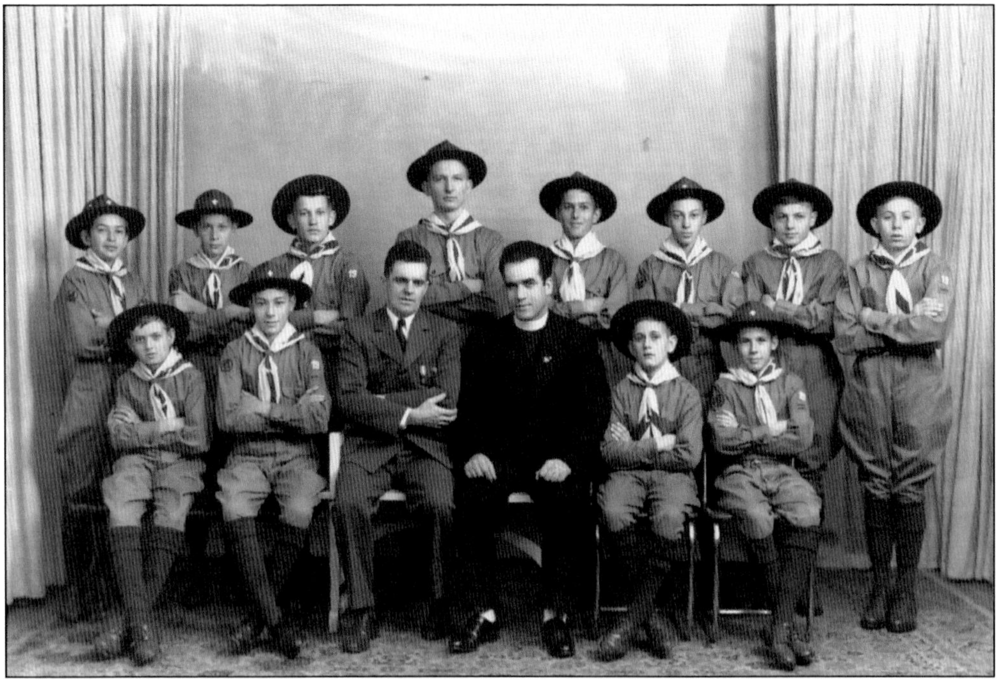

In 1942, Rev. Walter Bilynsky was transferred to Holy Ghost UCC in Chester. He saw the need for after-school activities for the youth. At his request, Gren Day organized the Boy Scouts of America Troop 19 in 1943. In the photograph, third from left, is Day, and next to him is Reverend Bilynsky.

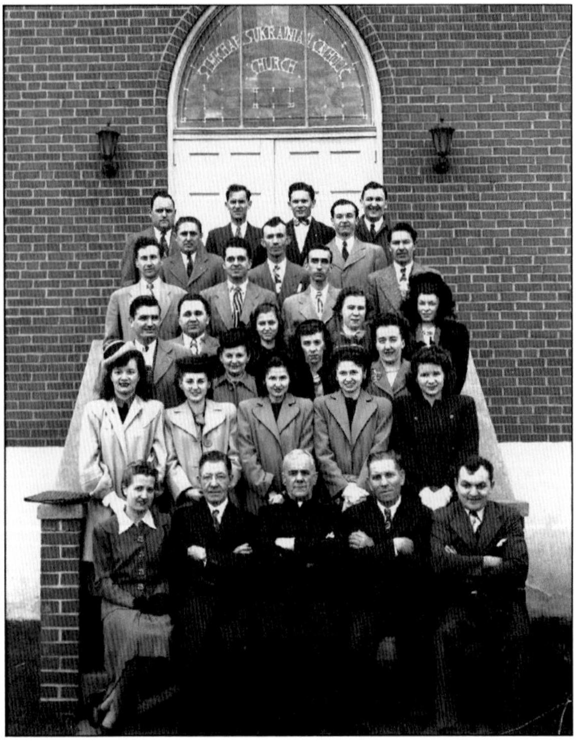

St. Michaels UCC choir in Pottstown was invigorated with the arrival of DPs into the area. Peter Martyniuk of Bridgeport was the choir organizer and director. The group poses happily in front of its church in 1948. Sitting second from left is Martyniuk, and to his right is Rev. Nicholas Baranetsky, the pastor.

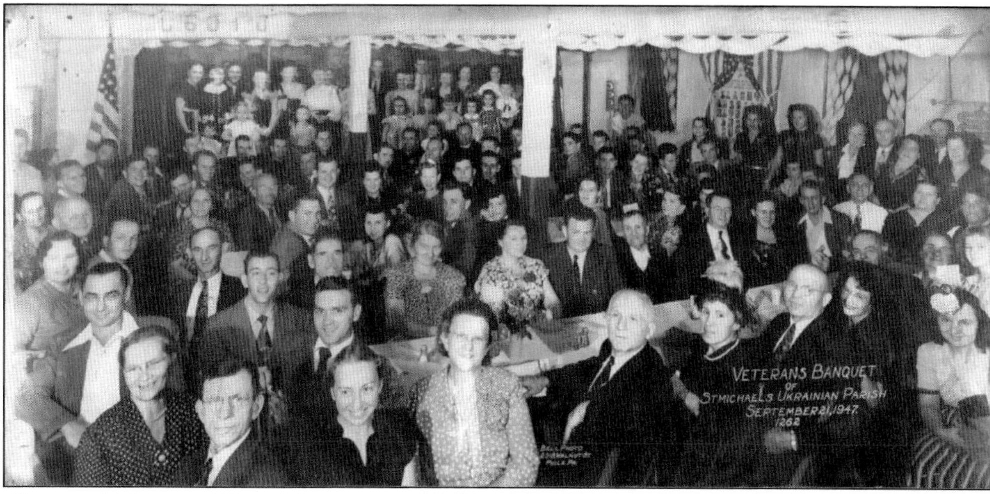

This is a "Welcome Home" banquet in 1947 for servicemen of St. Michael's UCC in Camden who served in the U.S. armed forces during World War II. The parish children who had performed are onstage behind the clergy.

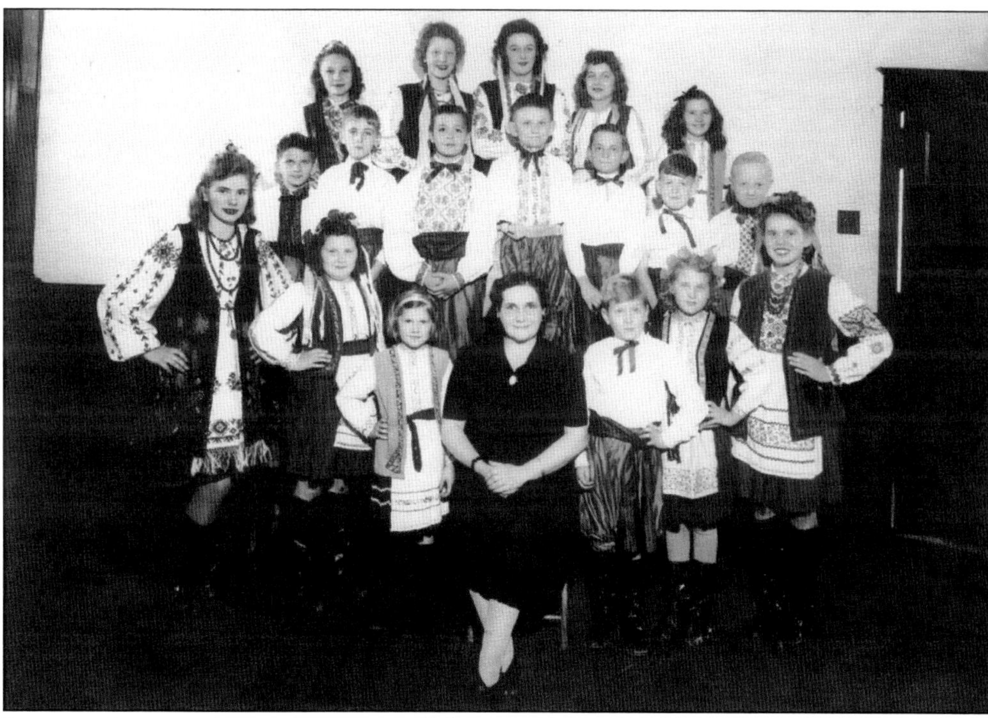

Between the wars, the primary source of Ukrainian heritage education was the evening classes held at the local parish. This was part of the Ukrainian heritage school system. Stephania Ulanitsky, wife of Rev. Antonin Ulanitsky, pastor of St. Josephat's UCC in Frankford, besides other heritage courses, instructed the group in Ukrainian singing and dancing in the 1940s.

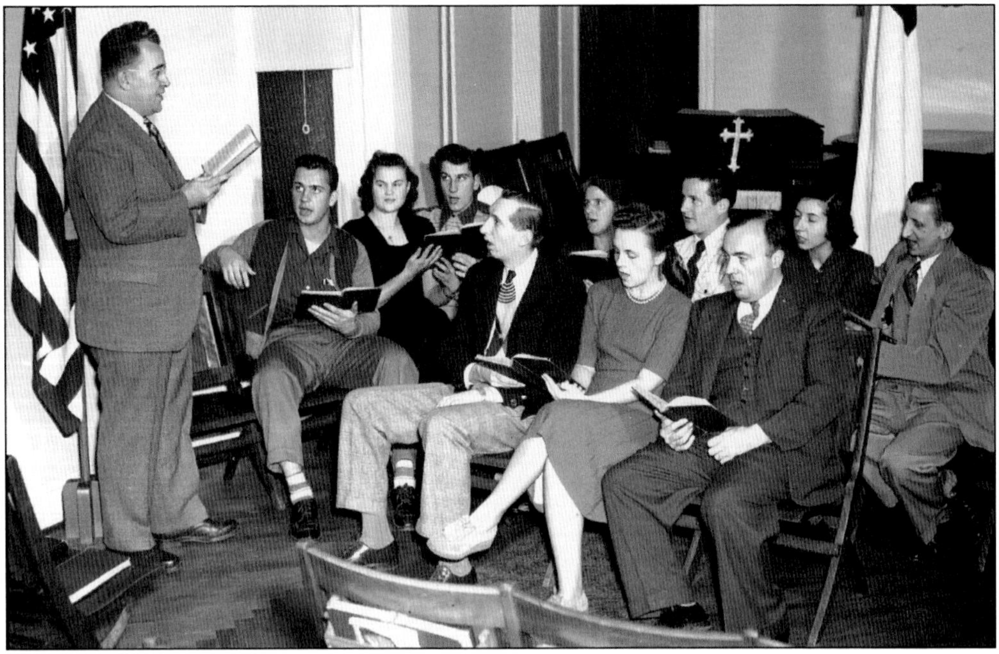

Singing is the highest form of venerating the Lord. Traditionally prayers are sung in the House of Prayer of the Ukrainian Baptists. Brother Constantine Lemcio is conducting choir rehearsals in 1948 in Chester.

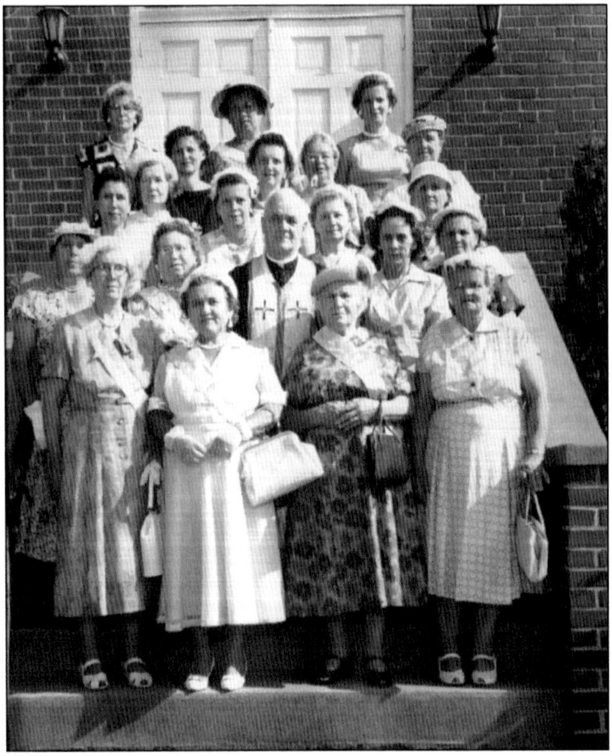

Pottstown community life centers about the church. During a mission in 1938, the Apostleship of Prayer was organized. This group organizes special church breakfasts or dinners, and they make *pyrohy*. All profits from these functions go toward the needs of the church. During its long history, the parish in Pottstown shared a priest either with Reading or Bridgeport. Rev. Nicholas Baranetsky (second row, center), himself a DP, was the first resident priest and is photographed with members of the Apostleship of Prayer in the early 1950s.

Three

IN PURSUIT OF HAPPINESS

In the worldwide struggle to preserve Western Christian civilization, Americans need Ukrainian friends who are concerned with America's problems, for many Ukrainian immigrants are related to Americans by blood.
—Rev. Isadore Nahayewsky, Phoenixville

After World War II, Ukrainians arrived by the thousands in Delaware Valley under the Displaced Persons Act, requiring sponsors to vouch for refugees until they found employment. Sponsors were not hard to find, especially in the Ukrainian communities of Chester, Bridgeport, Frankford, Phoenixville, Pottstown, and Reading, Pennsylvania, and Camden and Millville, New Jersey. Numerous industries were located in these areas, and farm work was available in Millville. The headquarters of the United Ukrainian American Relief Committee (UUARC) was in Philadelphia, leading many refugees to temporarily settle there and in port cities such as New York, Boston, and Baltimore.

In one fell swoop, existing fraternal, social, and cultural institutions doubled in size. However, many of the newly exiled Ukrainians, already overstressed by their war experiences, were unable to adapt to the American tempo of life. This sudden infiltration of new elements into the old Ukrainian diaspora way of life, especially in regard to language, caused much unfortunate friction and often ended in the establishment of separate institutions. The Catholic Church was the first to experience dilemmas because existing church buildings became too small, and the influx of Ukrainian-speaking priests arriving with the refugees were unable to preach in English. These scenarios were multiplied in youth organizations, schools, reading rooms, fraternal lodges, and other institutions almost all affiliated with local churches.

On the national level, diversity continued to rule the Delaware Valley's Ukrainian communities, as Ukrainians were isolated from the East European political arena. The "old immigrants," as they were referred to, were still not fully cognizant of their own nationality, whereas the newcomers, because of their experiences as displaced persons living in European camps after the war, were nationally conscious Ukrainians. The newcomers never fully comprehended the older Ukrainians' identity crisis, alienating many forever.

Nevertheless, old Ukrainian communities flourished, and new ones were founded. With the easy availability of cars, younger newcomers decided that living in Ukrainian communities in industrial centers was too stressful and established communities in New Jersey's Cherry Hill and Pennsylvania's Bristol, Melrose Park, Jenkintown, and Warrington. Perhaps their greatest accomplishment was their dedication to fostering and promulgating all Ukrainian traditions in any way they could, especially establishing Ukrainian resort areas.

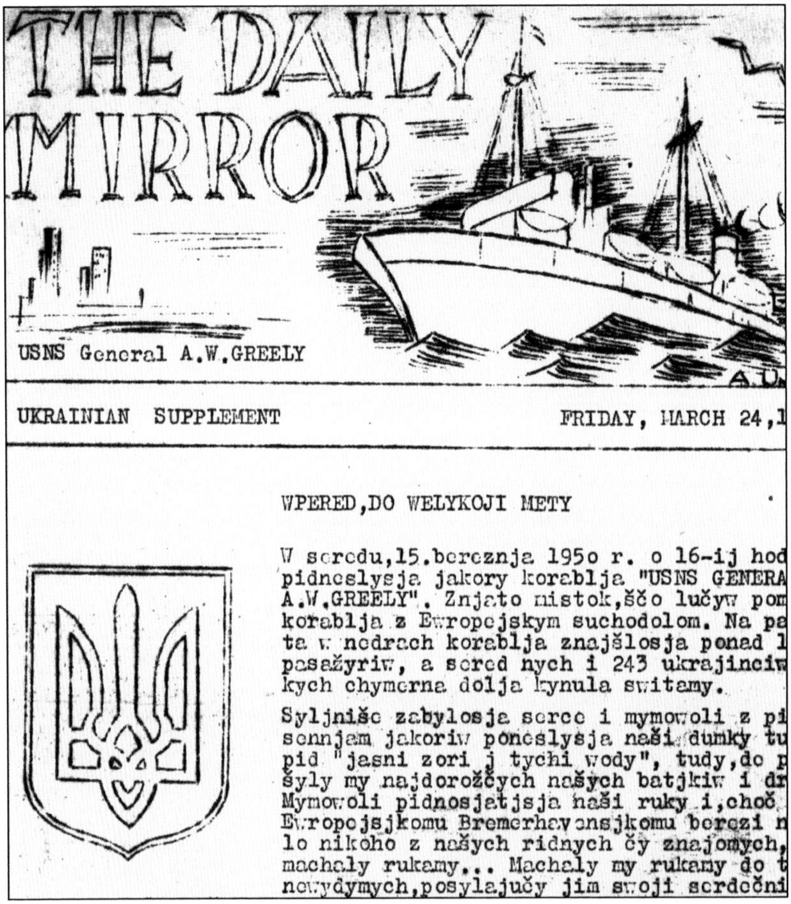

THE DAILY MIRROR

USNS General A.W.GREELY

UKRAINIAN SUPPLEMENT FRIDAY, MARCH 24,1

WPERED,DO WELYKOJI METY

W seredu,15.berecznja 195o r. o 16-ij hod
pidneslysja jakory korablja "USNS GENERA
A.W.GREELY". Znjato mistok,ščo lučyw pom
korablja z Ewropejskym suchodolom. Na pa
ta w nedrach korablja znajšlosja ponad 1
pasažyriw, a sered nych i 243 ukrajinciw
kych chymerna dolja kynula switamy.

Syljniše zabylosja serce i mymowoli z pi
sennjam jakoriw ponesly̌sja naši dumky tu
pid "jasni zori j tychi wody", tudy,do p
šyly my najdorožčych našych batjkiw i dr
Mymowoli pidnosjatjsja naši ruky i,choč
Ewropejsjkomu Bremerhawensjkomu berezi n
lo nikoho z našych ridnych čy znajomych,
machaly rukamy... Machaly my rukamy do t
newydymych,posylajučy jim swoji serdečni

On some of the American ships bringing DPs to their new homes in the United States, immigrants of all nationalities published daily newspapers in their own languages. Petro Stercho, who settled in Bridgeport, wrote one such newspaper on USNS *General A.W. Greely*, which was printed using the English alphabet recounting daily events.

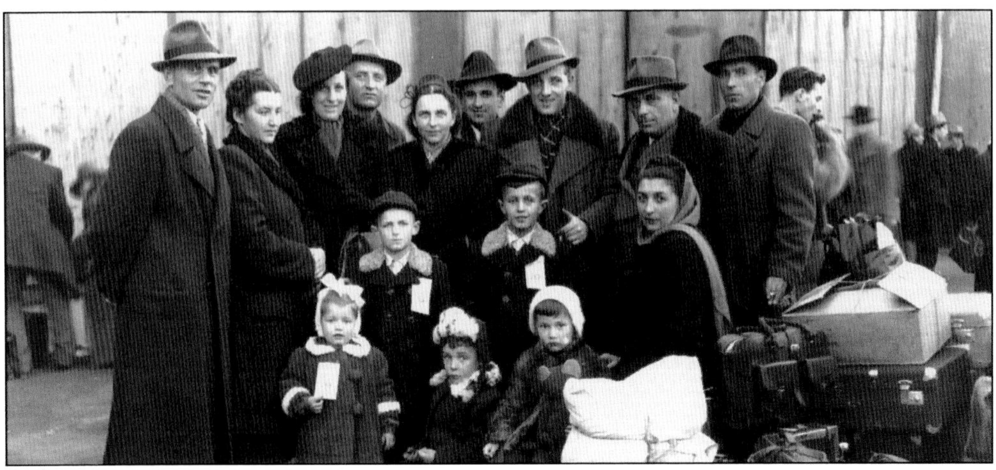

An often-repeated scene in the late 1940s and early 1950s on the streets of many port cities was the sight of refugees arriving to America happy to have reached their final destination. In the photograph are, from left to right, (first row) unidentified, unidentified, Myron Kyj, and unidentified; (second row) two unidentified children; (third row) Wasyl Kyj, Lydia Kyj, Yaroslava Kobryn, ? Melnyk. ? Melnyk, three unidentified, and Anastazij Kobryn, who have just disembarked from the USS *Haan* in 1949.

In 1944, the necessity to organize the United Ukrainian American Relief Committee (UUARC) to aid the thousands of Ukrainian DPs in Europe became obvious. The first phase of UUARC activity was to bring over 100,000 Ukrainian refugees to the United States, Canada, South America, and Australia. The second phase was to settle them here and to help those who remained in Europe. The smiling face of the new arrival in 1949 belongs to Larissa Lozynska of Wallingford.

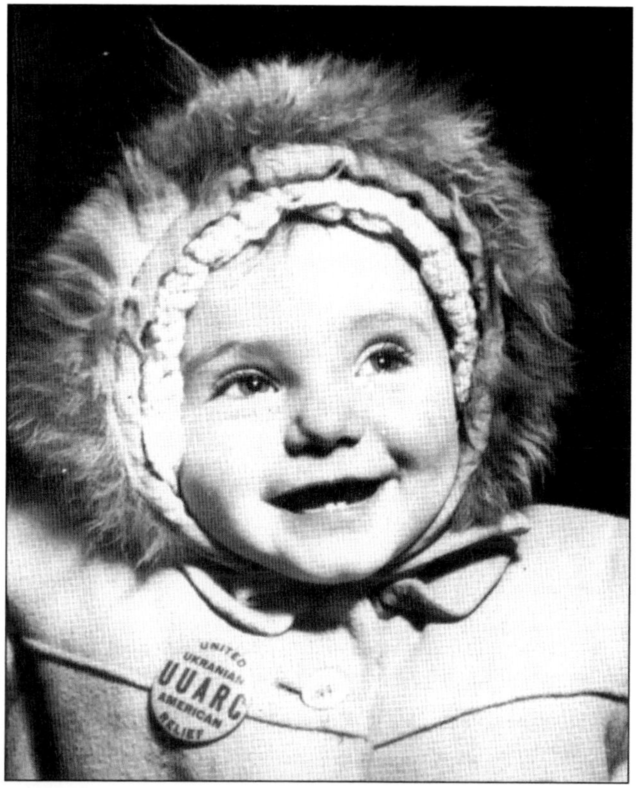

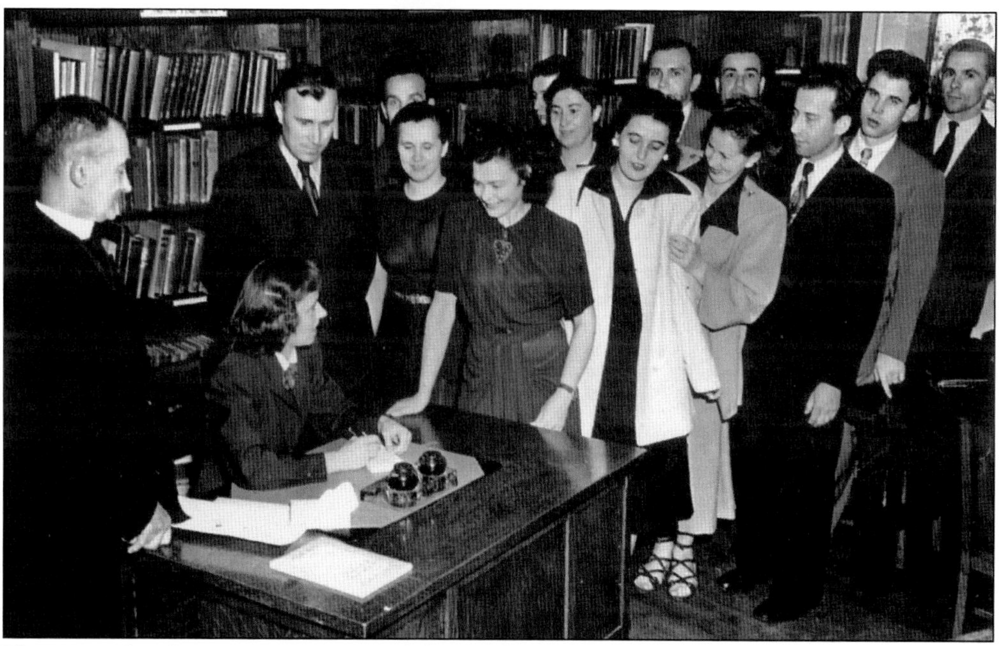

The arrival of so many non-English speakers necessitated the creation of evening English-language and citizenship courses throughout the Ukrainian communities. Signing up to learn are some members of the Wilmington community. Rev. Alexander Ulitsky is on the left, and sitting at the desk is teacher Mary Bukay.

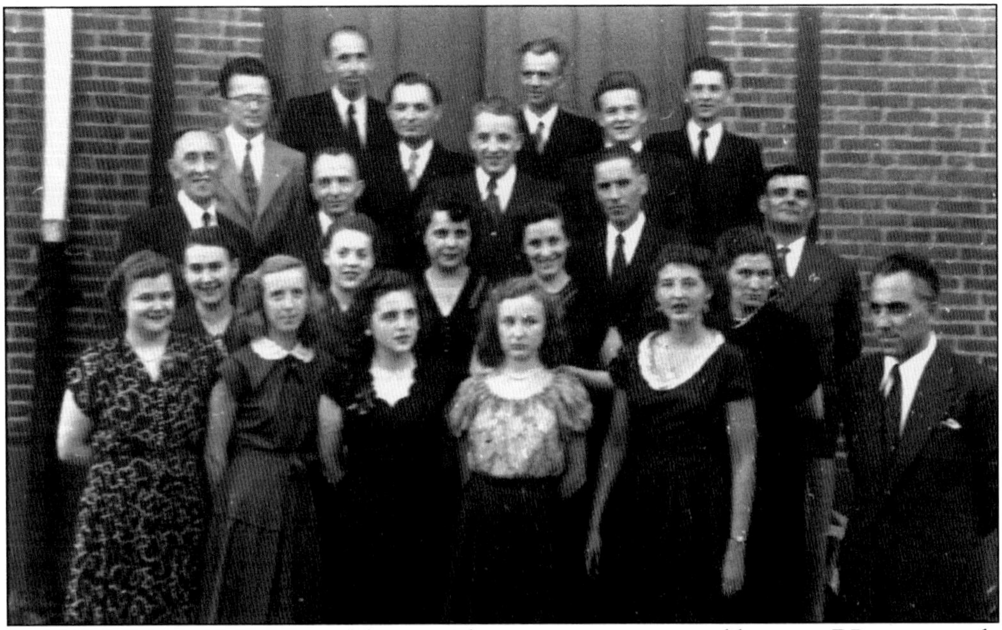

The new arrivals were a resourceful group. Their war experiences and living in DP camps made them adaptable to their new life. They formed Holy Ghost UCC Choir in Chester, under the leadership of Wolodymyr Korchynsky, illustrating that they already comprehended the importance of advertising. The postcard is from 1949.

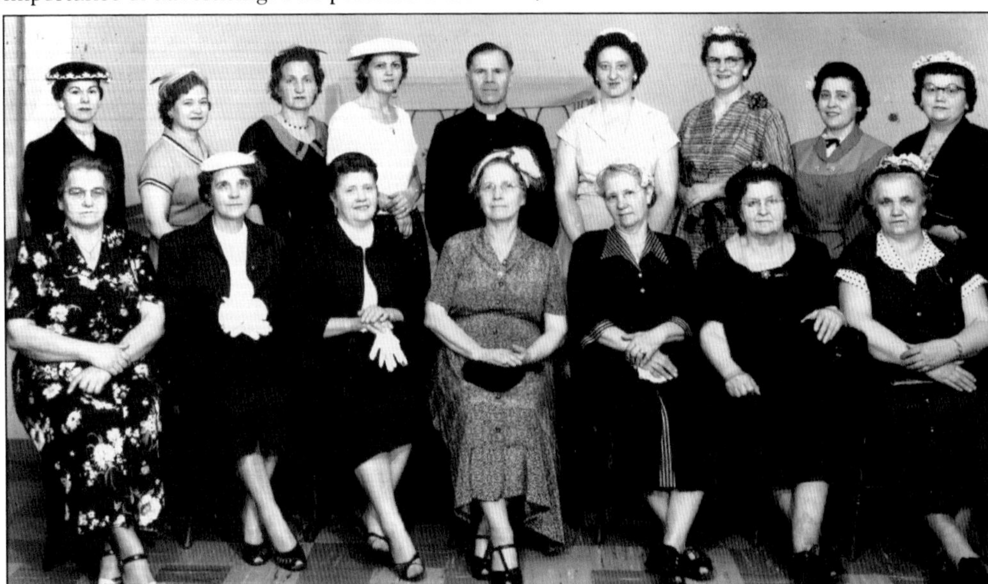

The ladies who make pyrohy sold for the upkeep of the church are the financial backbone of every parish. This Ukrainian tidbit of potatoes and cheese stuffed into dough and cooked is the beloved food of many. From left to right are (first row) Anastasia Senishen, Mary Stremba, Julia Senishen, Xenia Jurasinska, Stella Duda, Eva Tacyn, and Mary Kilyk; (second row) Sophie Wloczewski, Anna Tacyn, Anna Pawlyk, Josephine Valgus, Rev. Wolodymyr Kowal, Anna Weber, Anna Katriniak, Mary Yedynak, and Stella Phillipczak. They all belong to Nativity UCC in Reading. The photograph is from the early 1950s.

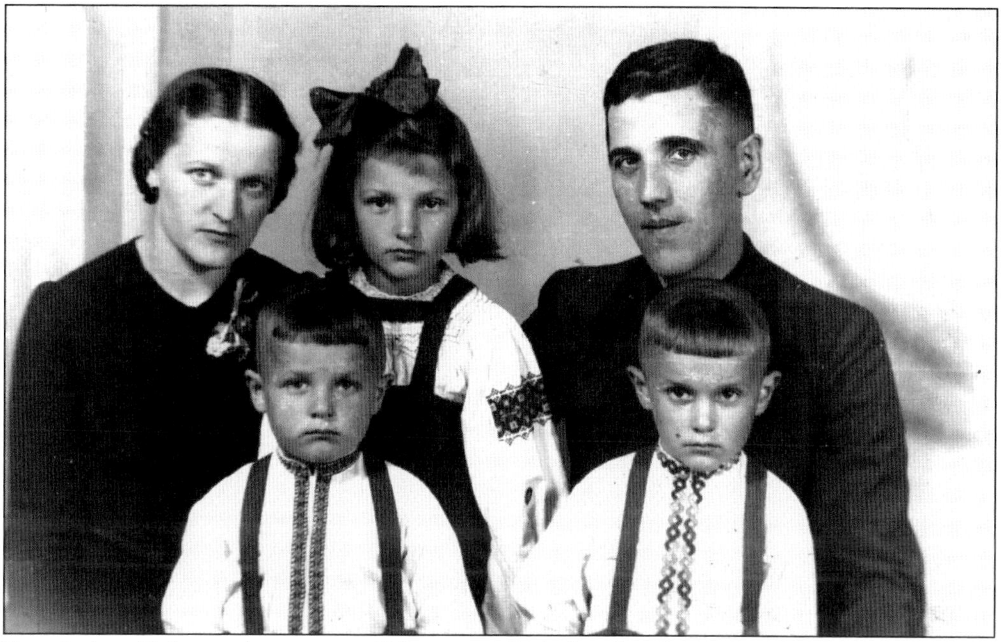

Rev. Isidore Nahayewsky, pastor of Ukrainian Catholic churches in Camden, Williamstown, and Phoenixville, was a renowned scholar, prolific writer, historian, and artist. In the family photograph are, from left to right, his wife Olha née Cependa, who fostered Ukrainian culture by organizing numerous choirs, dramatic clubs, and orchestras in the parishes where her husband served; Oleh; Irene; Reverend Isidore; and Zenon.

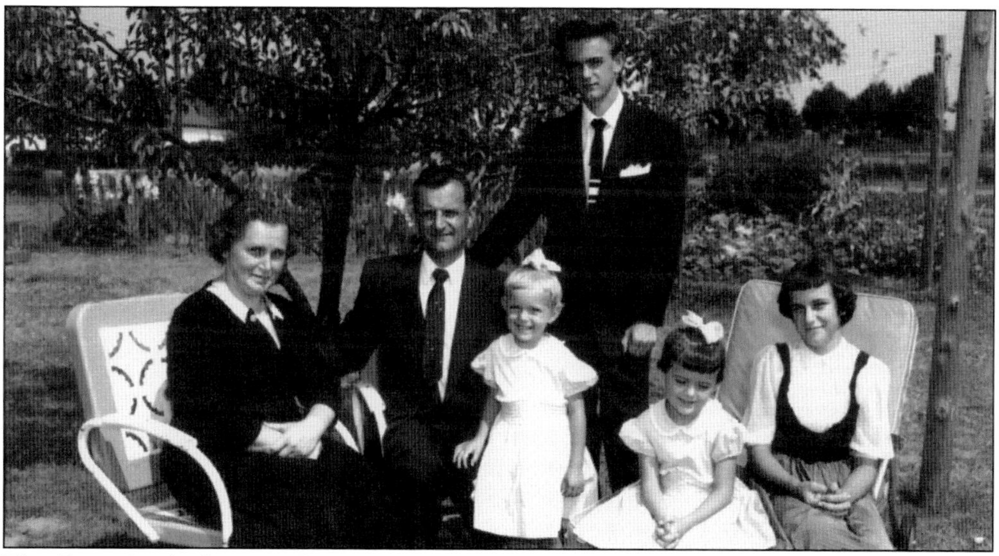

The Zguta family for over 50 years perpetuated Ukrainian culture in the Phoenixville area. Stefan Zguta, a music professor, was the choir director and cantor for 49 years at SS. Peter and Paul UCC in Phoenixville. Rev. Nicholas Baranetsky of Pottstown sponsored his family as DPs in 1949. Zguta taught future cantors in Philadelphia, and for his loyalty to the Catholic Church, he was awarded the Pro Ecclesia et Pontifice medal by Pope John Paul II in 1988. In this 1956 family photograph are, from left to right, (seated) Pauline, Stefan, (standing) Oksana, Jaroslaw (Russell), (seated) Christine, and Maria.

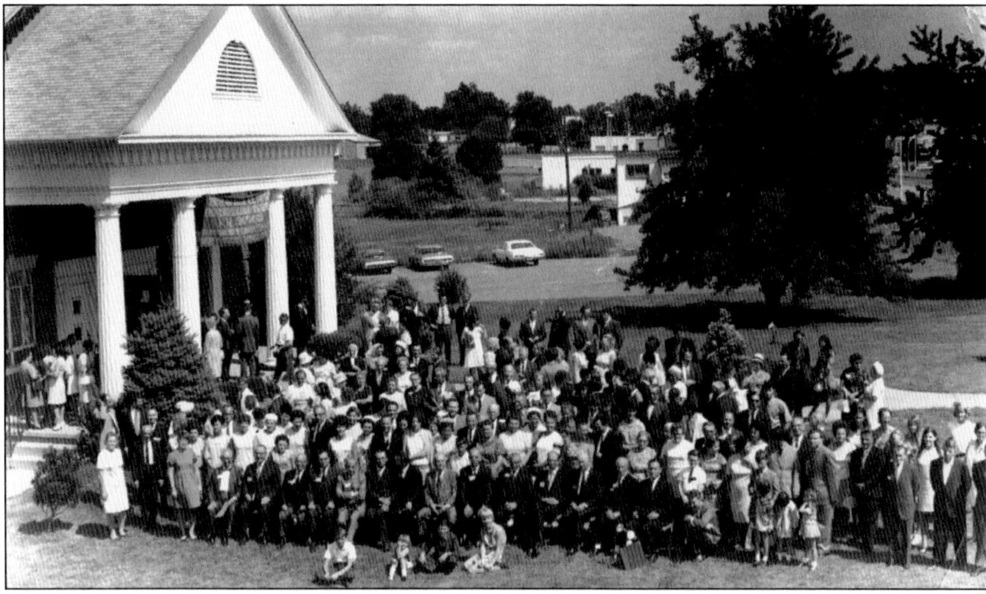

The center of the Ukrainian Baptist Society's activities shifted from Philadelphia to Chester with the arrival of post–World War II refugees. One of the first fraternal conferences was held in 1951 in Parkside, near Chester.

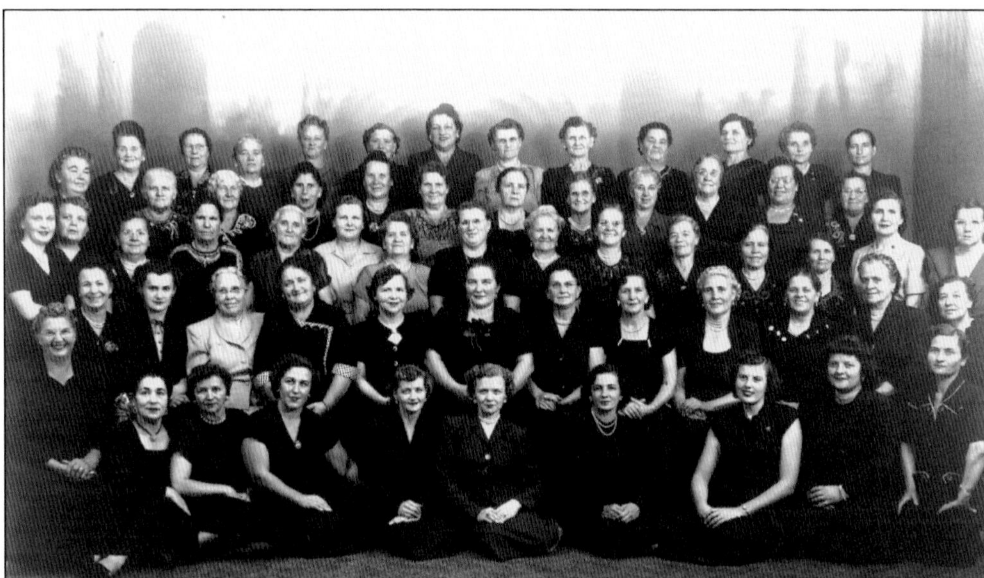

Chester's Branch 2 of Ukrainian National Women's League of America (Soyuz Ukrainok) was formed in 1927 to help Ukrainian causes. By 1937, membership increased to 87. Financially they aided the UANH and sent economic assistance to the homeland. They supported UANH and St. Mary's UOC. The 1951 membership is pictured above.

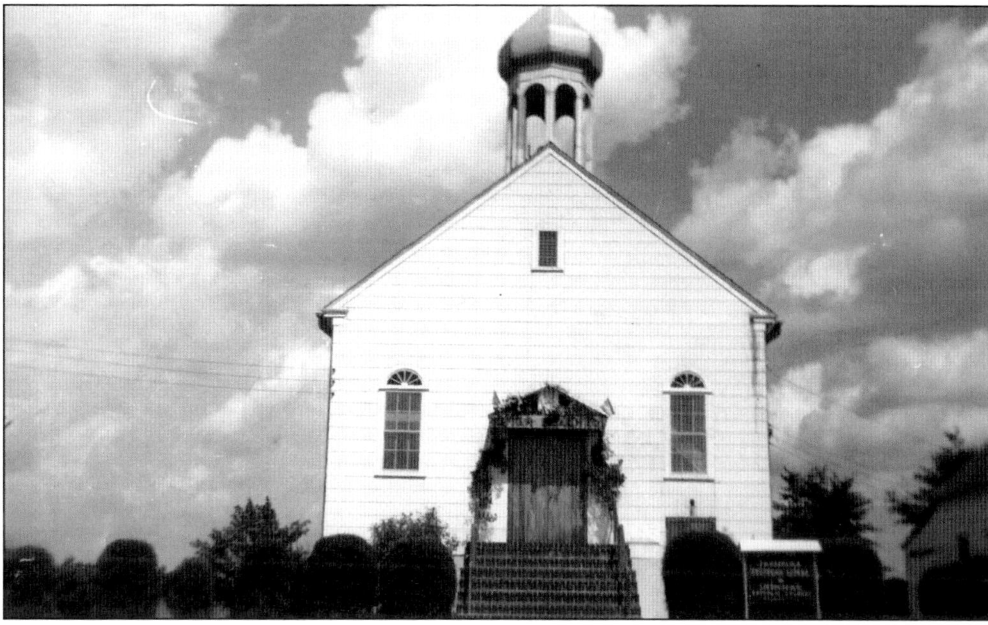

The Millville-Vineland area was farmland first settled by Ukrainians around 1910. They came from Bibka, Rohatyn, Sanyk, and Kolomya in western Ukraine. As late as the 1970s, Ukrainian newspapers still advertised farmland for sale in this area. By the 1930s, UNA was instrumental in organizing two churches: Ukrainian Catholic and Ukrainian Orthodox. In both churches, theatrical groups, choirs, reading rooms, and youth organizations were formed. At some point a national home was built. The photograph is of St. Nicholas UCC in the 1960s in Millville.

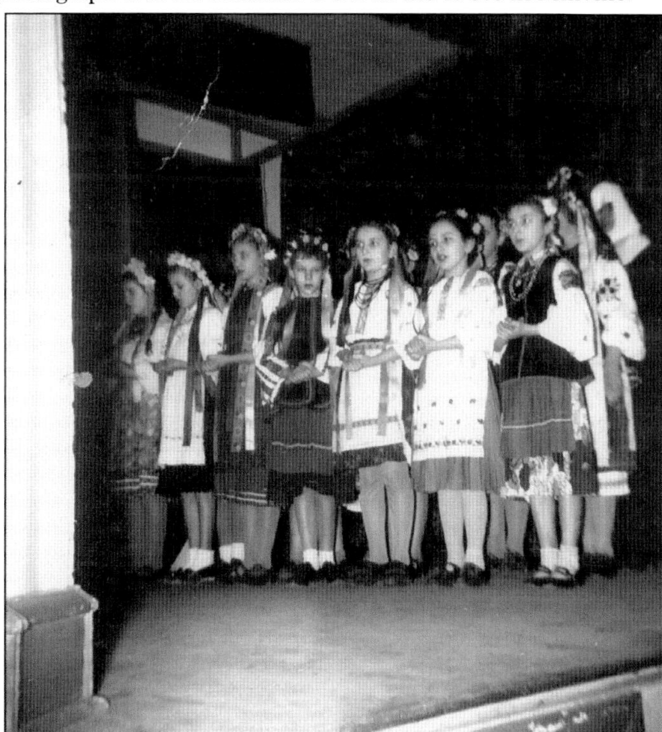

The Millville-Vineland area was energized with the arrival of the DPs preserving Ukrainian language and culture. Children attended Ukrainian Saturday schools conducted by the parishes. In 1952, schoolchildren of St. Nicholas UCC participated in a concert honoring Taras Shevchenko with their songs.

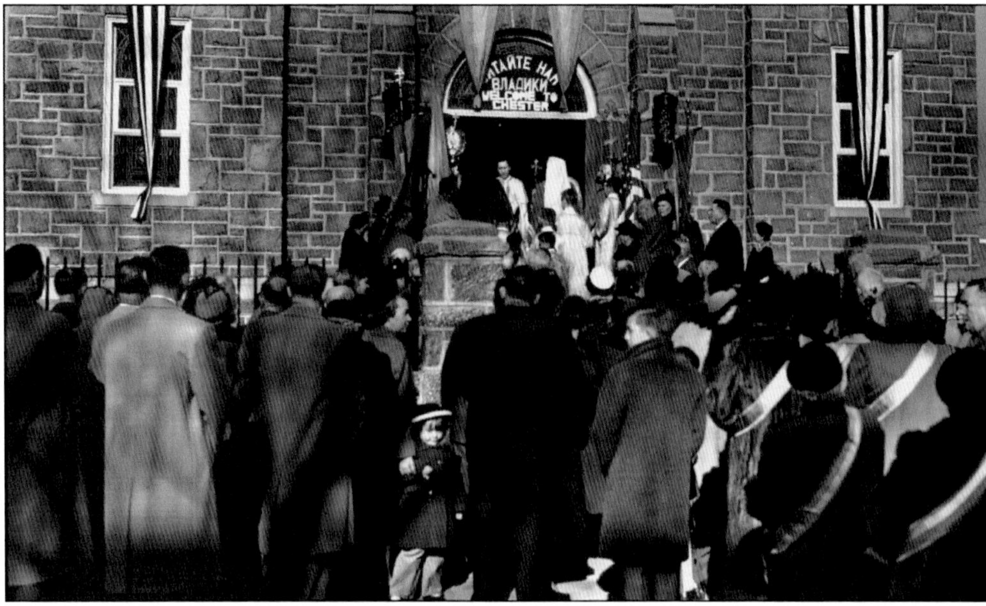

Some parishioners, believing that Holy Ghost UCC in Chester was becoming too Latinized and too Americanized, founded St. Mary's UOC in 1928. First they built the UANH, and to sustain their religious beliefs they erected a magnificent church in 1944. The Chester Orthodox community organized itself to such an extent that it became the prime force of Ukrainian national revival. The pontifical visitation of Archbishops John and Mstyslav in 1951 is seen above.

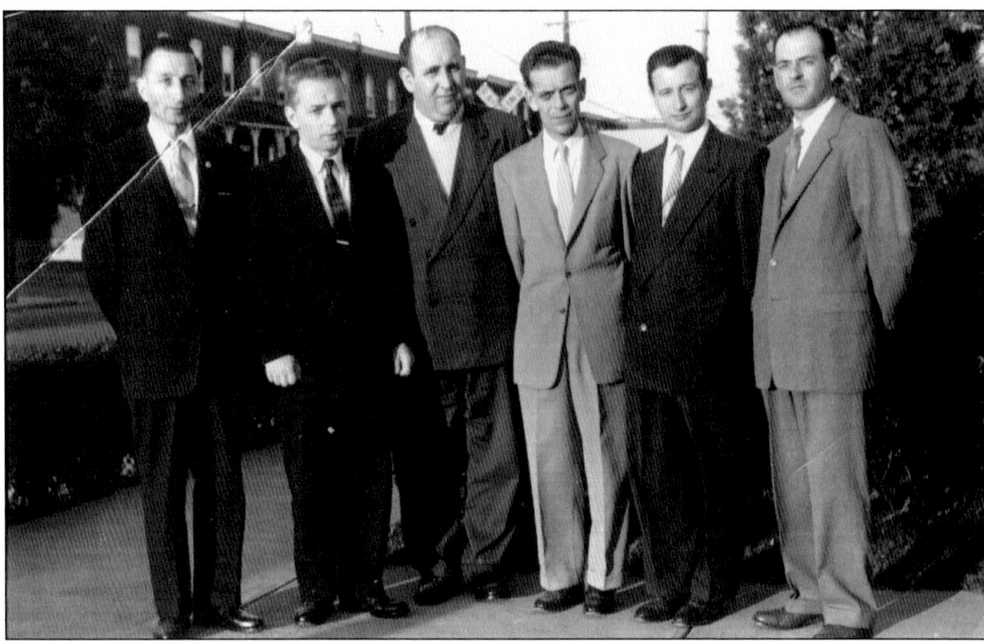

Chester, with its booming economy, attracted many talented people who upon arrival formed a self-help economic relief institution called Samopomich to aid other new arrivals. The organizers, from left to right, are Franko Hrabij, Mychajlo Mychajlewsky, Yaroslaw Tarnowsky, Omelian Rylko, Alexander Kobasa, and Yaroslaw Kushnir.

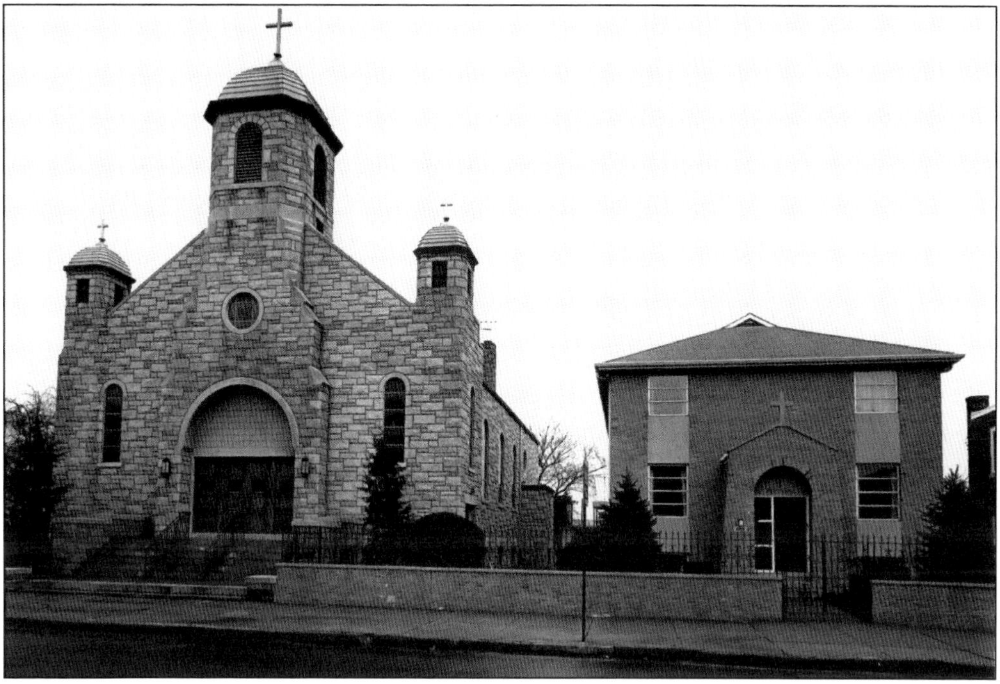

The new Holy Ghost UCC was built in 1953 and the rectory in 1969. The old rectory was remodeled and converted into the parish convent for the Sisters of St. Basil the Great who taught in the school. The old church, which was directly opposite the new, was used for choir practice, organizational meetings, and a library.

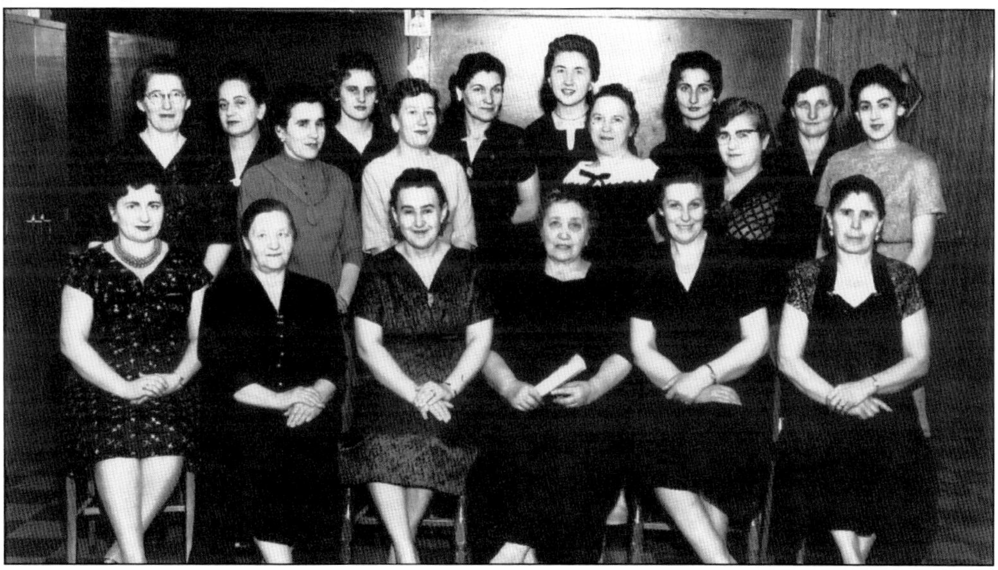

Branch 13 of Soyuz Ukrainok in Chester was organized in 1952. They supported church projects including money for scholarships and sending packages to the needy in Ukraine. From left to right are (first row) Anna Wizniak, Julia Mykyta, Yaroslava Zbyr, Natalia Mochnacka, Yaroslava Kobryn, and Eva Bijanska; (second row) Anna Mykyta, Lydia Gawdiak, Maria Rylko, Oksana Gawdiak, Anna Baszta, Evhenia Korchynska, Halyna Mykyta, Leontyna Minchak, Stefania Sarachman, Anna Minchak, Anna Sarachman, and Taisa Zbyr.

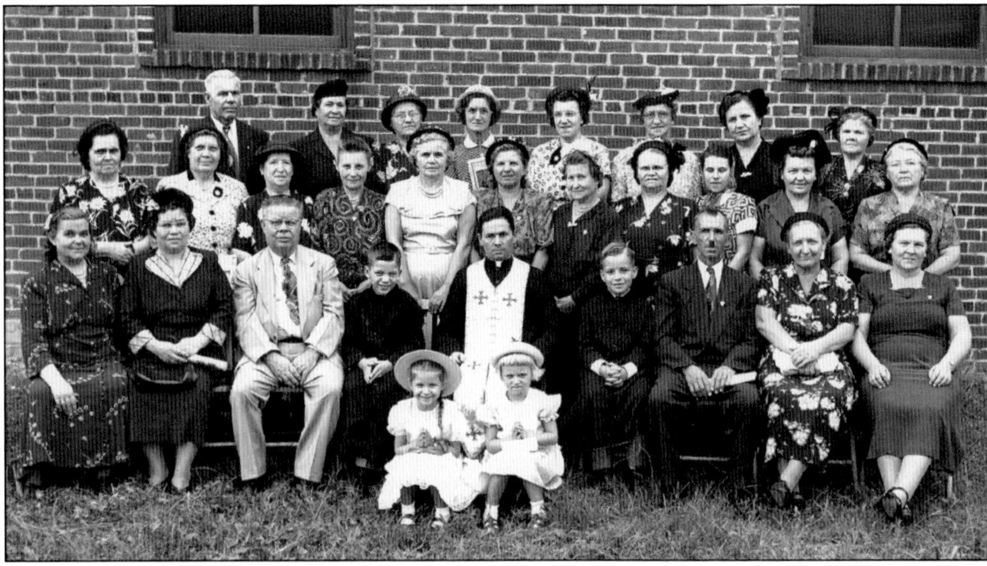

In 1949, Ukrainian Catholics who lived far from Clifton Heights separated and founded a new church. Protection of the BVM UCC was located on the outskirts of southwest Philadelphia. One generation later, as the number of parishioners dwindled, the parish was closed, and they rejoined SS. Peter and Paul UCC in Clifton Heights. The first parishioners are seen with Rev. Peter Lypyn, their pastor in 1952. The two little girls are Anna Budwisky (left) and next to her, Katherine Dupriak.

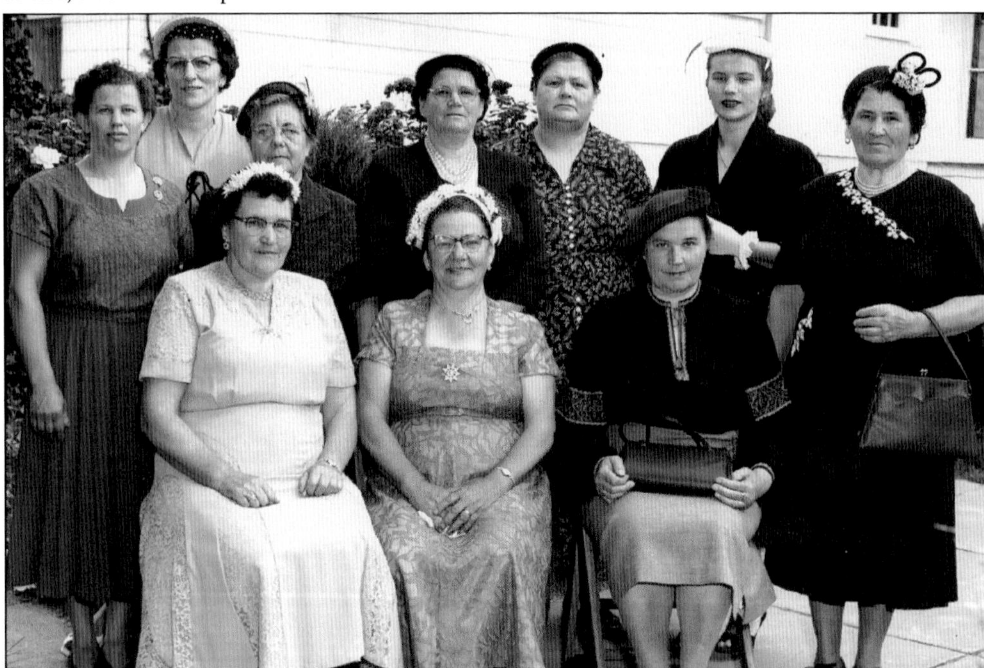

Soyuz Ukrainok of Millville belongs to the New Jersey Regional Council of Ukrainian National Women's League of America. In 1953 are, from left to right, (first row) Maria Horyn, Catherine Marmash, and Praxeda Yasinska; (second row) unidentified, Pauline ?, two unidentified, Sophia Staruch, Maria Murowana, and Catherine Kindzorska.

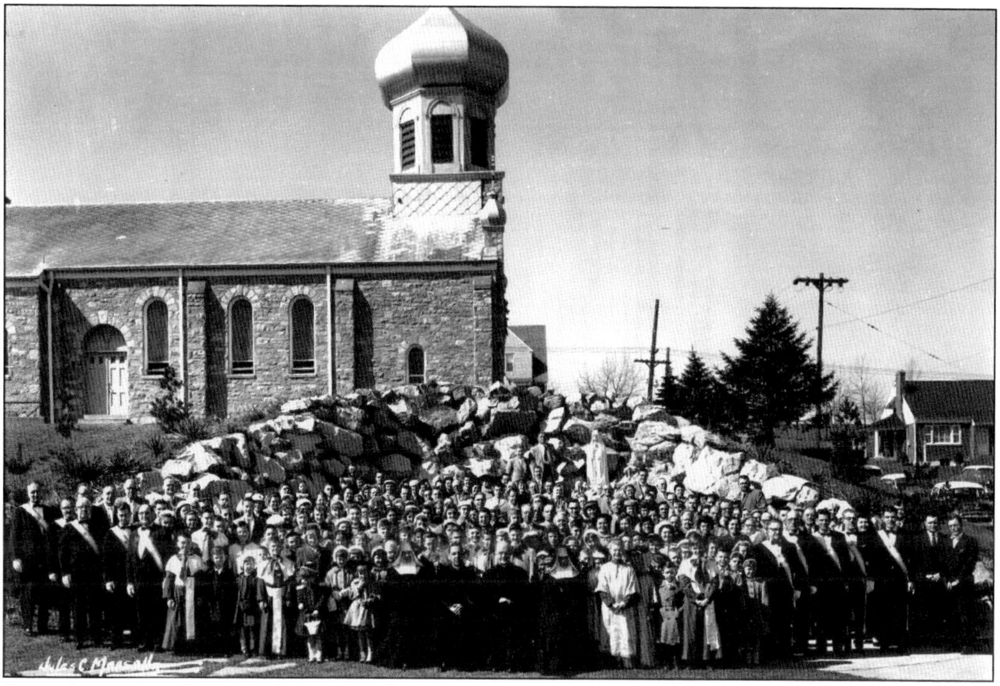

Seen here are the parishioners of SS. Peter and Paul UCC with Bishop Constantine (Bohachevsky), seated center left, on the occasion of his visitation to Bridgeport in 1953. Rev. Basil Sheremeta is on his right. Both are flanked by the Sisters of St. Basil the Great, who taught at the school.

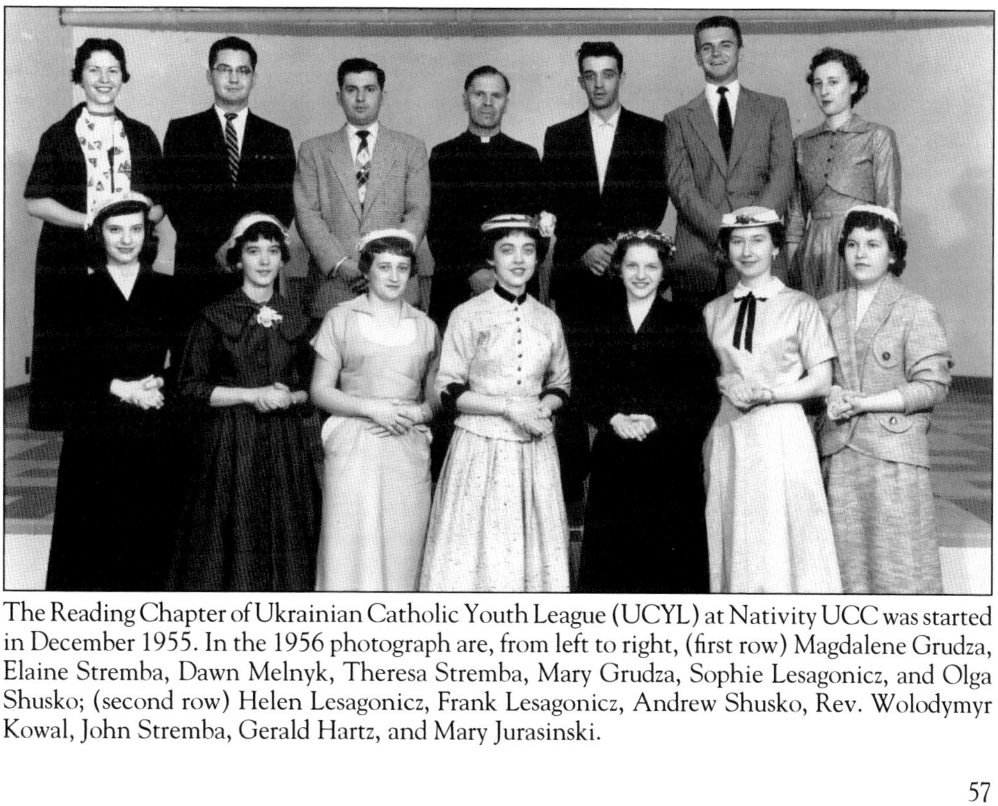

The Reading Chapter of Ukrainian Catholic Youth League (UCYL) at Nativity UCC was started in December 1955. In the 1956 photograph are, from left to right, (first row) Magdalene Grudza, Elaine Stremba, Dawn Melnyk, Theresa Stremba, Mary Grudza, Sophie Lesagonicz, and Olga Shusko; (second row) Helen Lesagonicz, Frank Lesagonicz, Andrew Shusko, Rev. Wolodymyr Kowal, John Stremba, Gerald Hartz, and Mary Jurasinski.

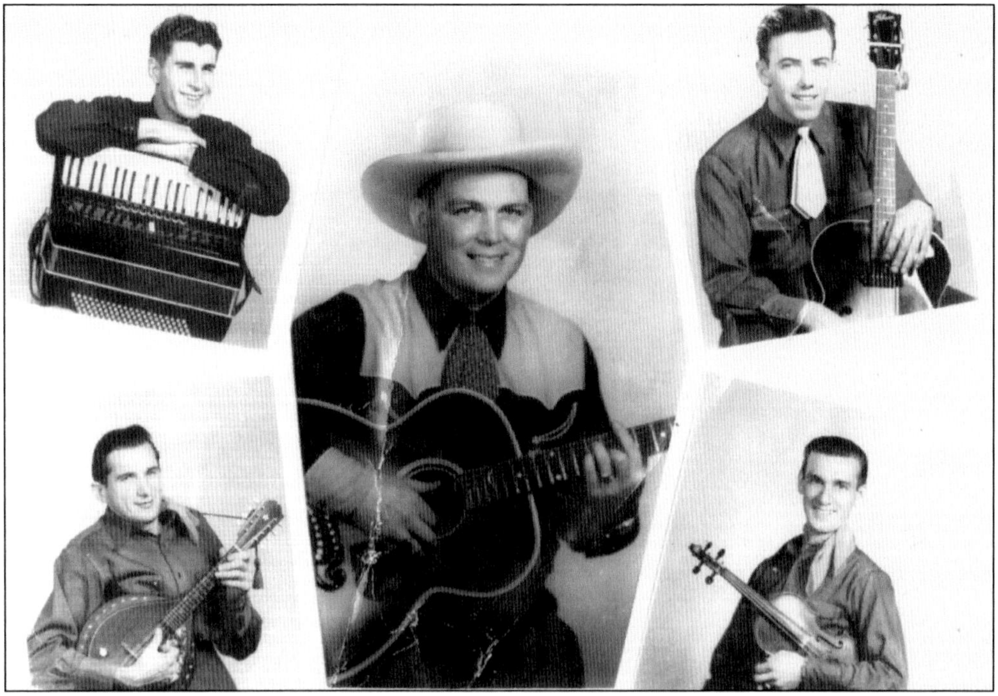

The Ukrainian band Sons of Song from Millville performed every week on WSNJ out of Brighton, from 1938 to 1953. They sang and played western swing, country music, and Ukrainian folk songs. Seen are Philip Aldrich (center) and (clockwise from top left) Anthony Murowany, John Lubonki, Joseph Patten, and Bohdan Nayda.

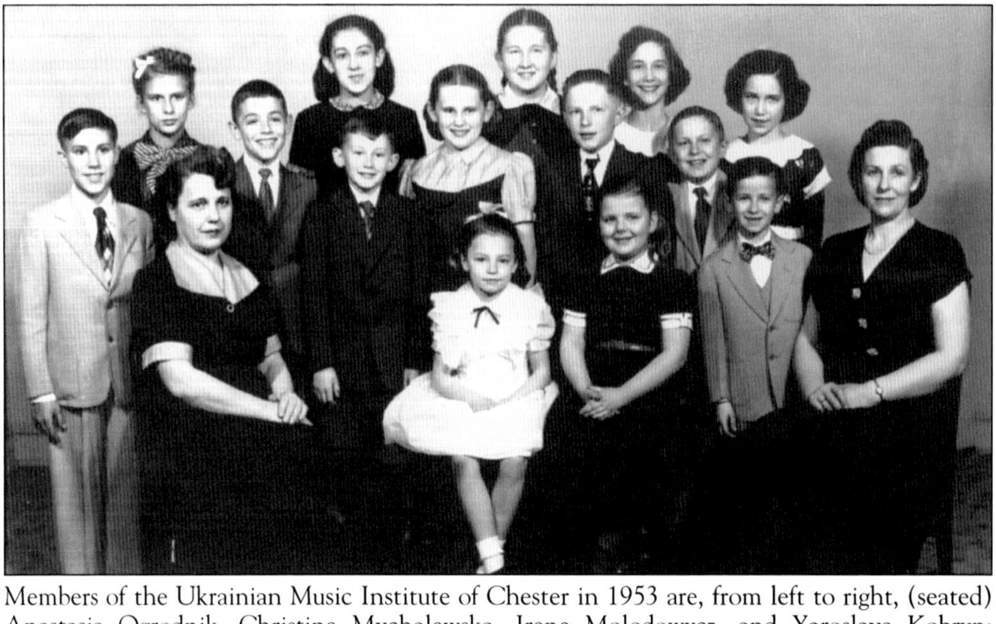

Members of the Ukrainian Music Institute of Chester in 1953 are, from left to right, (seated) Anastasia Ogrodnik, Christine Mychalewska, Irene Molodowycz, and Yaroslava Kobryn; (standing) Basil Bijanskyj, Halya Sodowska, George Kobryn, Taisa Zbyr, Myroslaw Kyj, Oksana Gavdiak, Halya Mykyta, Roman Minczak, Maria Roberts, Walter Matkiwsky, Michelle Roberts, and Ihor Kobasa.

Ukrainians settled Reading, known as Dutch Country, in 1902. These primary settlers were from the Carpathian Mountains and Lemko County and had migrated from the coal-mining regions of Pennsylvania. Being religious, they attended the local Polish Catholic church until 1906, when they purchased a house and converted it into a chapel that served them until 1953, when the new church was built.

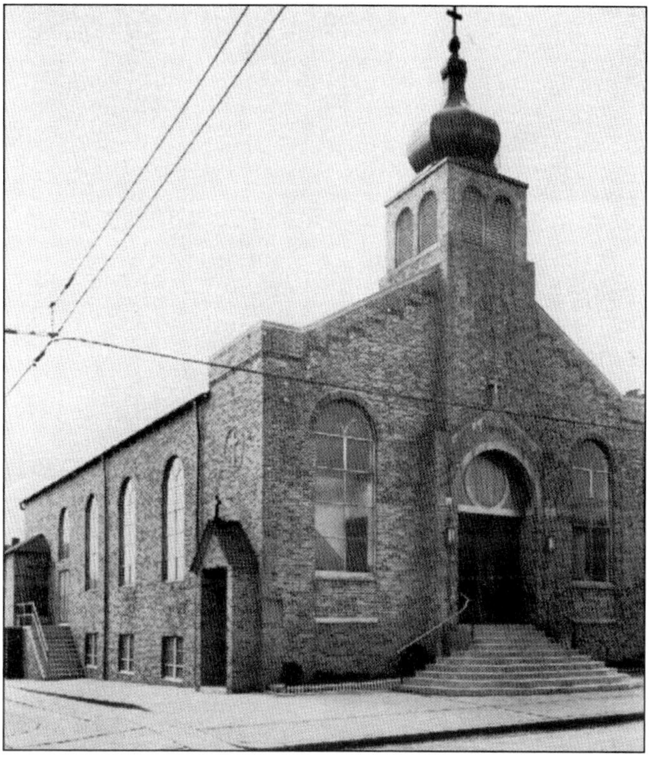

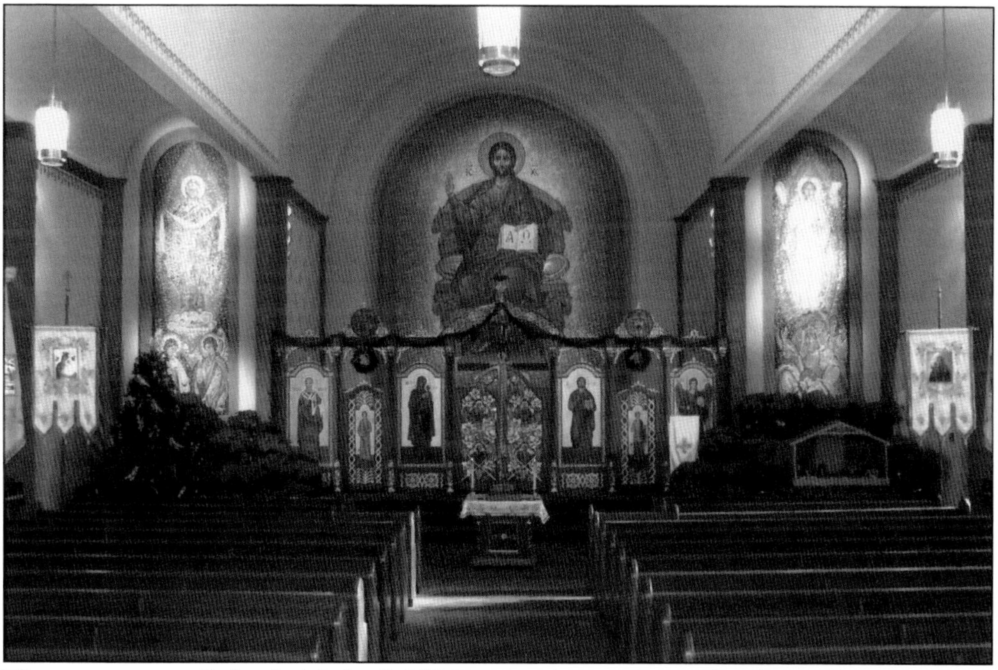

The iconostas installed in St. Michael's UCC in Camden was designed and carved by Rev. Isadore Nahayewsky, pastor of the church in the 1950s. He also painted the icons on the central doors. Michael Vakula painted the remaining icons. When the church moved to Cherry Hill, the iconostas was also moved. In 1993, Daria Haluk-Kulchytsky restored the iconostas.

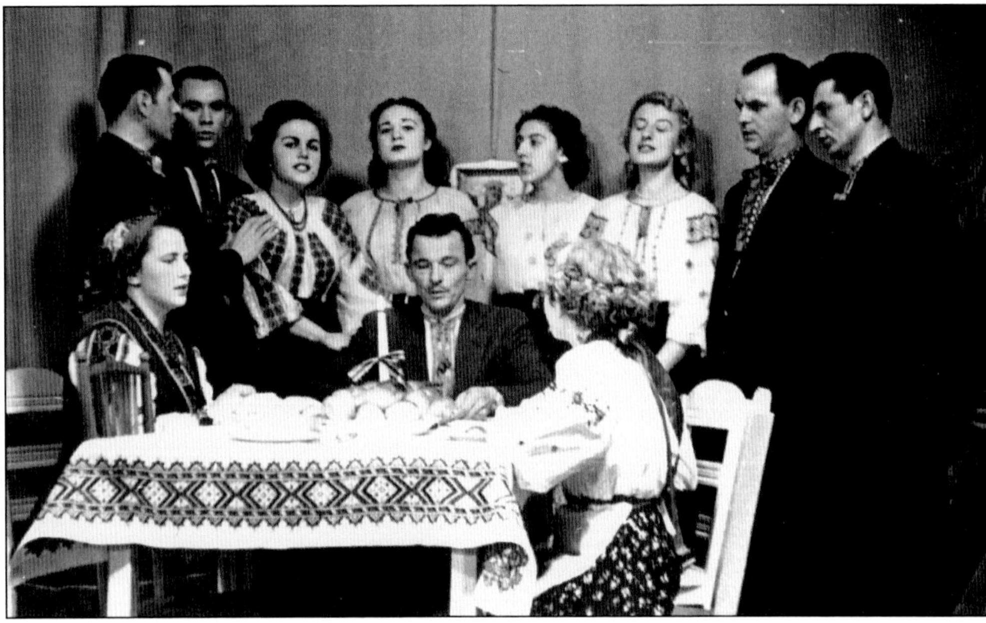

Periodically Wilmington television station Channel 12 presented a sketch of immigrant life. *A Ukrainian Christmas Eve* was presented in 1954. Seated at the table are, from left to right, Sophia Cybak, Bohdan Malecky, and Nadia Balanczuk. The carolers are, from left to right, Yaroslaw Kushnir, Alexander Korotko, Daria Minczak, Tania Zabrodsky, Taisa Zbyr, Nusia Kiczula, Lubomyr Kociuba, and Michael Kiczula.

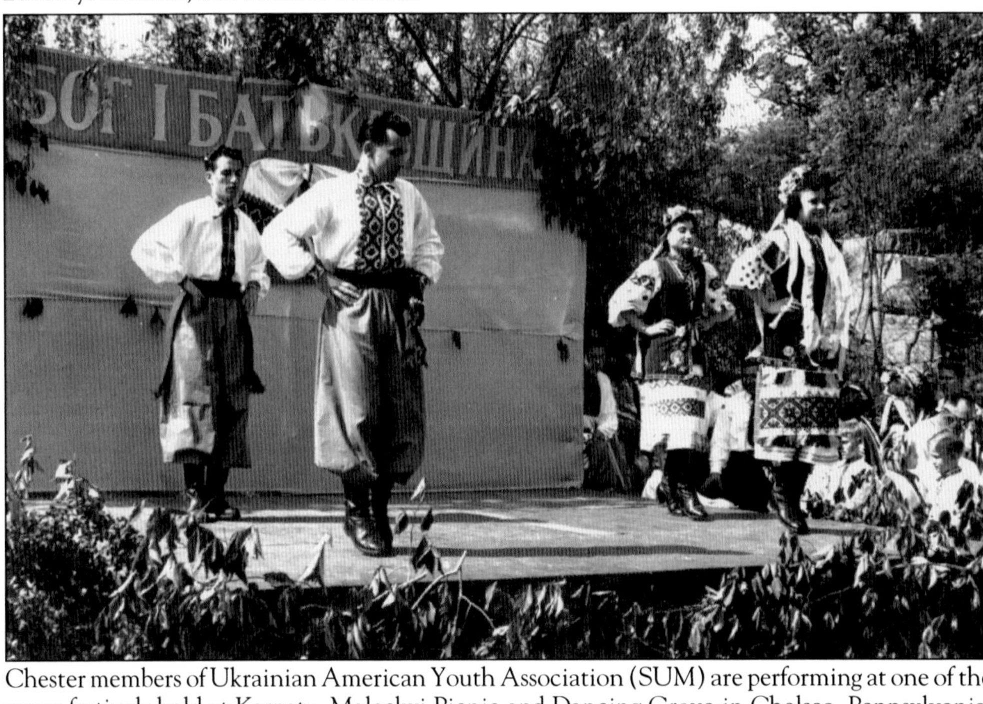

Chester members of Ukrainian American Youth Association (SUM) are performing at one of the many festivals held at Karpaty, Maleckyj Picnic and Dancing Grove in Chelsea, Pennsylvania, in 1953. From left to right are (first row) Anatol Huzva and Myroslava Brodycz; (second row) Ihor Smolij and Linda Bezlyk.

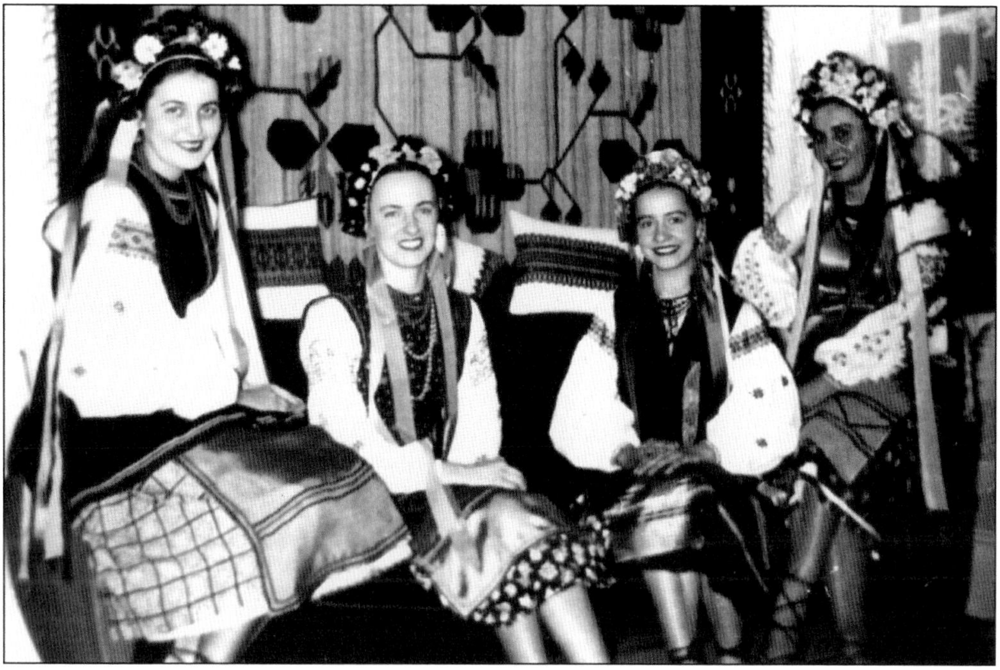

Ukrainian dancing was one way of showcasing their culture since the times of the early immigrants. The Ukrainian Dance Ensemble in 1954 in Wilmington was made up of , from left to right, Lidia Harwanko, Mary Bukay, Maria Petesz, and Irene Malanchuk.

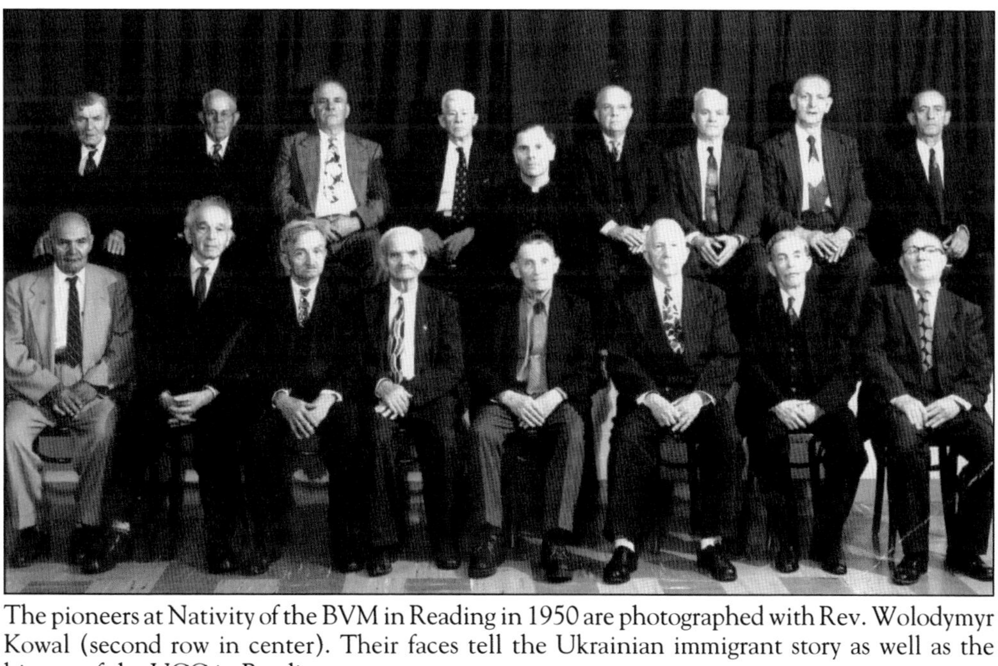

The pioneers at Nativity of the BVM in Reading in 1950 are photographed with Rev. Wolodymyr Kowal (second row in center). Their faces tell the Ukrainian immigrant story as well as the history of the UCC in Reading.

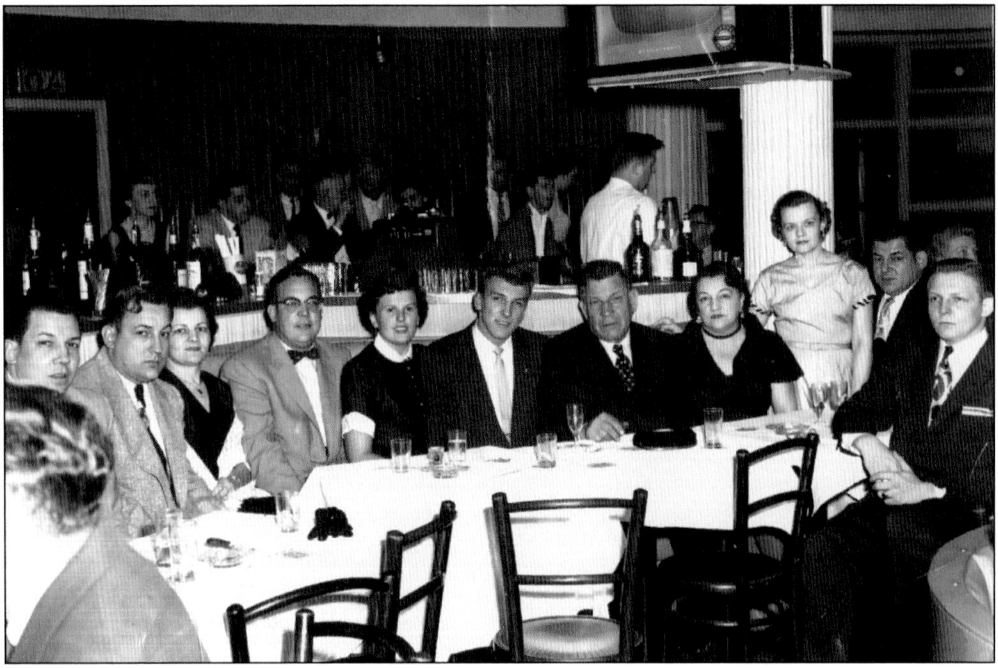

The Orthodox community constructed UANH in Chester. Literally, stone by stone, the structure was built one block long and two stories high. Upstairs the hall was multipurpose; downstairs a clubroom was available for relaxation. It was dedicated in 1929. Pastuszek family pioneers and patrons enjoyed a family party at the club in 1955. From left to right are Harry; Joseph and his wife, Mary; William and his wife, Dozia; Andrew, an entertainer on cruise ships; Michael Sr. and his wife, Mary; and Olga, wife of Marty; Marty; and Michael Jr.

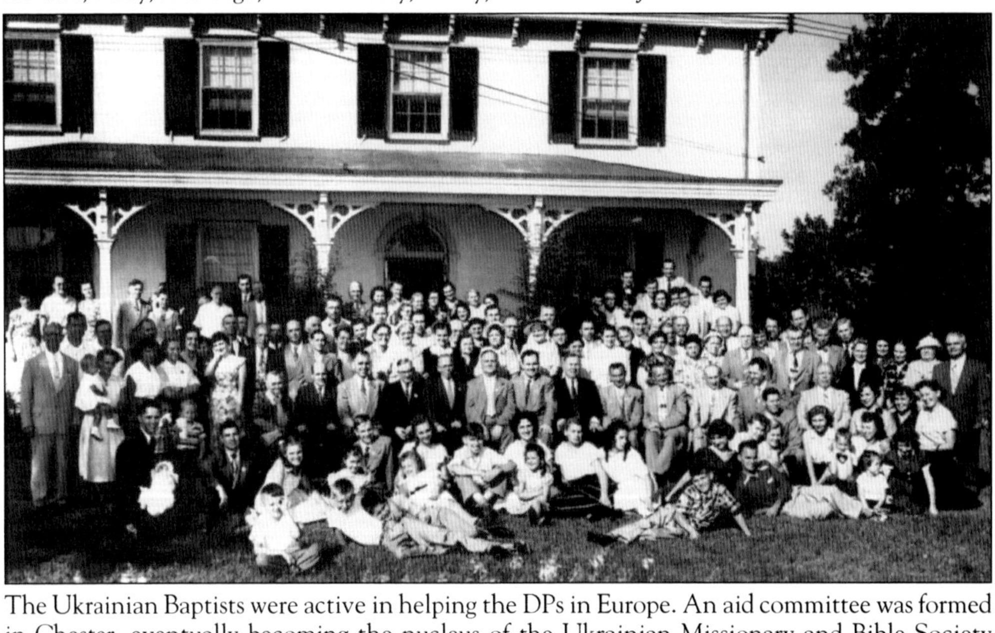

The Ukrainian Baptists were active in helping the DPs in Europe. An aid committee was formed in Chester, eventually becoming the nucleus of the Ukrainian Missionary and Bible Society around which the Association of Ukrainian Evangelical Baptists Churches in the United States was formed. The seventh convention was held in 1954 in Brookhaven, near Chester.

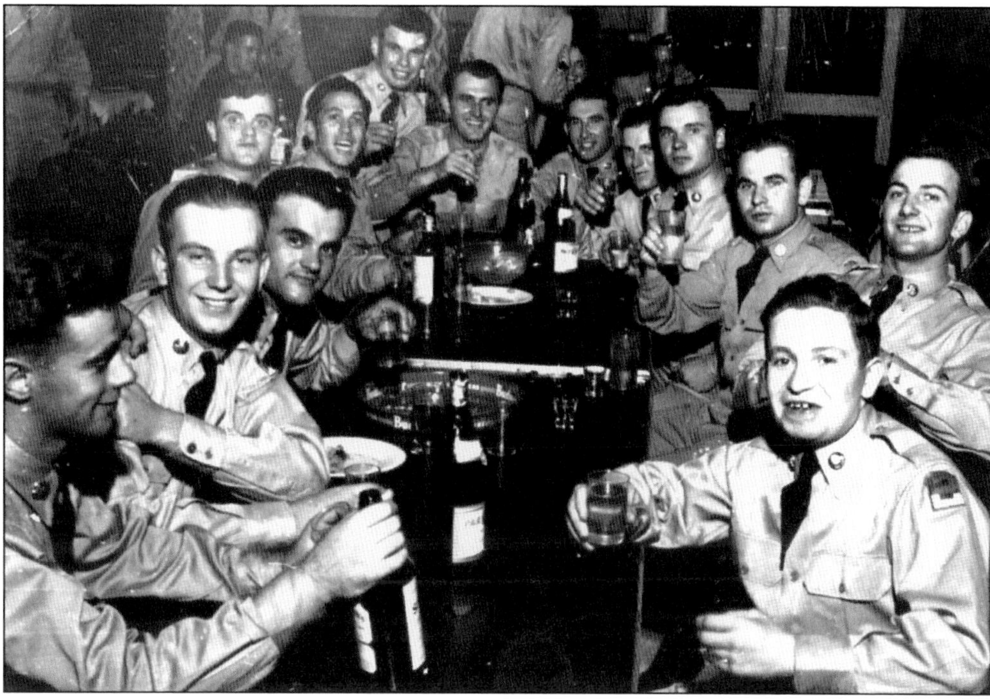

During the Korean Conflict, many newcomers, who had experienced the yolk of communism and were fluent in multiple languages, were selected for Army Military Intelligence Service at Fort Meade, Maryland. In 1952, their choir was invited to the White House to sing in Ukrainian. They were from the Delaware Valley and across the United States. Here they are clearing their throats after the performance. Around the tables are, from left to right Orest Rudyj, two unidentified, Semen Krywusha, two unidentified, Oles Worobec, two unidentified, Gregory Iwaskiw, Mychaylo Lotocky, Taras Halushka, and Karlo Dobriansky.

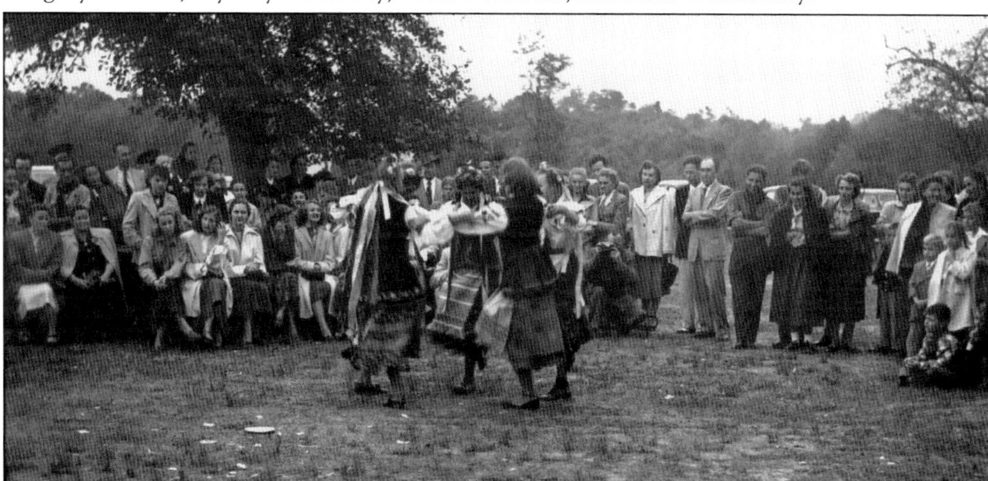

In 1951, Ukrainians of the Delaware Valley, New Jersey, and New York City areas purchased land in Cream Ridge, New Jersey, which was central to all. It was named Chercha, after the resort in Ukraine known for its healing waters. Numerous groups used the facilities at Chercha. Besides the picnic grounds, eventually a swimming pool, soccer field, and dance area were built. In 1952, onlookers enjoyed Ukrainian folk dancing.

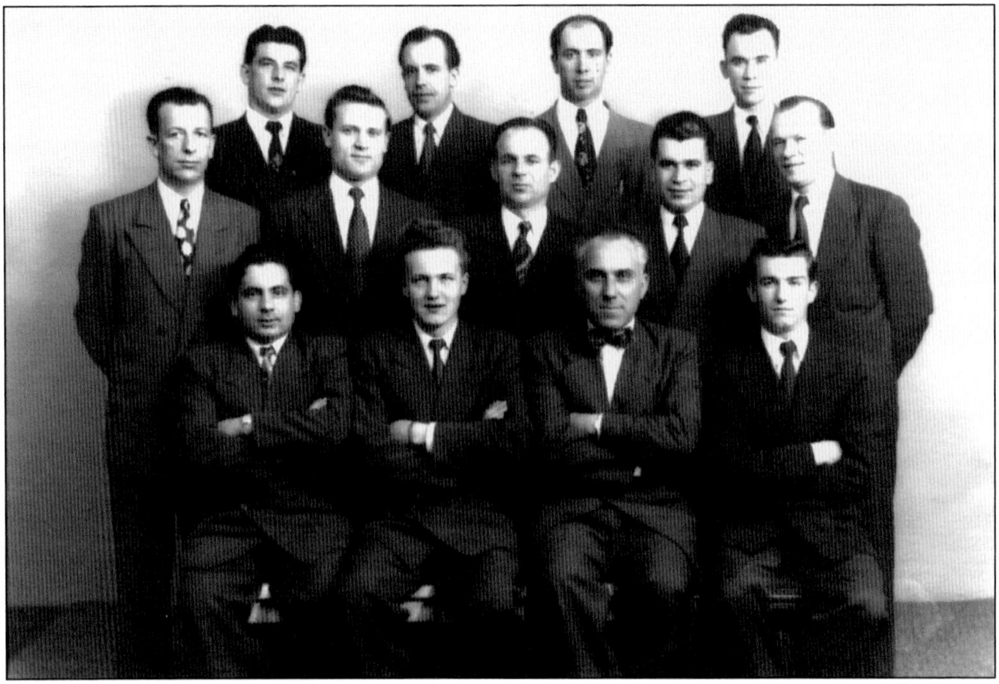

Officers of SUM in Chester in 1954 are, from left to right, (first row) Ivan Bezlyk, Zenon Matkiwsky, Wolodymyr Korchynsky, and Ihor Smolij; (second row) Wolodymyr Wacykewycz, Jaroslaw Kluka, Petro Brodycz, Andrij Zabrodsky, and Mykola Maksymyk; (third row) Mykola Cichanowsky, Wasyl Yagla, Harasym Makowsky, and Alexander Korotko.

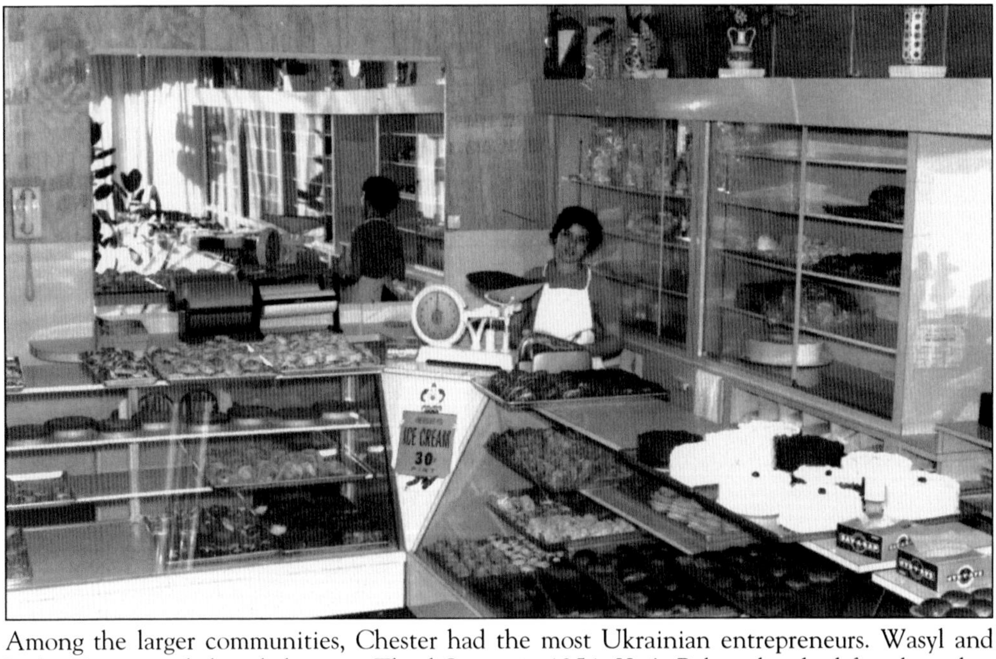

Among the larger communities, Chester had the most Ukrainian entrepreneurs. Wasyl and Lydia Kyj opened their bakery on Third Street in 1954. Kyj's Bakery has had four branches scattered throughout Delaware County. Their daughter Christine is pictured in the original store with a display of their delicious selections.

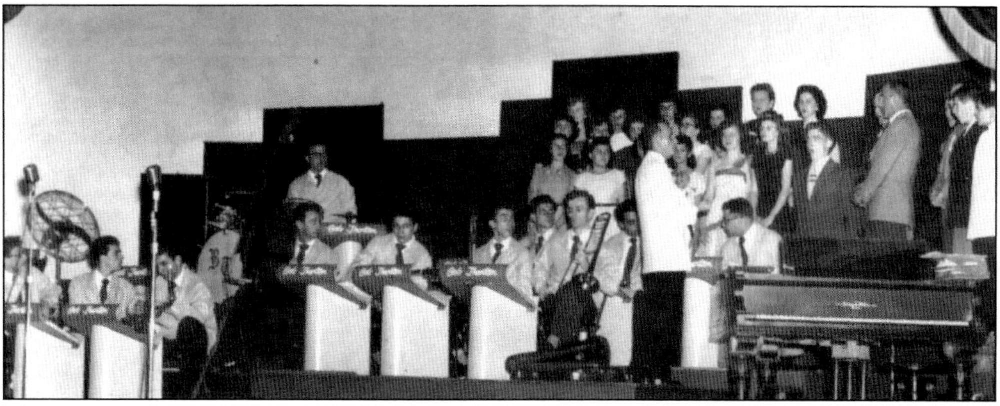

The choir director of Nativity UCC in Reading, Bob Taptich appeared as Bob Thornton and his Big Band in a concert at Sunnybrook in the early 1950s. This concert included singing by the parish choir. In the first row the singers are, from left to right, Anna Misura, Olga Shusko, unidentified, Elaine Stremba, and at the end of the first row Rose Spolski; the others are unidentified.

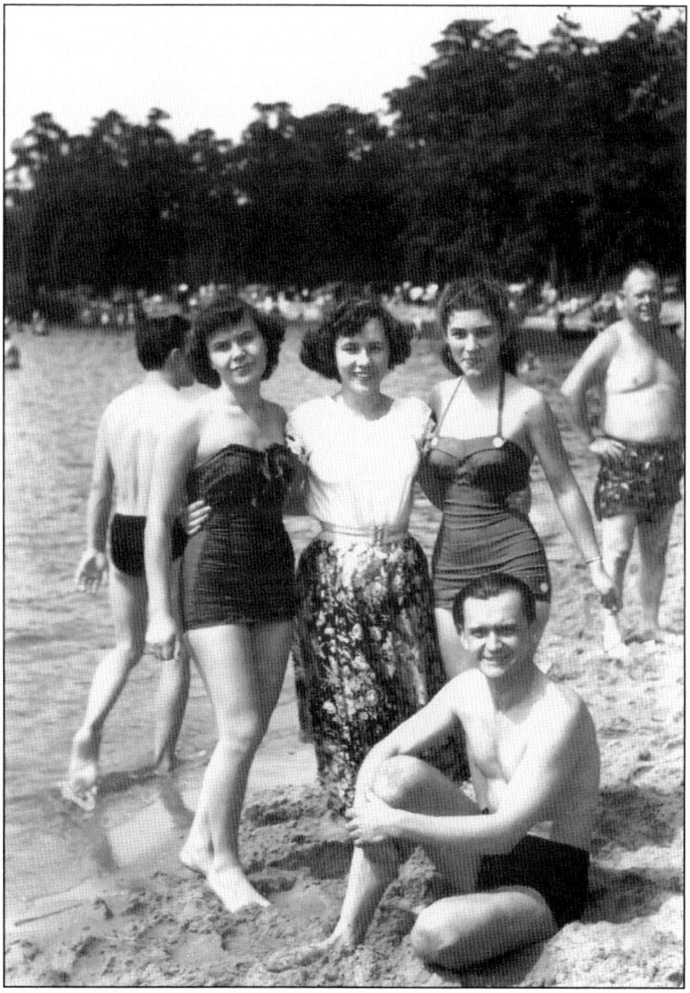

Millville Lake, because of its proximity to Philadelphia, was a popular destination for Ukrainian students during the 1950s and 1960s. Enjoying the lake and the beach are, from left to right, (sitting) Theodore Zareba; (standing) two unidentified and Larissa Chatyrka.

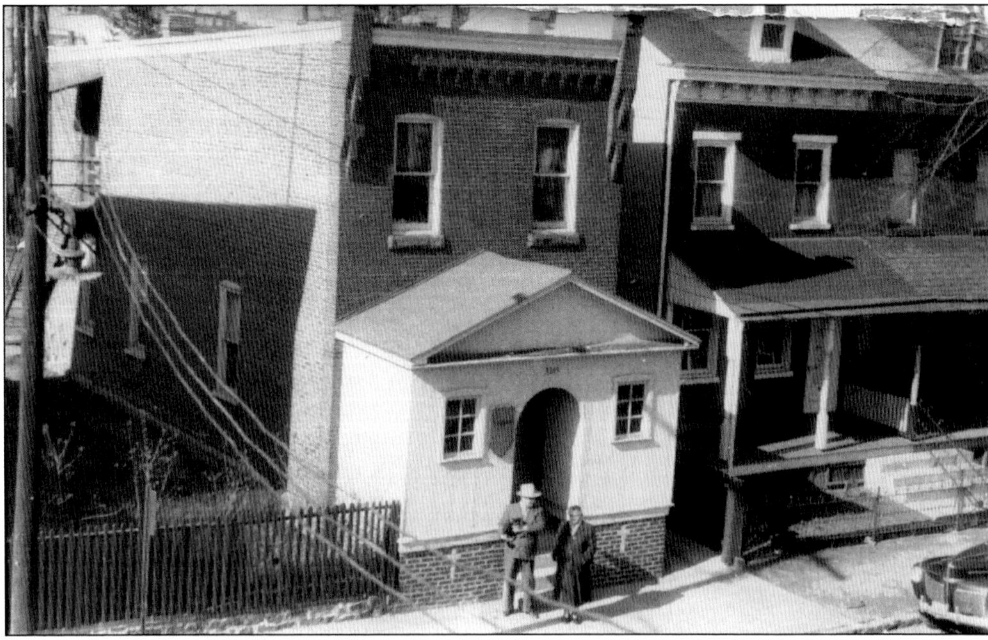

Standing in front of the House of Prayer of the Ukrainian Mission and Bible Society in Chester are newly arrived Pastor Leon Zabko-Potapowicz with his wife, Natalia, in 1950. For many years, he was the editor of the monthly *Messenger of Truth*. The publishing house also printed many hymnals and religious books.

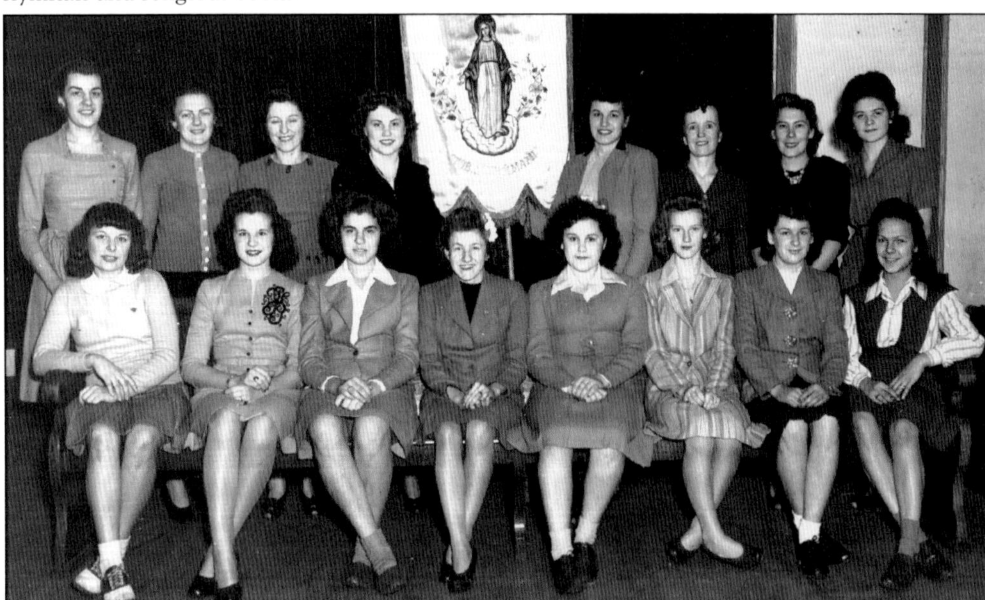

Membership in the Sodality of the Blessed Virgin Mary at St. Michael's UCC in Camden dispersed when the parish moved to Cherry Hill. Some went to Cherry Hill, some joined the UCC in Williamstown, and still others moved away. Seen here in 1955 are, from left to right, (first row) Anna Zawoyski, Mary Haday, Catherine Haday, Catherine Hetz, unidentified, Olga Zurinski, and two unidentified; (second row) Julia Haday, unidentified, Mary Cole, unidentified, Stephanie Haday, Margaret Cole, unidentified, and Catherine Lajioka.

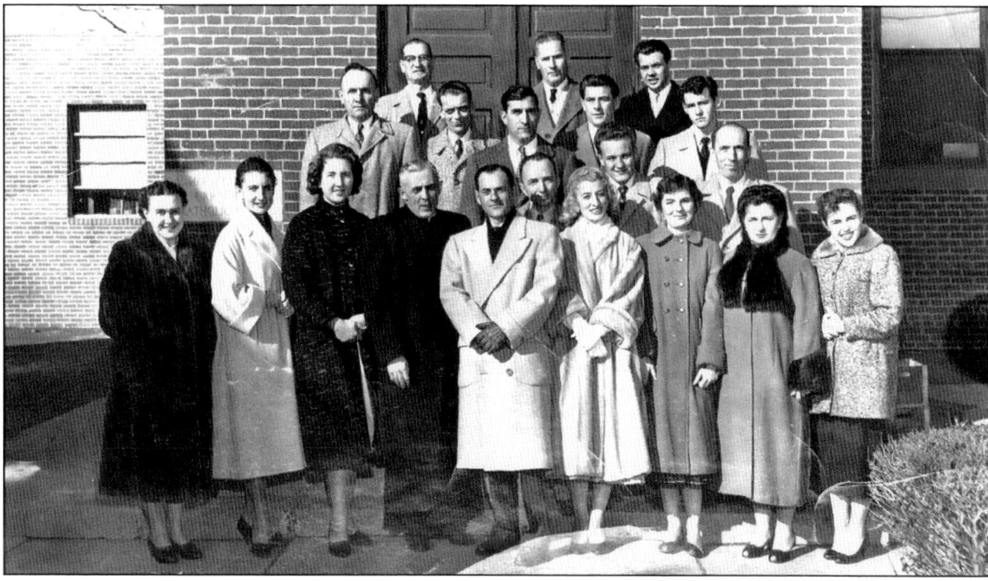

Holy Ghost UCC Choir in 1956 consisted of the following: from left to right (first row) Jaroslawa Zbyr, Stephanie Sarachman, Halia Mykta, Rev. Nicholas Zbyr, Jaroslawa Kusznir, Anna Kiczula, Halia Szabatura, Anna Wizniak, and Daria Minchak; (second row) Zenon Mychajlewsky, Zenon Matkiwsky, and Roman Zawycky; (third row) Osyp Sarachman, Omelian Rylko, Wolodymyr Olexander, Mykola Cichanowsky, and Ihor Kiziuk; (fourth row) Michael Betz, Atanas Kobryn, and Gregory Wolos.

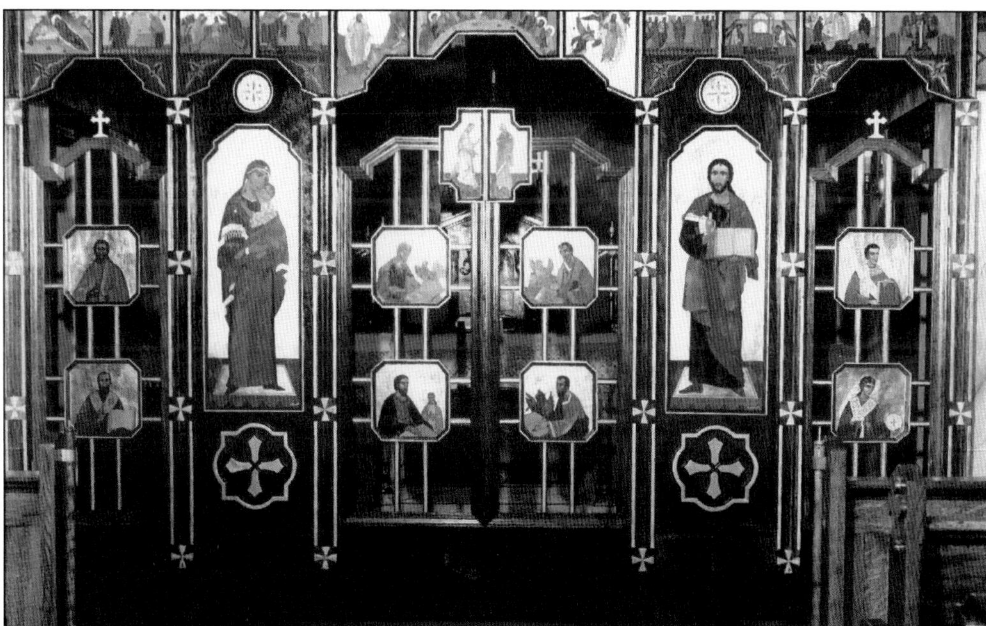

The iconostases (altar screens) were designed and painted by well-known artists throughout the United States after World War II in Ukrainian churches. Rev. Victor Pospishil, an eminent Ukrainian theologian and scholar, designed this iconostas in 1956 in St. Michael the Archangel UCC in Pottstown.

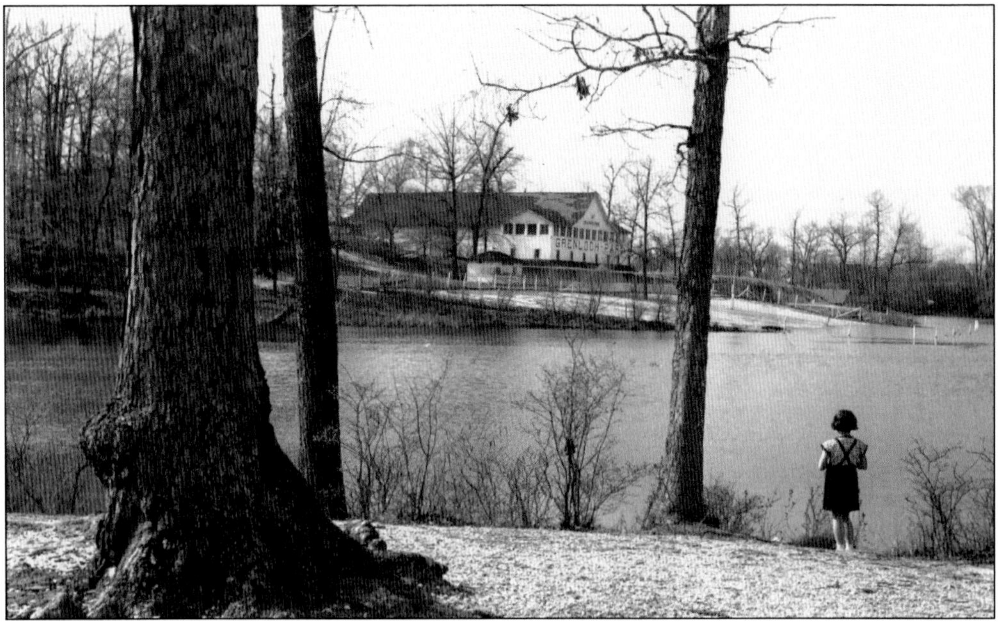

Ukrainians purchased Glenlock Park, 10 miles south of Camden, in 1950. Veselka, as it was named, began as a multipurpose club with sport activities and prospered due to its proximity to the large Ukrainian populations in Philadelphia and the surrounding areas. As attendance dwindled down, because organizations began to buy property, Veselka went into decline and was sold in 1956.

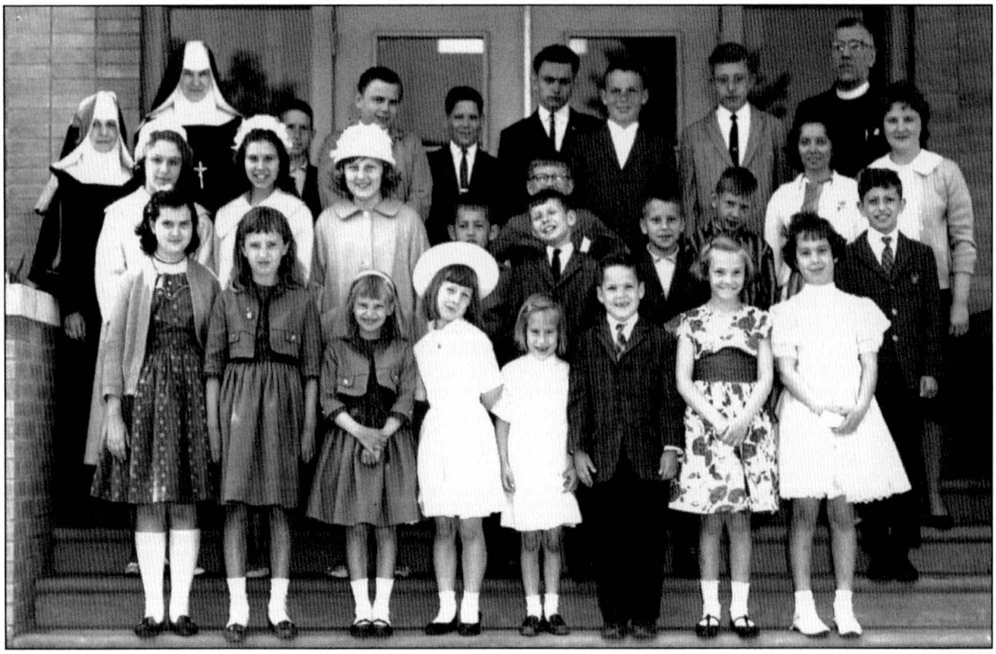

In the 1950s, newcomers resumed the tradition of offering courses of Ukrainian studies to instruct the youth in their culture, language, and religion. In 1955, the Sisters of St Basil the Great taught at St. Michael's UCC Saturday school in Camden.

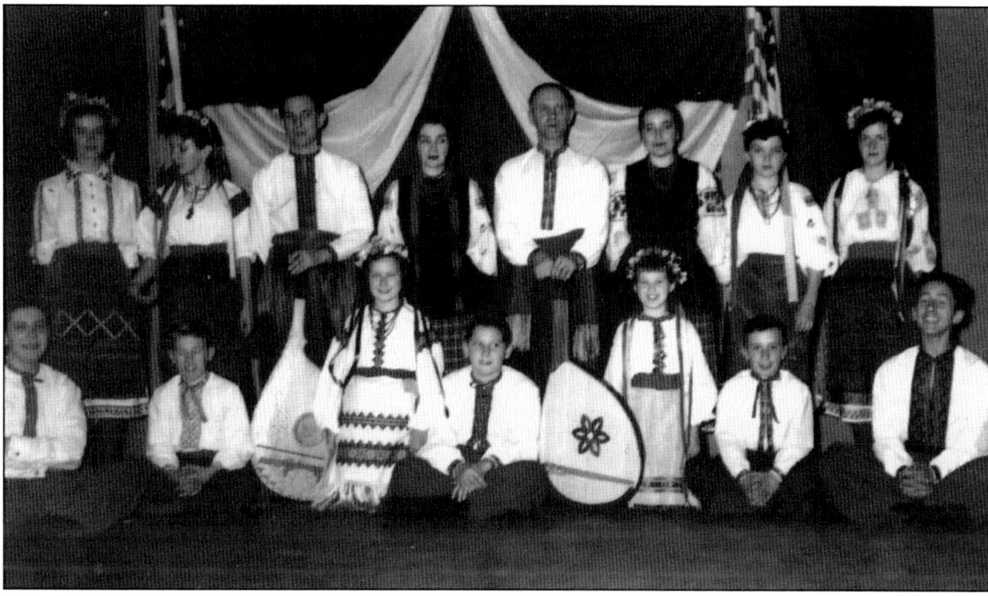

The homegrown dance group in Bristol performed at church and civic occasions and was applauded by all. The annual Thanksgiving dinner and dance not only supplied food and dancing but also cultural diversity. Performers for this 1956 occasion are, from left to right, (first row) Michael Kravchak, unidentified, Patricia Kravchak, Paul Kravchak, Patricia Krysak, William Krysak, and Michael Krysak; (second row) Paula Romanko, Kathleen Ferko, unidentified, Katherine Suchenko, two unidentified, Chrystyna Tatomyr, and Martha Tatomyr.

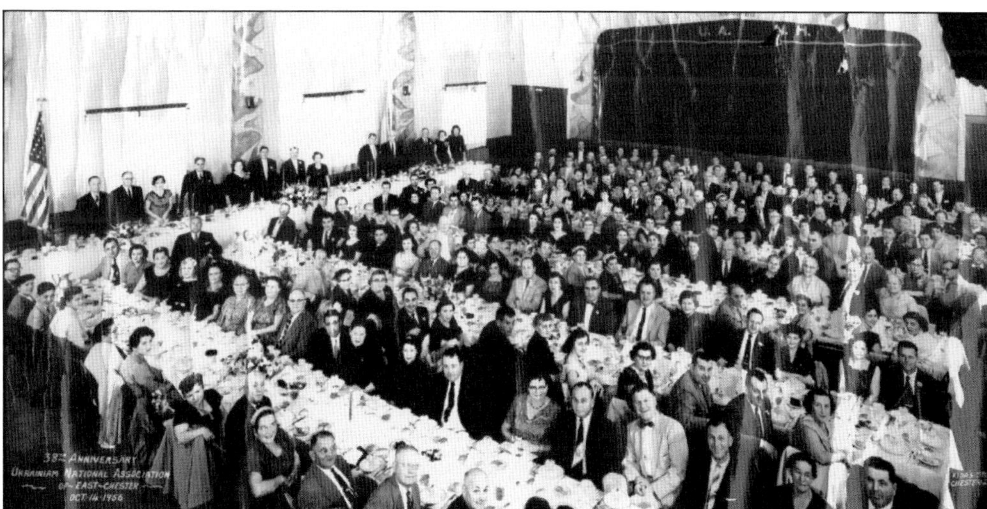

By the mid-1940s, the Ukrainians in Chester had three major organizations, each with their own clubs. All were in different localities, with one at the east end, another at the west end, and UANH in the middle. The 1956 banquet of the East End UNA celebrated its 38th anniversary in the upper rooms of UANH.

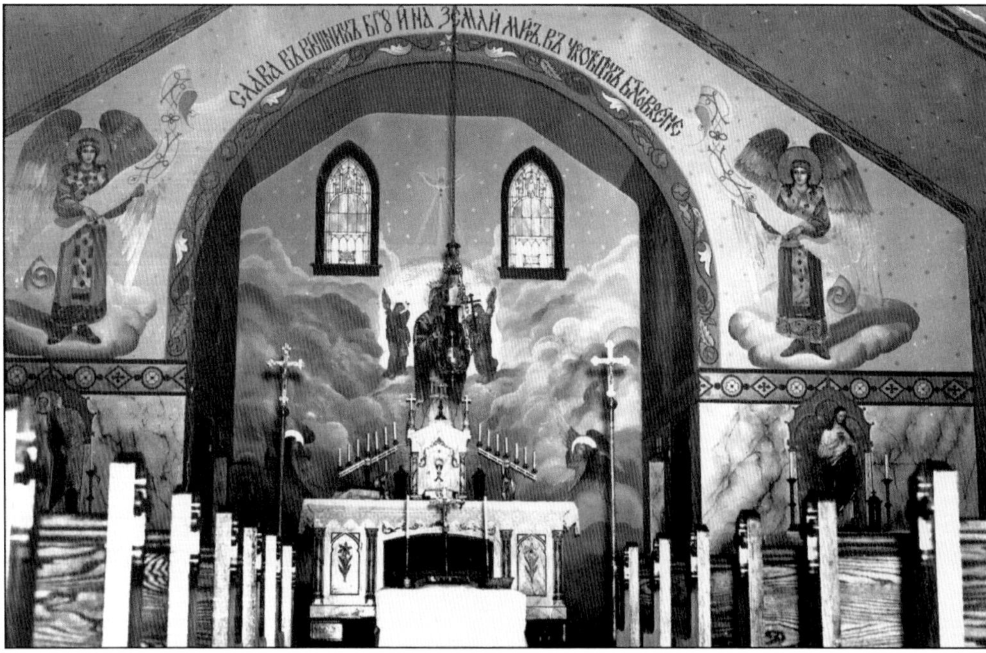

In Eastern churches, the iconostas, a partition with icons, separates the sanctuary from the rest of the church. With the expense of building a church, sometimes it took a while to completely decorate the church, and statues, a less expensive alternative, were used. This led to disagreements with the arriving DPs. This was the interior of St. Michael's UCC in Pottstown in 1956, before the installation of the iconostas.

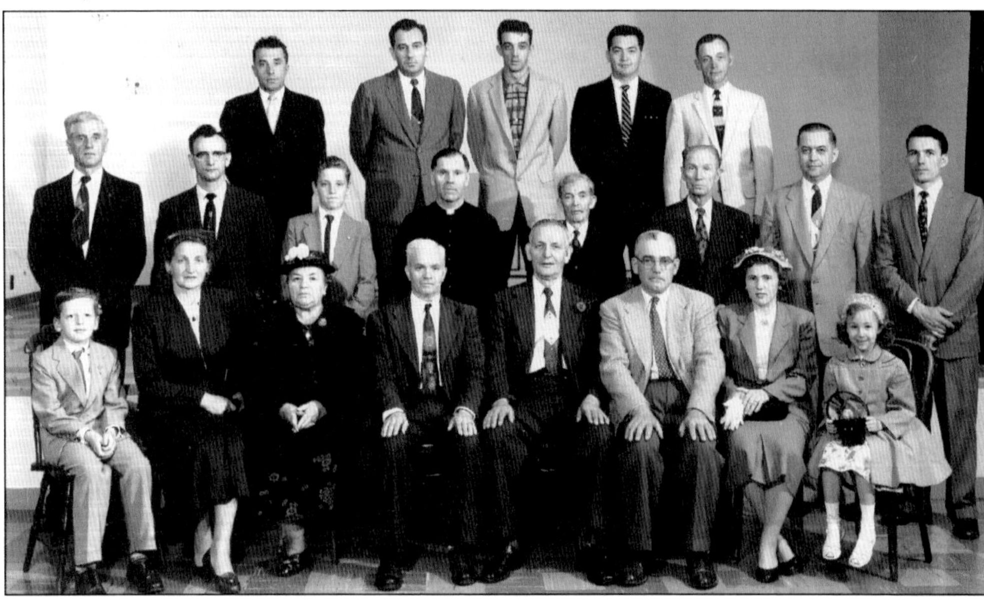

Nativity UCC was located among other Slavic communities in Reading. Some believed that the competition from finer-looking churches, especially the Russian Orthodox, caused a number of parishioners to leave. Reading's Providence Branch, founded in 1915, worked to help the UCC thrive. Providence members in 1956 are photographed with their pastor, Rev. Wolodymyr Kowal (second row, fourth from left).

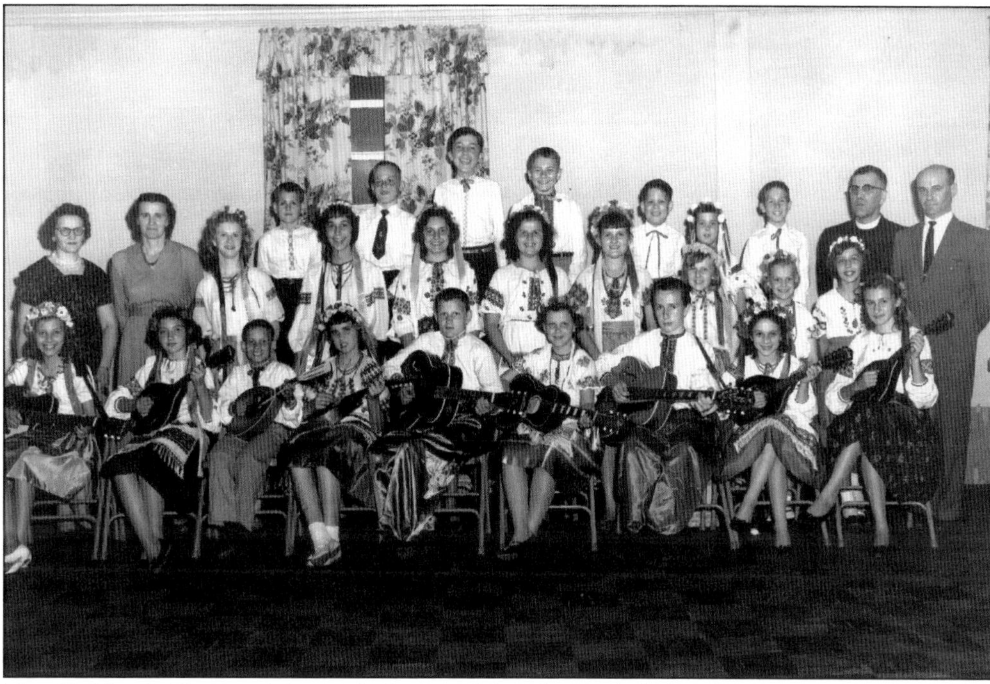

The Children's Choir and String Orchestra of Camden included students who attended evening and Saturday classes in 1956. The adults in the photograph are, on the left, Olha Nahayewska, musical director, and Maria Romach, head of the parents association; on the right are Rev. Isadore Nahayewsky and Michael Romach, principal of the school.

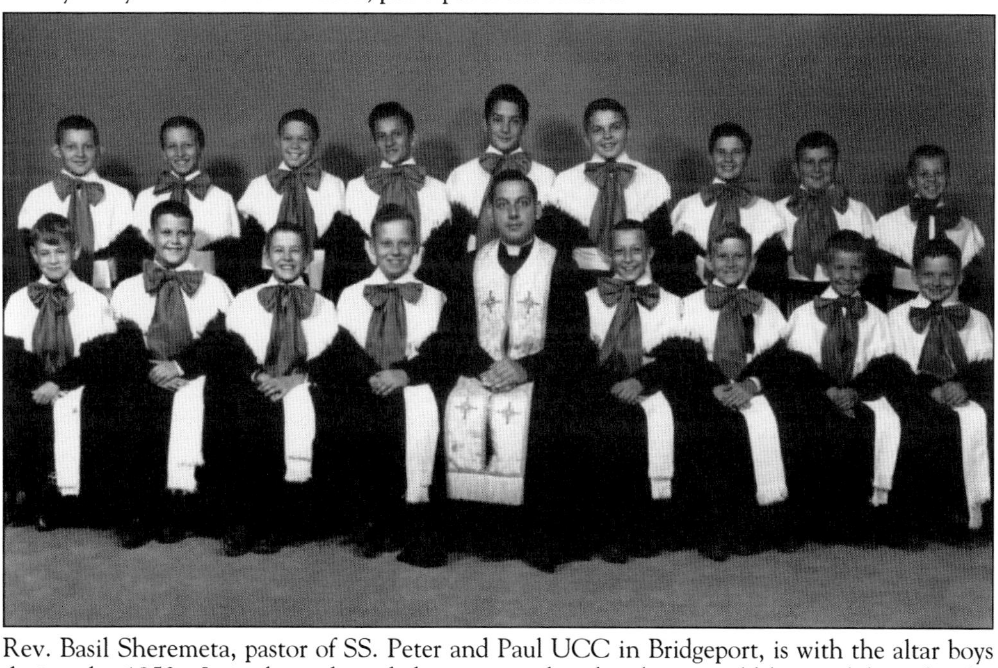

Rev. Basil Sheremeta, pastor of SS. Peter and Paul UCC in Bridgeport, is with the altar boys during the 1950s. It is always hoped that among the altar boys would be candidates for the priesthood. Customarily in the Eastern Church, they are garbed in black cassocks; however, Reverend Sheremeta chose to decorate their attire.

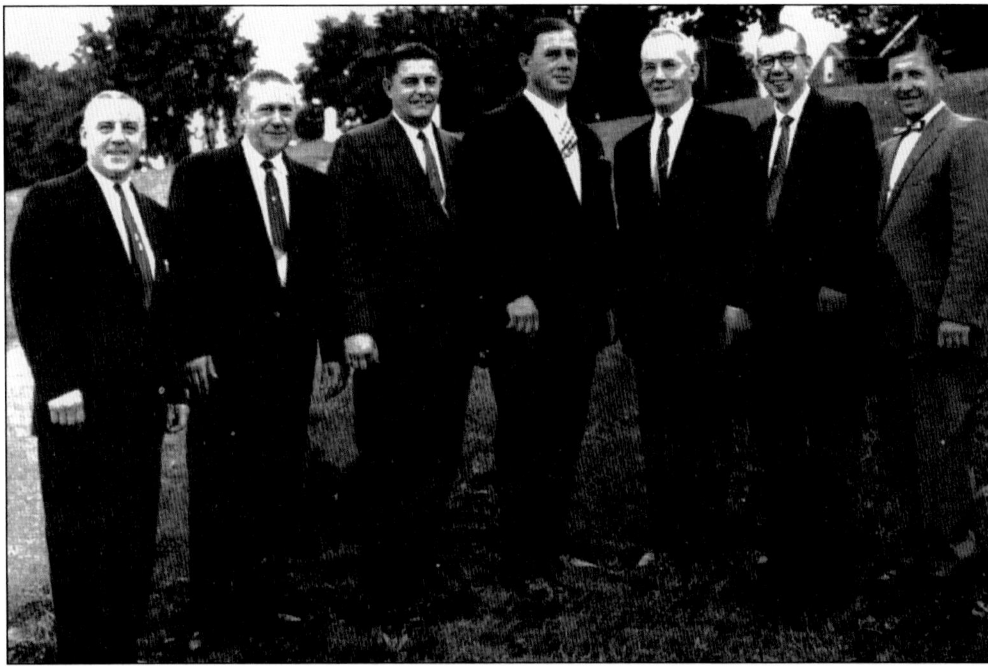

Since the 1920s, major Ukrainian communities formed Ukrainian American Citizens' Clubs (UACC), having their own buildings where civic activities were held. Officers of the Bridgeport UACC in the 1950s are, from left to right, Joseph Saboe, Edward Rotay, Michael Bukata, Andrew Smulley, Luka Sarabun, John Shewchuk, and Stephen Shewchuk.

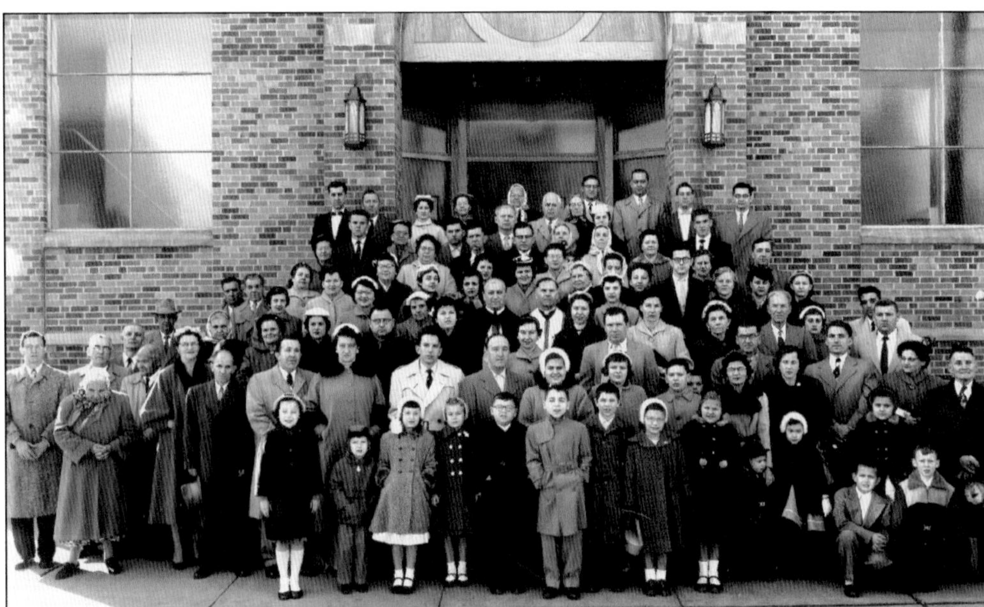

It was customary for parishioners to be photographed after a Lenten mission. This moment was embedded in a memory card that parishioners were given. Rev. Nicholas Kohut OSBM conducted the 1955 mission at Nativity UCC in Reading. Reverend Kohut is in the third row center, and on his left is the pastor Rev. Wolodymyr Kowal.

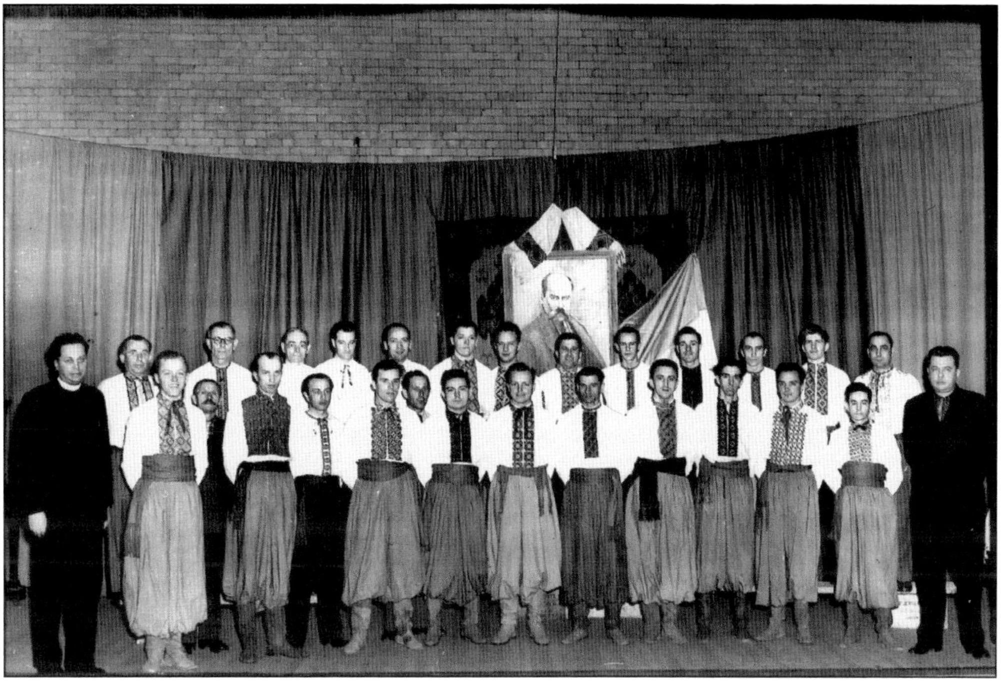

With the arrival of post–World War II refugees, church halls and citizens' clubs became too small. In 1950, the Shevchenko Concert was held at the Wilson Elementary School auditorium. In Camden, all generations of immigrants formed the choir. Rev. Leo Adamiak is on the left.

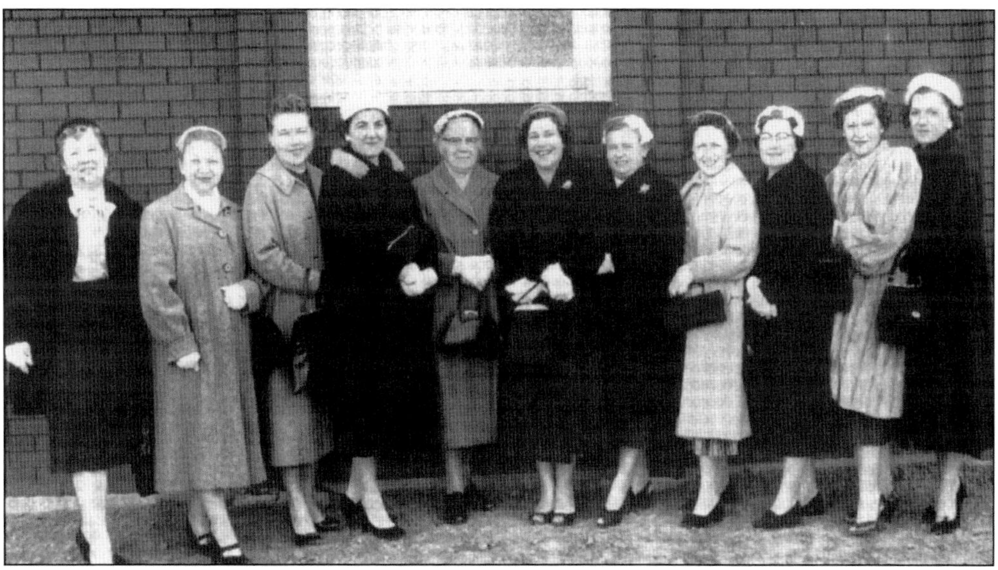

Throughout its 90-year-plus interesting history, SS. Peter and Paul UCC in Clifton Heights managed to survive. The most influential group in the community toward beautifying the church and rectory was the Citizens' Club Auxiliary. The 1957 members are, from left to right, Mary Gardner, Esther Anderson, Anne Phillips, Ann Androsko, Anastasia Kondryc, Catherine Wozny, Mary Swecz, Ann DiAntonio, Anna Newmaster, Mary Small, and Olga Cienki.

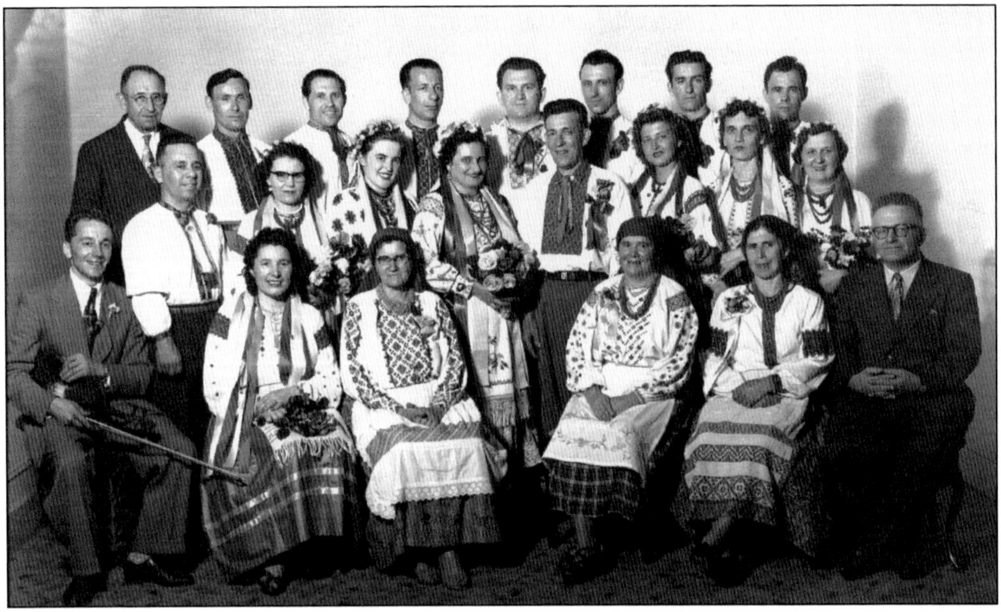

Amateur theater flourished in Ukrainian communities from the start of their immigration because they continued the practice from home. This form of entertainment was a perfect way to preserve customs and heritage as well as to convey new ideas. A traditional Ukrainian wedding was ideal because it supplied words as well as music. Pictured in the early 1950s is such a play, in Chester, with bride and groom in the middle of the second row.

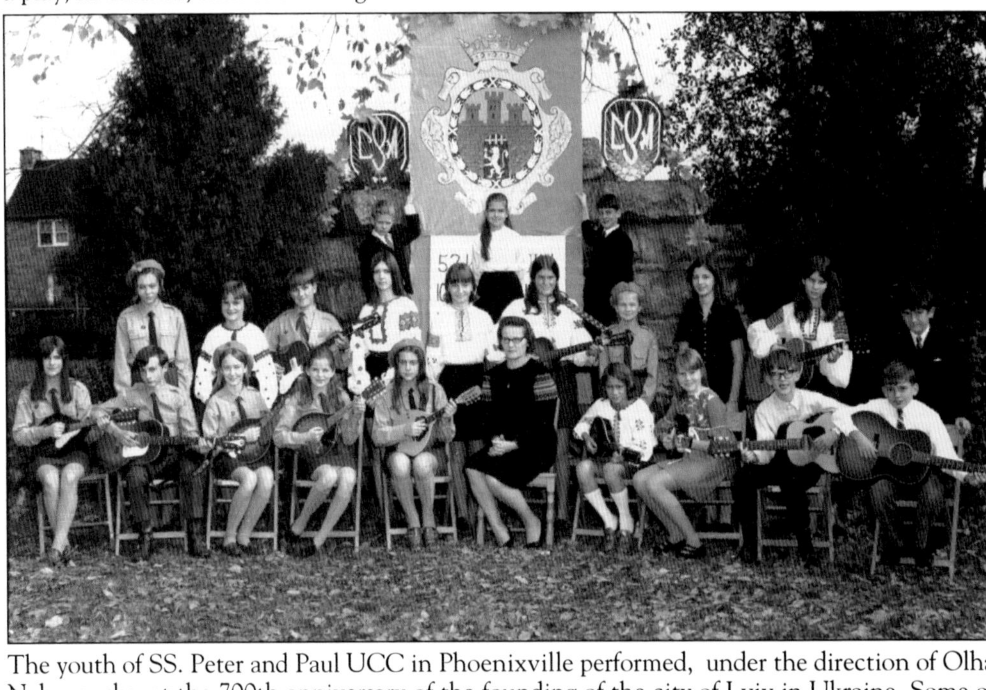

The youth of SS. Peter and Paul UCC in Phoenixville performed, under the direction of Olha Nahayewska, at the 700th anniversary of the founding of the city of Lviv in Ukraine. Some of the musicians belonged to SUM, and others were parishioners. On Saturdays, for three years, they traveled to Philadelphia to attend the Ukrainian School of Arts and Sciences, a school where classes were formed based on knowledge, not age.

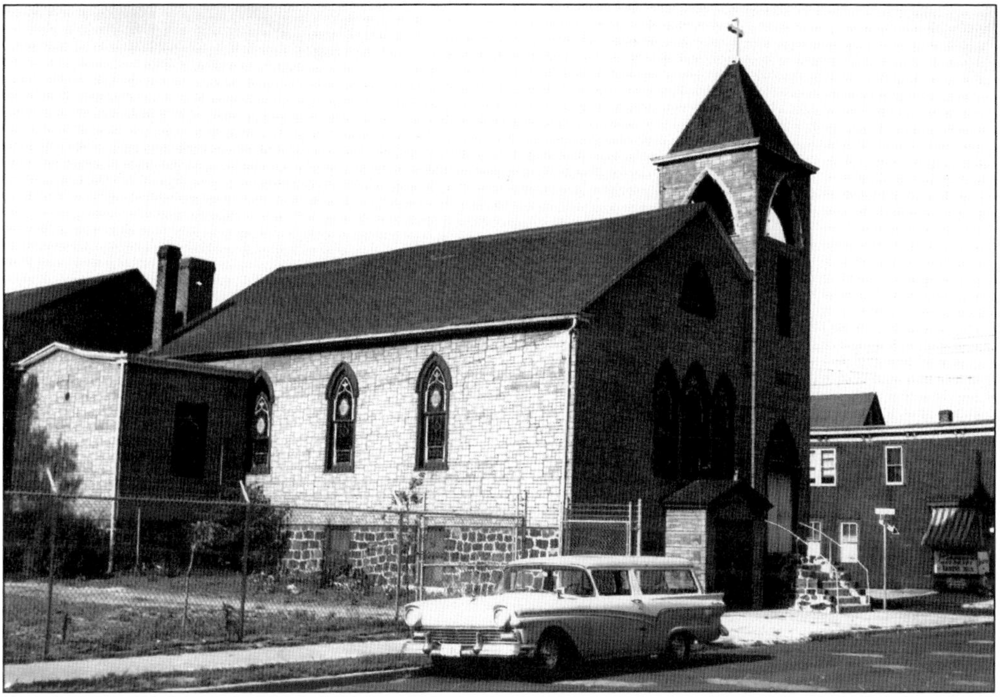

St. Michael's UCC in Camden, incorporated in 1924, gained a new lease on life with the arrival of refugees. In 1958, a hall was built and the parish flourished under the pastorate of Rev. Isadore Nahayewsky. By 1968, the majority of parishioners had left Camden, and it was apparent that the church would also have to change locations. This was accomplished in 1976 when a new home was found in Cherry Hill.

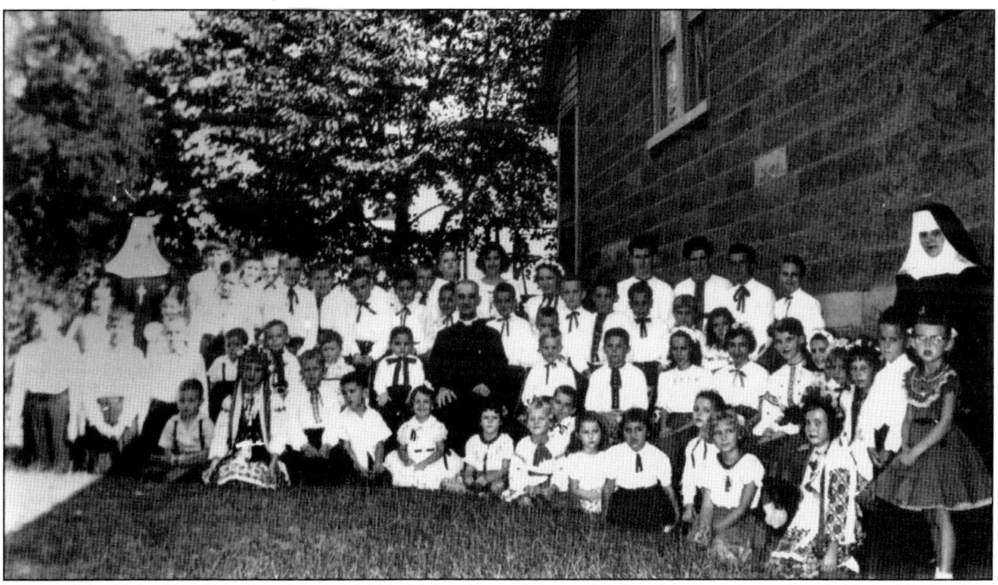

It was imperative for the post–World War II generation to send their children to Ukrainian summer schools, where they reinforced and broadened their knowledge of Ukrainian culture and religious traditions. This school at St. Nicholas UCC in Wilmington in the 1950s was under the direction of the Sisters of St. Basil the Great.

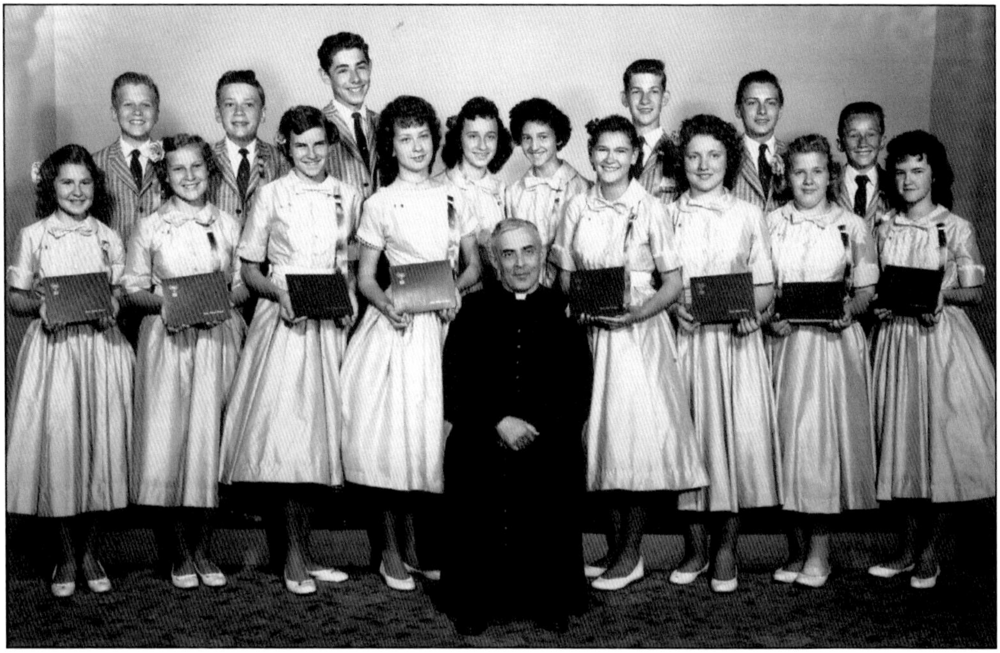

Holy Ghost Ukrainian Catholic School of Chester was the oldest Ukrainian elementary school in Delaware Valley. The graduation class of 1958 includes, from left to right, (first row) Bohdanna Trondowska, Nina Bandrowska, Caroline Druchyk, Sonia Wayda, Rev. Nicholas Zbyr (seated), Anne Kasper, Eve Soroka, Suzanne Hoynych, and Caitlin Gates; (second row) Michael Skrebut, Ihor Nazarewych, George Kobryn, Patricia Kowalchuk, Dorothy Zeliak, Stephen Wozny, Ronald Satsko, and James Murray.

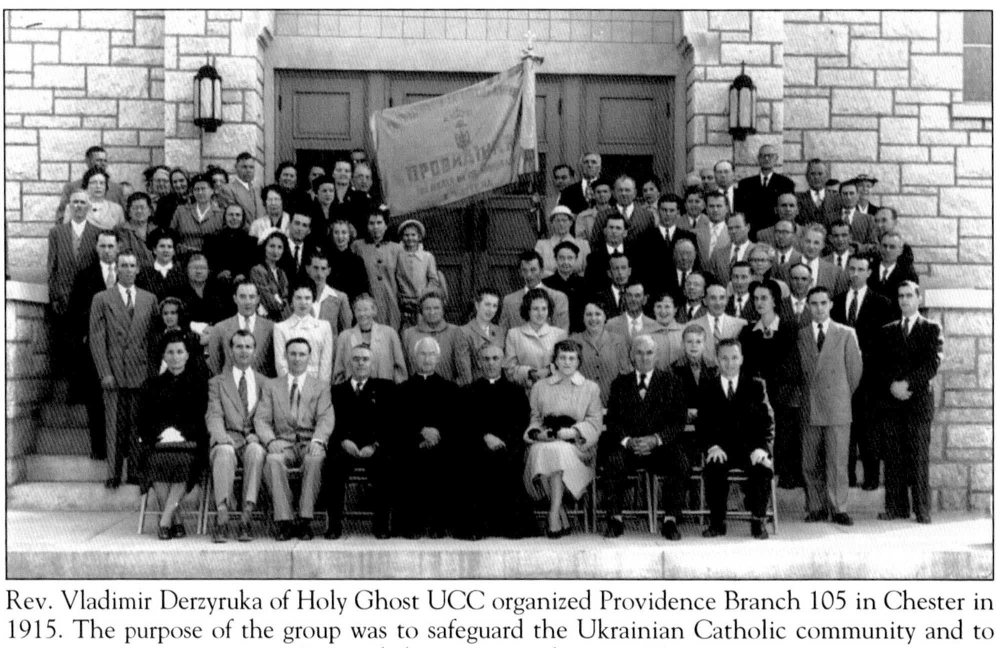

Rev. Vladimir Derzyruka of Holy Ghost UCC organized Providence Branch 105 in Chester in 1915. The purpose of the group was to safeguard the Ukrainian Catholic community and to support various institutions. Pictured above are members in 1958.

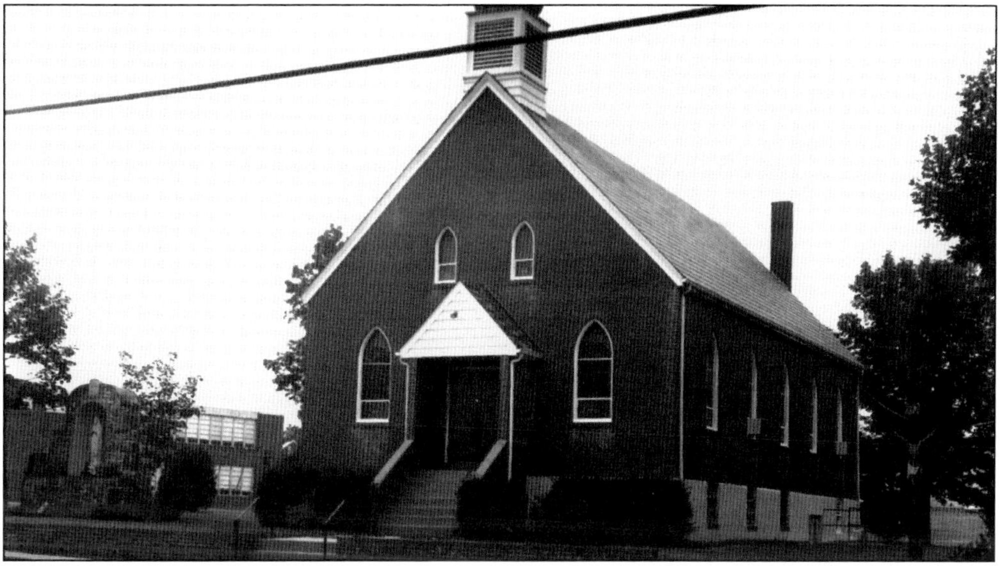

It was customary in the old country to beautify church grounds with a cross and a grotto. To the right at St. Michael's UCC in Pottstown, a cross was raised in 1954 at the conclusion of the Holy Mission. On the left a grotto was constructed honoring the Blessed Virgin Mary at the conclusion of the Marion Year in 1958.

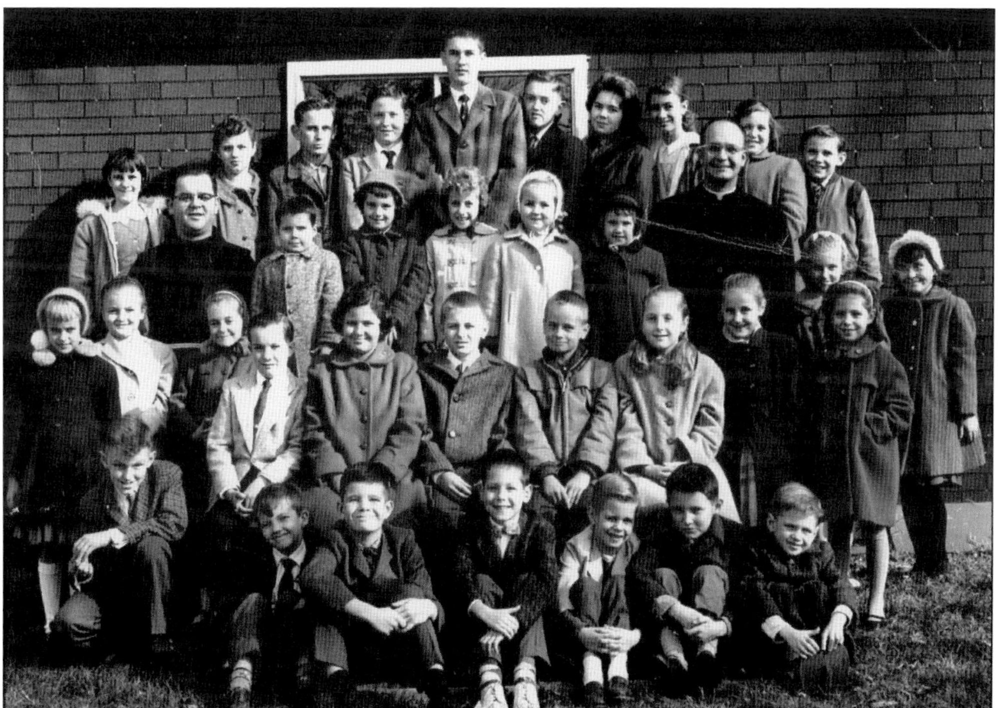

The beginnings were turbulent at St. Mary's UCC in Bristol. There were misunderstandings and strife between the generations of Ukrainians. Finally unity was achieved in 1963 when the schools were combined. Pictured here are children who attended the courses at the Bath Street School House in 1958.

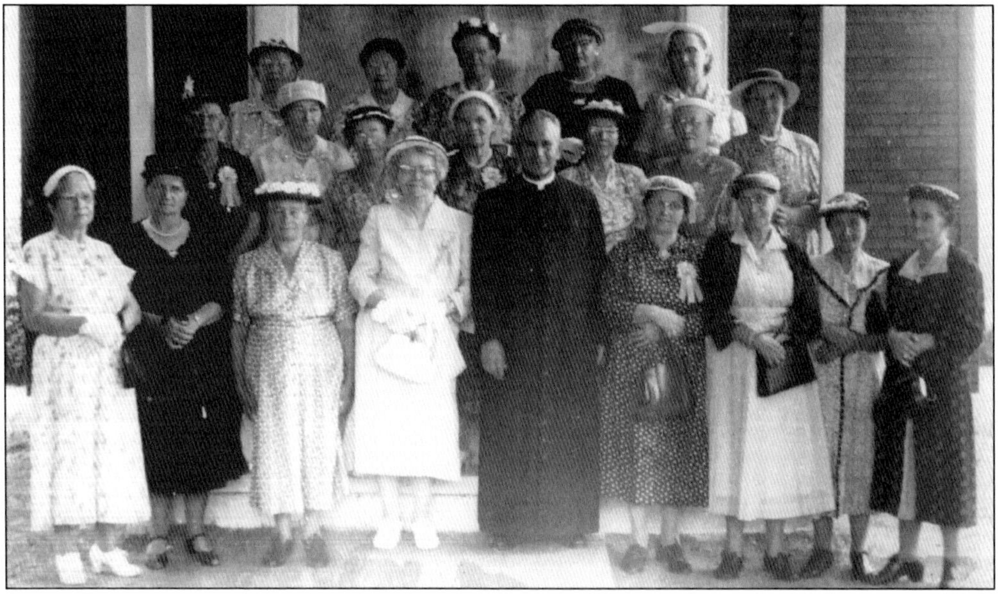

The 1959 Sodality of the Blessed Virgin Mary members from Chesapeake City pose by their church. From left to right are (first row) Martha Luzetsky, Lena Wasylczuk, Anastasia Shestock, Julia Losten, Rev. Ivan Lebedowych, Teckla Blendy, Tessi Shreiber, Anna Maksyn, and Maria Statkavige; (second row) Catherine Breza, Anna Tycki, Pauline Hrabec, Mary Trush, Kathleen Malinowsky, Sophie Lysak, and Pauline Yonko; (third row) Rose Kulic, Mary Swyka, Anna Harasymtzuk, Mary Basalyga, and Catherine Kutz.

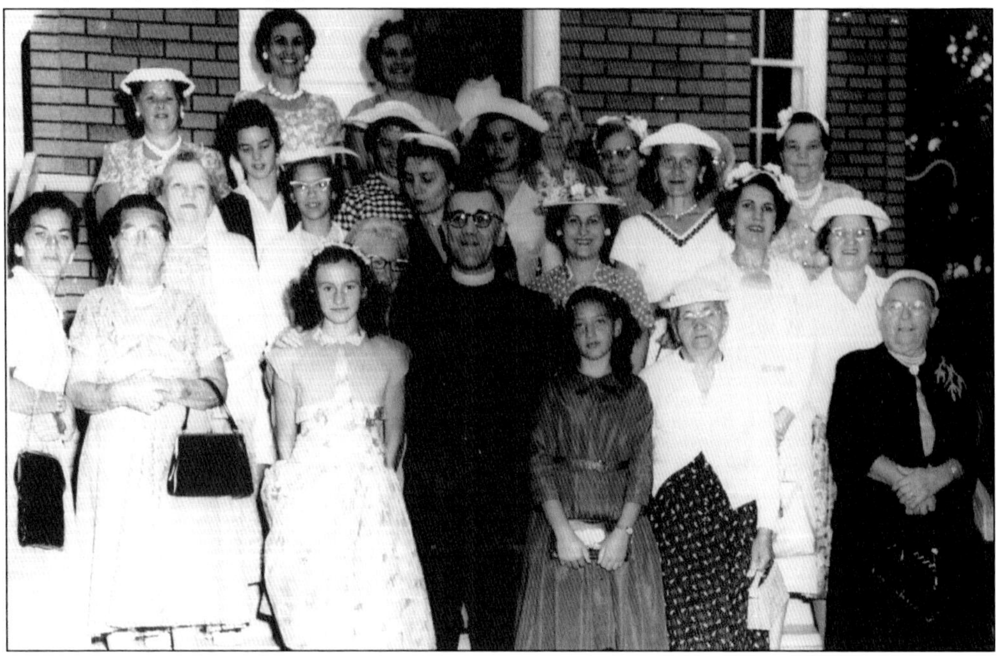

Since its inception the community in Williamstown, because of its rich farmlands, has been steadily growing. UNA started St. George's Branch in 1916. In 1918, the Apostleship of Prayer was organized. Both were influential in building SS. Peter and Paul UCC. In 1959, the pioneers and their descendants surround Rev. Isadore Nahayewsky in front of the old church.

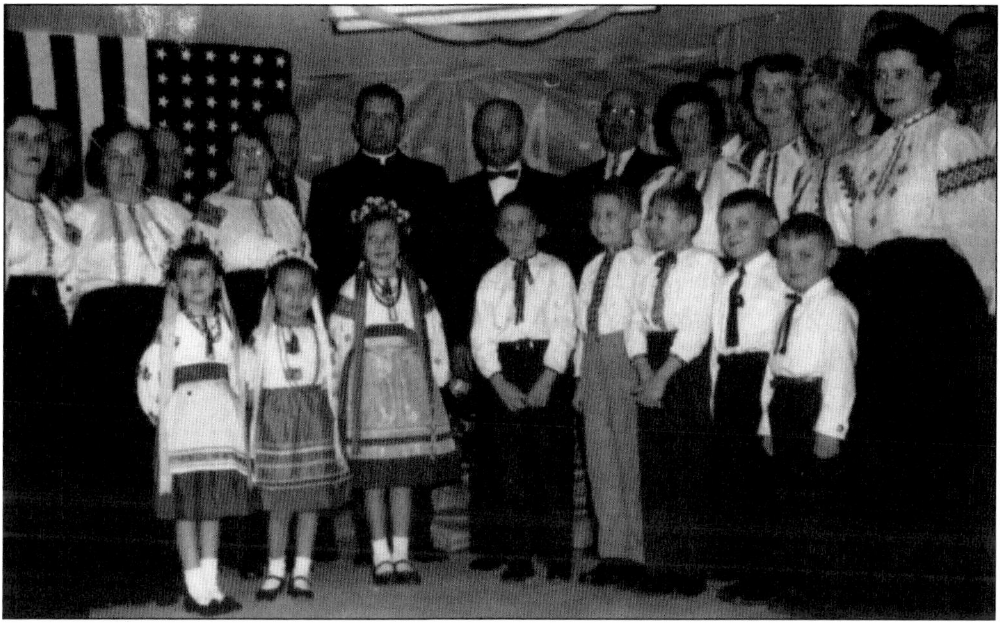

For the newcomer in the 1950s, a camera was a treasured possession. To interrupt a performance with the flash of a bulb was considered ill-mannered. St. Mary's UCC Choir from Bristol in 1957, with other program participants, poses for the obligatory photograph after the presentation.

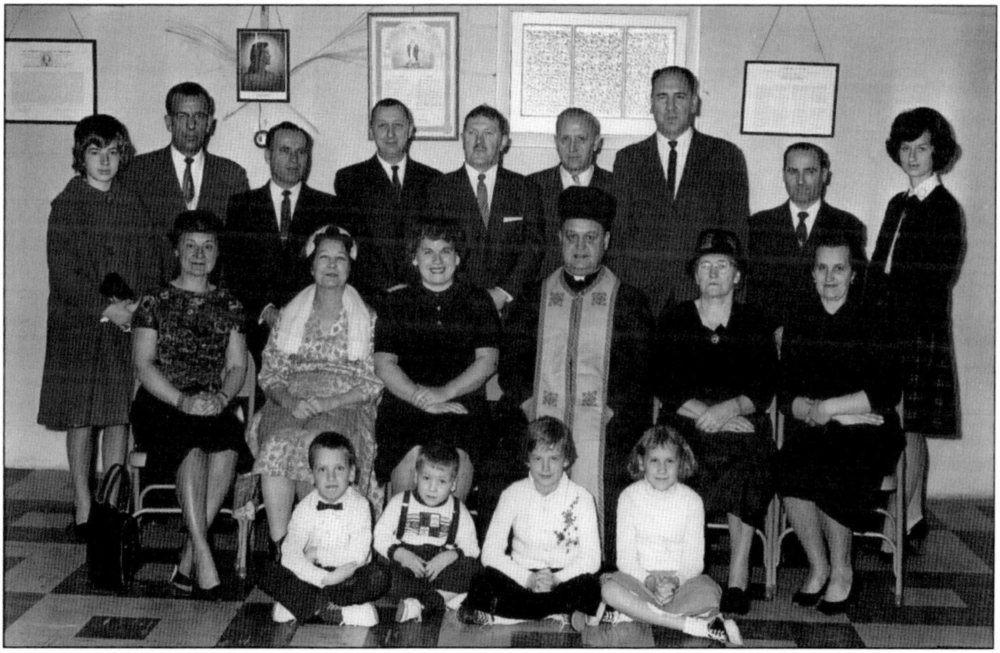

Providence Branch 110 was organized in 1956 at SS. Peter and Paul UCC in Clifton Heights. From left to right are (first row) Michael Boyko, William Boyko Jr., Stephanie Wasykewicz, and Barbara Boyko; (second row) Catherine Wascavage, Anna Newmaster, Mary Boyko, Rev. Henry Sagan, Rose Mandick, and Stephanie Wasykewicz; (third row) Ann Sehinsky, Walter Wasyke, Stefan Nych, William O'Hearn, Nicholas Robak, John Swecz, William Boyko, Michael Nych, and Irene Wasykewicz.

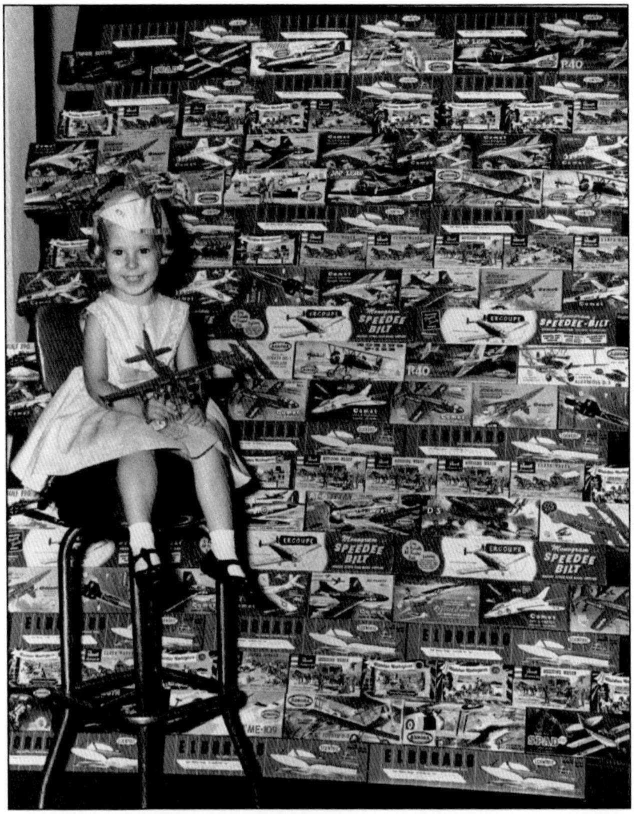

Frankford's St. Josaphat's UCC Post 371 Catholic War Veterans sponsored Operation Purple Heart in taking model kits to the Coatesville Veterans Hospital in 1959 under the leadership of Past Post Commander Peter Krawczuk. The photograph displays the model kits with Krawczuk's daughter Faith Ann holding a model of the navy's 2PV-7.

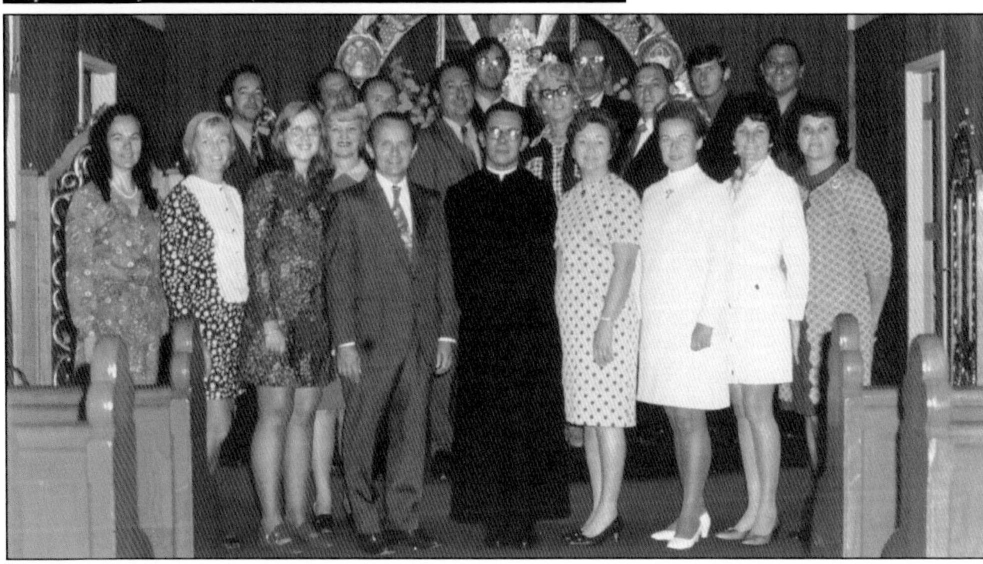

When Rev. Robert Moskal started the UCC in Warrington the first church organization was St. Anne's Choir. Members in 1970 are, from left to right, (first row) Ann Colombo, Patricia Chern, Tina Fransois, Ann Demusz, Stephen Sikora, Reverend Moskal, Christina Meckes, Sonya Gol, Dorothy Bercowy, and Helen Orzechowski; (second row) George Izak, Arthur Rohach, Ray Melnik, George Bercowy, Stephen Meckes, Sally Hudick, William Charuk, unidentified, Tim Fransois, and Steven Soroka.

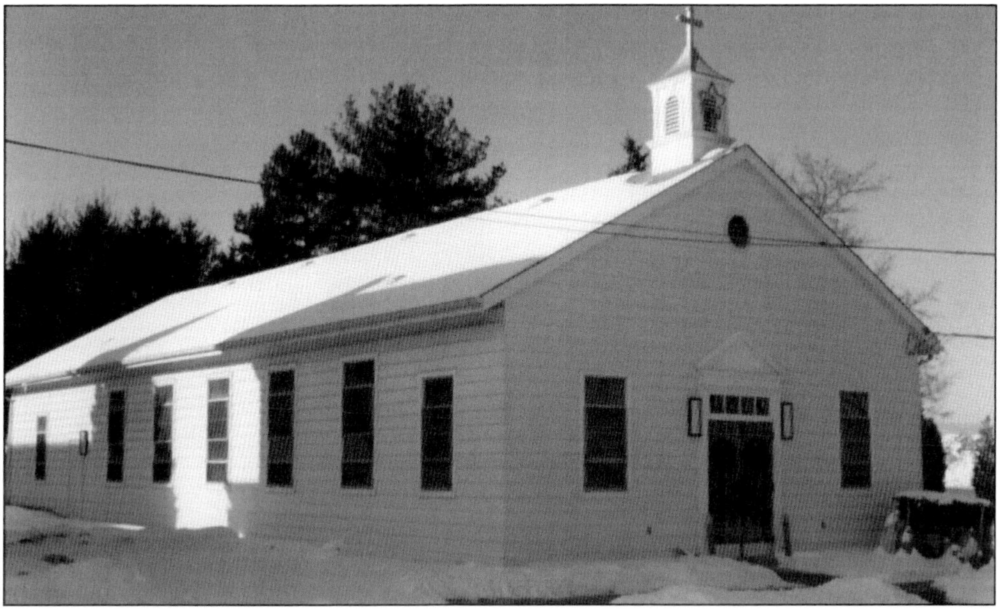

In the 1960s, some of the oldest Ukrainian farming families, descendants of Philadelphia pioneers who moved to the suburbs, upstaters who came south searching employment, and individuals who migrated from various parts of Pennsylvania and New Jersey populated the area around Warrington. For the purpose of building a diocesan high school, 16 acres of farmland was purchased. Instead St. Anne's church was built in 1964, not only for the Ukrainians but also for the Rusins and Slovaks.

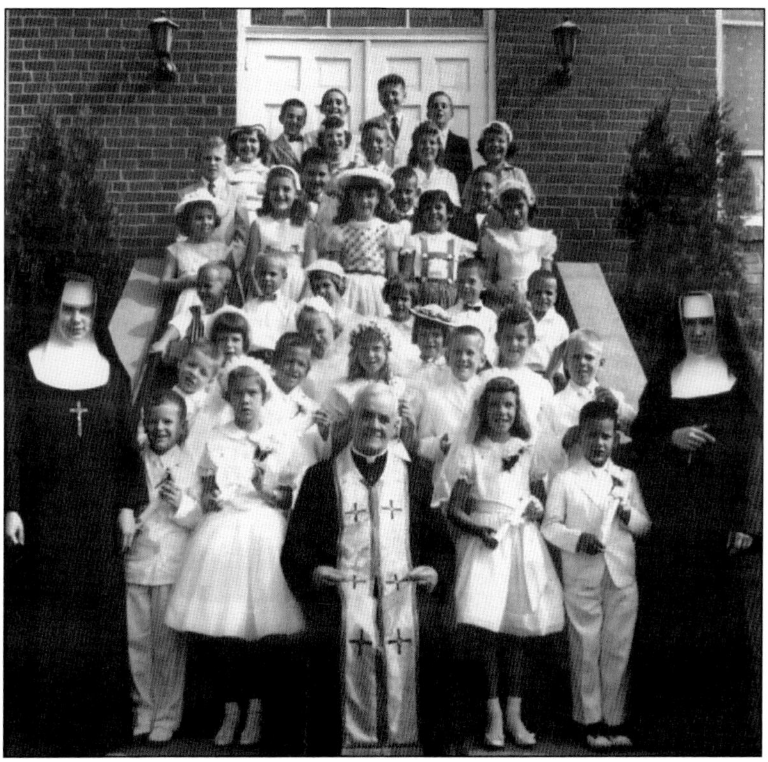

The community of St. Michael's UCC in Pottstown was also blessed by many newcomers. Rev. Nicholas Baranetsky requested the Sisters Servants of Mary Immaculate to help with religious instructions. Reverend Baranetsky is seated in the center. The first three rows of children made their First Holy Communion while others are participants of the summer school program in 1960.

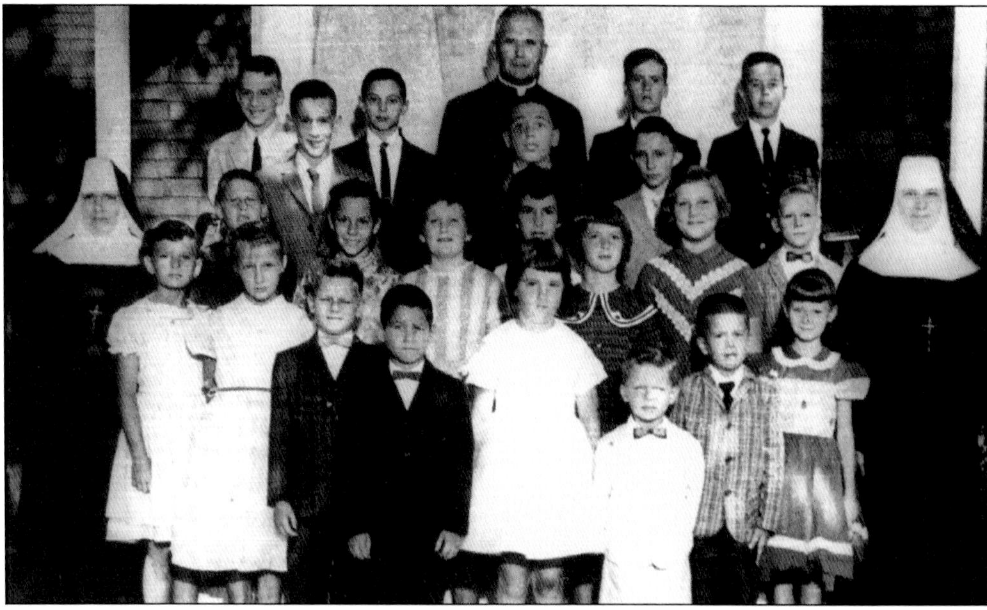

Participants at Ukrainian Summer School in Chesapeake City in the early 1960s, from left to right, are (first row) Nicholas Wasylczuk, James Jensen, Carol Krochak, Michael Wasylczuk, Paul Hrabec, and Katherine Wasylczuk; (second row) Sister Daniel OSBM, Helen Critchley, John Jensen, Katherine Loller, Linda Caruso, Catherine Vaughn, Rosemary Krochak, Christine Krochak, Mary Jane Bowers, Ralph Bowers, and Sister Christine OSBM; (third row) Robert Swyka, Jerry Swyka, Ronald Luzetsky, Rev. Ivan Lebedowych, Mark Alcorn, Raymond Hrabec, Jerry Caruso, and Robert Loller.

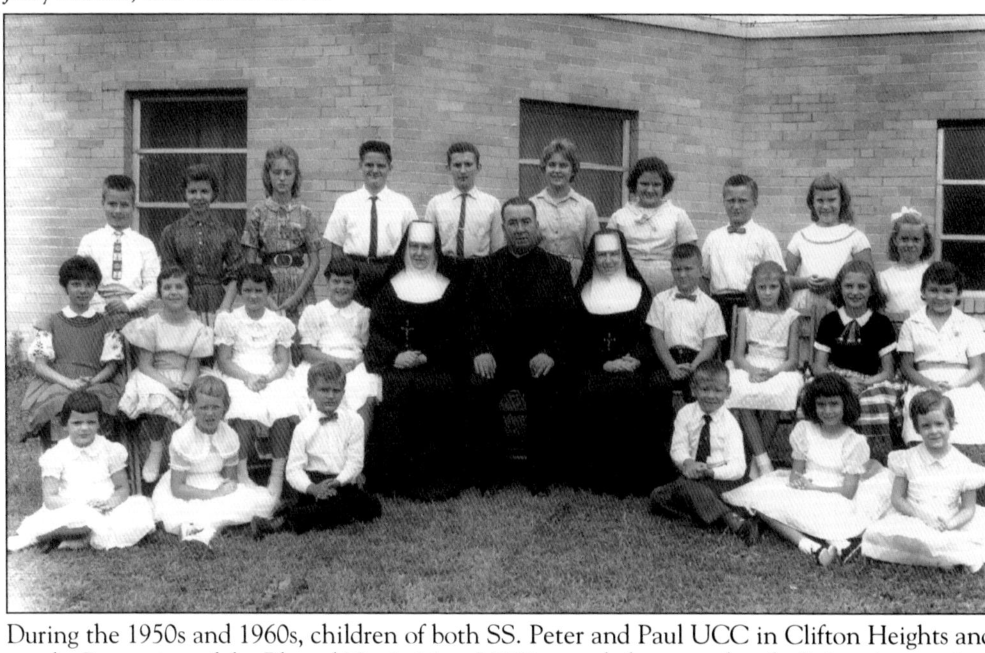

During the 1950s and 1960s, children of both SS. Peter and Paul UCC in Clifton Heights and nearby Protection of the Blessed Virgin Mary UCC attended two weeks of religious instruction. In 1960, the students are photographed with their teachers, Sister Servants of Mary Immaculate and Rev. Michael Pyrih in the center.

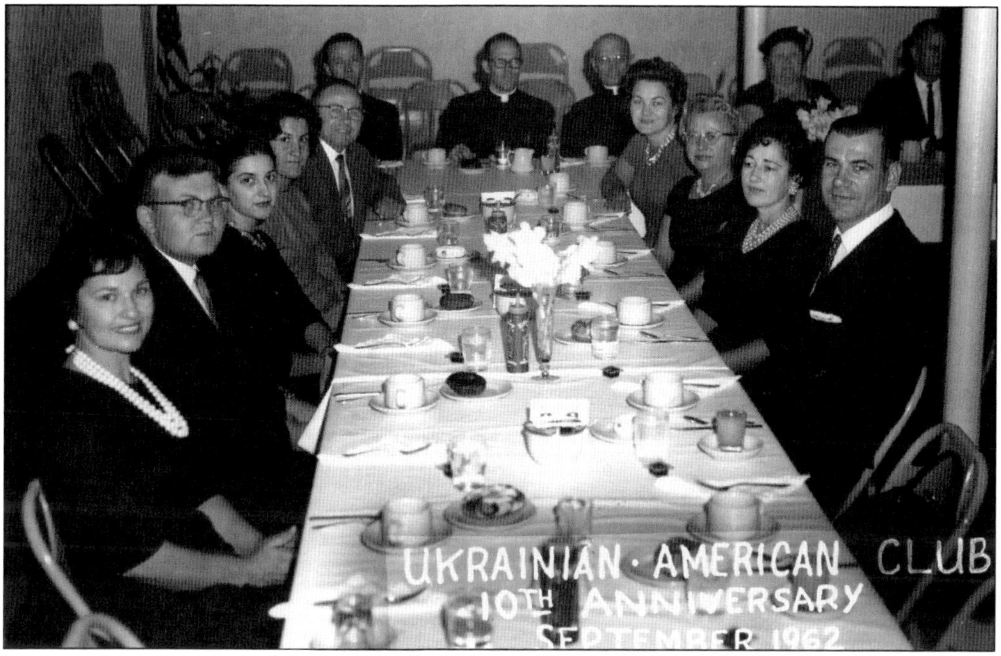

Members of St. Nicholas UCC in Millville and some Ukrainian Orthodox church members started the Ukrainian-American Club in 1952. Besides nurturing Ukrainian heritage in the community, they participated in church activities. In 1962, they celebrated their 10th anniversary.

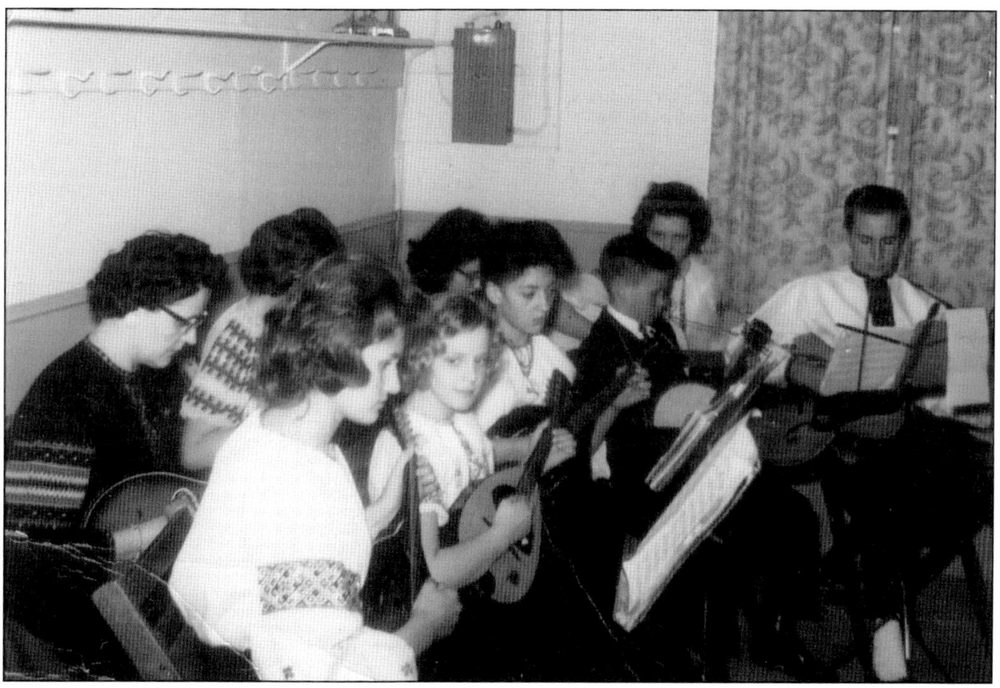

In 1941, a youth society named Ukraina was organized in Williamstown and formed an orchestra. In 1956, Providence Branch 174 under the patronage of St. Olha revived the orchestra. Olha Nahayewska directed the orchestra in 1961.

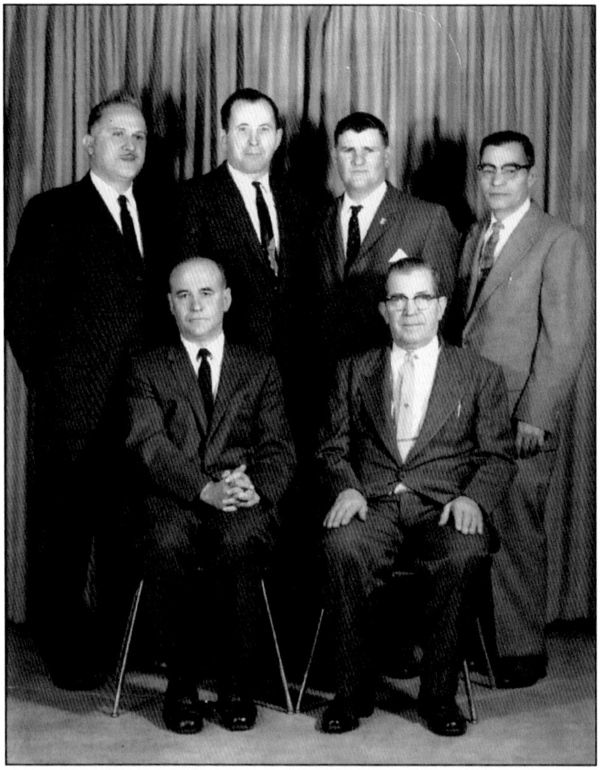

The transition of St. Michael's UCC from Camden to Cherry Hill created many difficulties. With hard work from Providence Branch 52, the transition proved to be successful. Officers of Camden's Providence Branch 52 in 1962 are, from left to right, (first row) Michael Romach and Stephen Haday; (second row) Mykola Rudnytsky, Stefan Panasiuk, Yurij Policzuk, and Stefan Solowy.

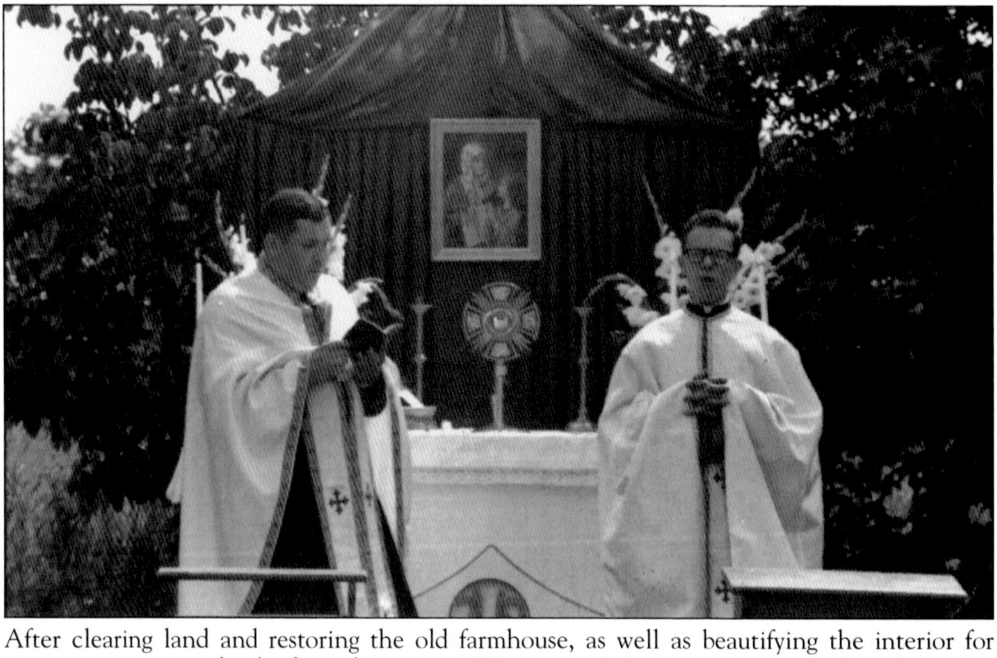

After clearing land and restoring the old farmhouse, as well as beautifying the interior for services, it was time for the first pilgrimage to Warrington's St. Anne's Mission Chapel in 1963. A miraculous icon of St. Anne as well as some of her relics were exposed for veneration. From left to right are Rev. Myron Kozmoski and Rev. Robert Moskal (the first pastor) conducting a Moleben service outdoors. Dancing in the barn that evening ended the festivities.

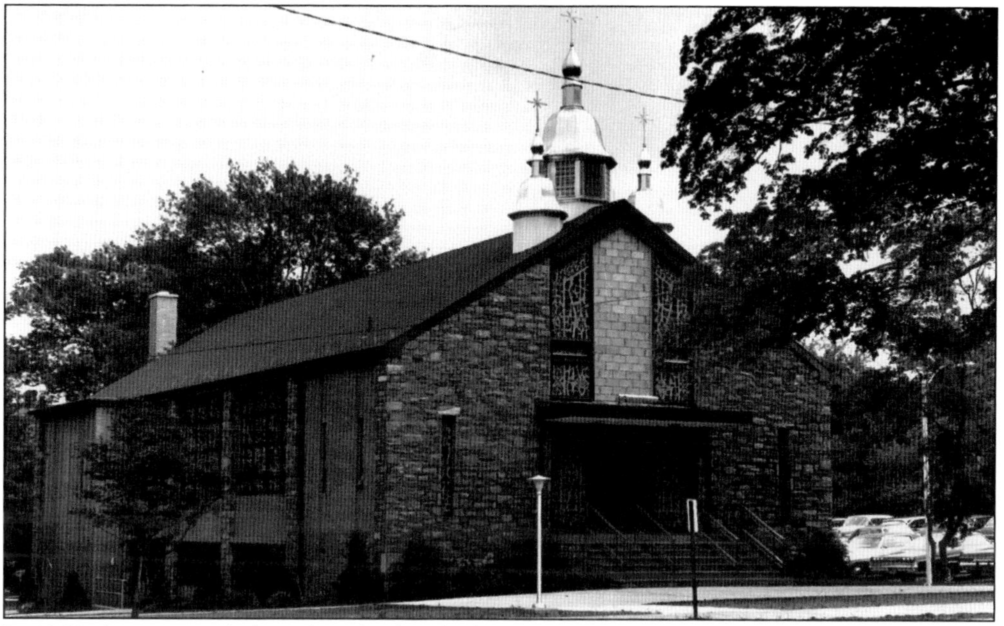

In 1962, there was a shift to the suburbs; the hierarchy of the UCC saw the need for parishes in these new areas. Annunciation of the Blessed Virgin Mary in Melrose Park, an affluent suburb, was one such case. At first a home was purchased and remodeled into a chapel, and 18 years later, after a series of financial woes, this church was built. This is the church in 1985.

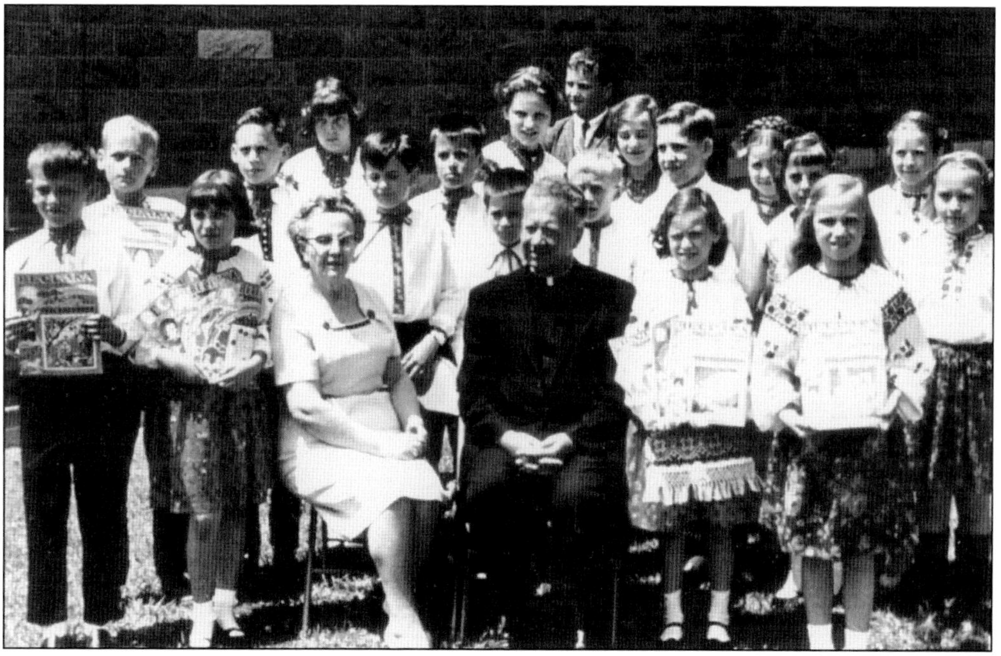

From the beginnings, Ukrainian parishes conducted evening classes to foster traditions and culture among the youth. With the arriving DPs, classes were held at the Catholic churches on Saturdays and at the Orthodox churches on Sundays with the same intent. Above is the St. Nicholas UCC class picture from 1964 to 1965 in Wilmington with teacher Olha Harwanko and Rev. Stephen Hotra seated in the center.

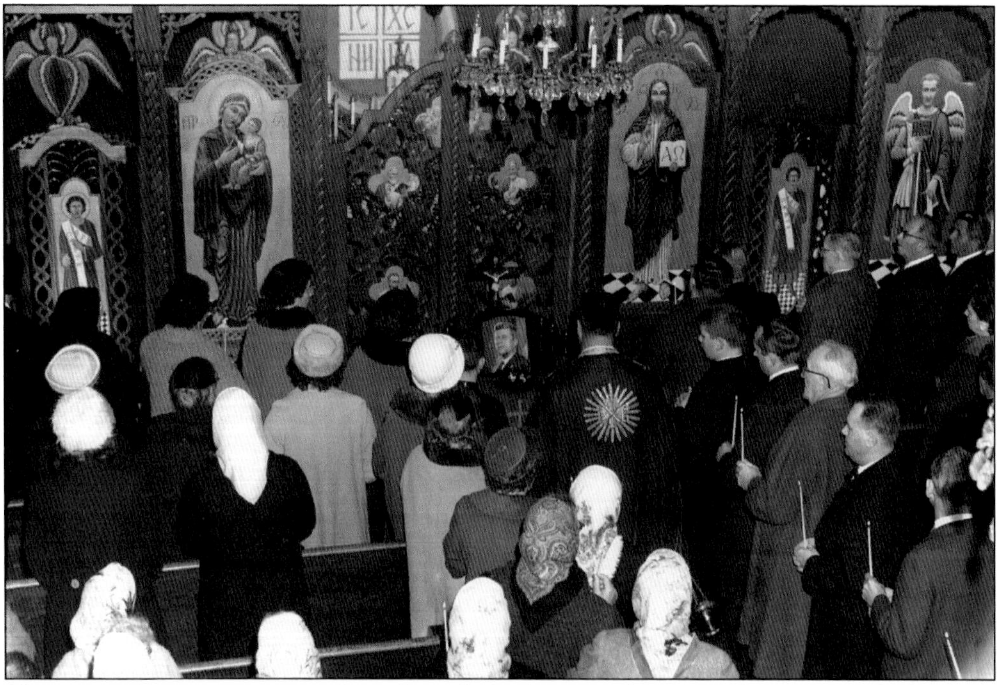

Ukrainian religious institutions throughout the Delaware Valley not only maintained Ukrainian traditions they also promulgated American patriotism. St. Michael's UCC in Camden conducted a memorial service observing the first anniversary of the death of Pres. John F. Kennedy in 1965.

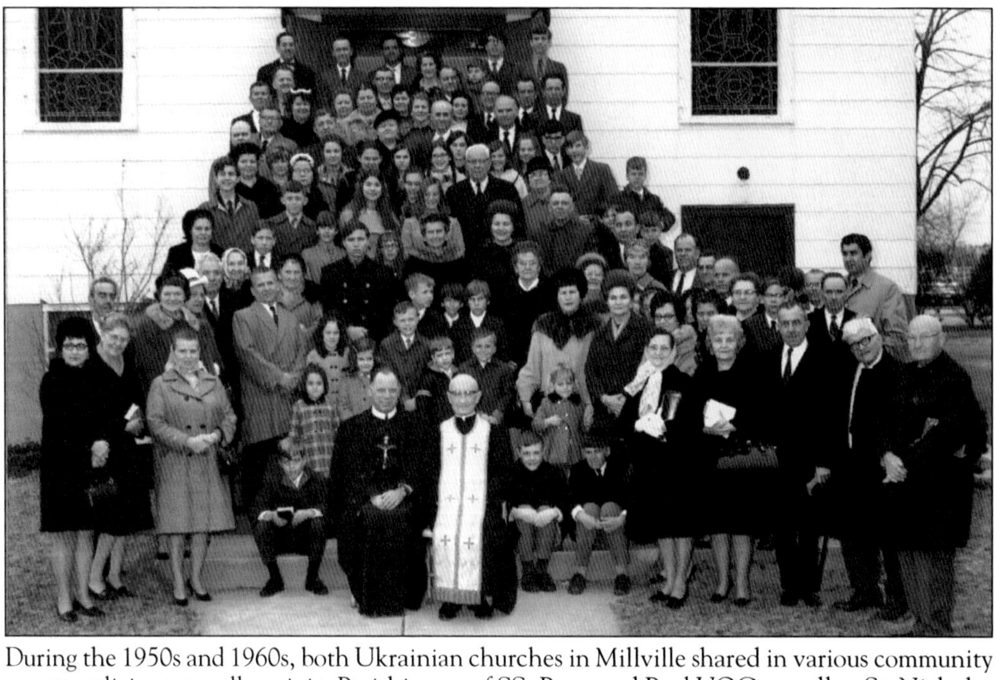

During the 1950s and 1960s, both Ukrainian churches in Millville shared in various community events, religious as well as civic. Parishioners of SS. Peter and Paul UOC as well as St. Nicholas UCC attended an annual mission in 1964 and were photographed after the event in front of St. Nicholas UCC.

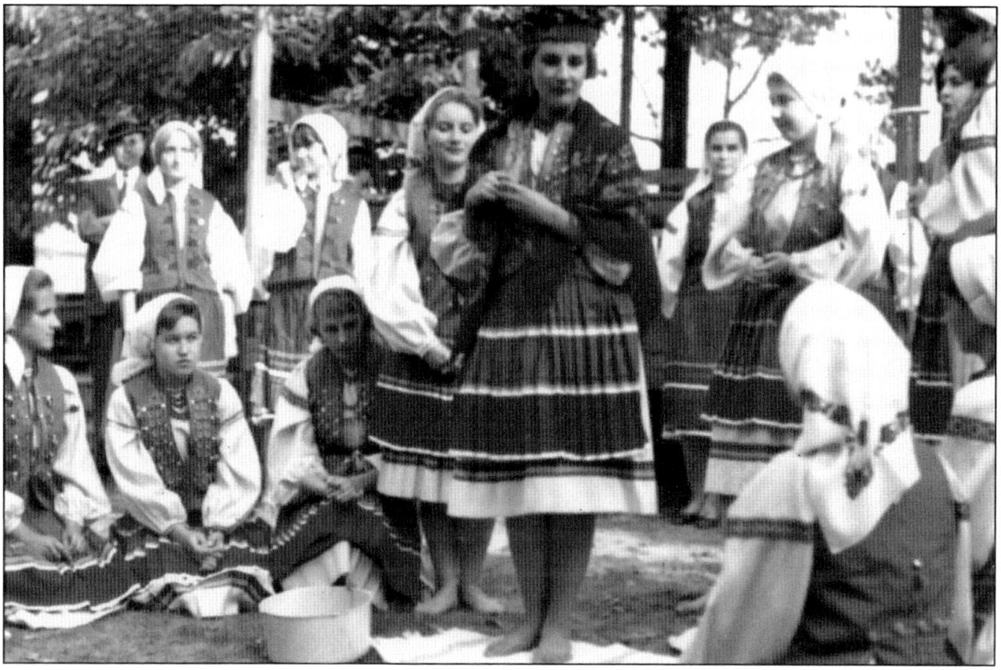

In the early 1950s, newly formed youth organizations held their outings on Ukrainian farms or picnic grounds. Standarowich's farm, located in Torresdale, was a favorite. Members of Plast Ukrainian Youth Organization of America display the folk dress of Lemkivchyna. Their parents sewed the costumes. Stephania Mycak (behind) and Halyna Sagata are standing in the center.

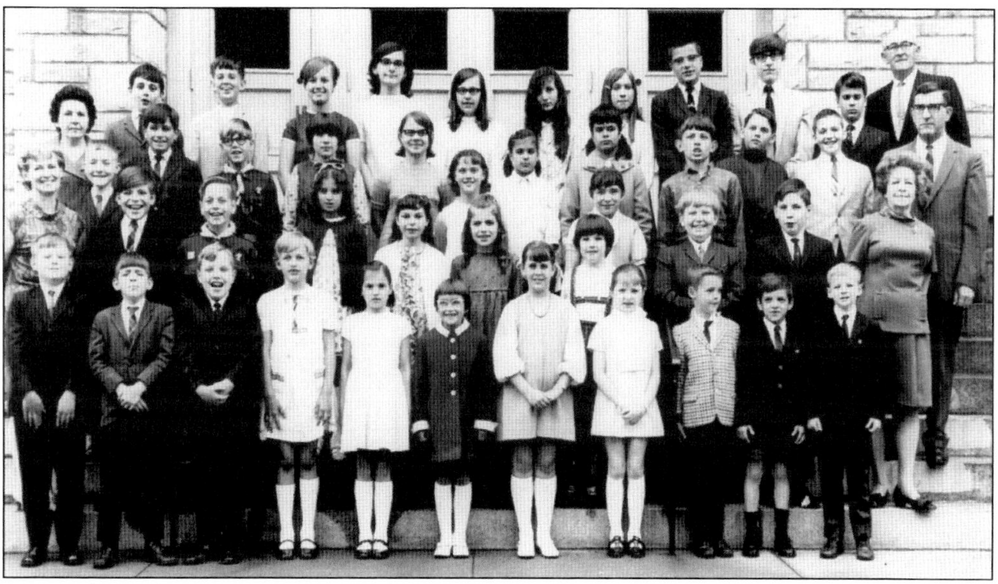

Soyuz Ukrainok Branch 13 organized Ukrainian Heritage School held on Saturdays in Chester in 1961 where students studied language, history, and culture. This 1968–1969 photograph shows the faculty and students. On the extreme left are teachers Irene Kuzyk in the second row and Lidia Hrabova in the third row. On the far right in the second row is Dora Sawchek, in the third row is Wolodymyr Alexander, head of the parent teacher's association, and in the fourth row is the principal Stephen Mykyta.

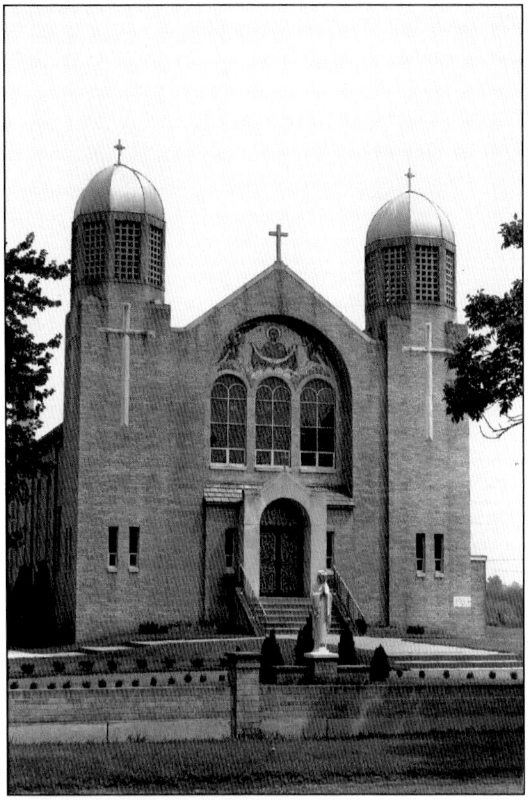

Ukrainians from Philadelphia, Chester, and Frankford purchased farmland in the 1920s around Bristol. By the 1940s, about 30 families lived in the area. By the mid-1950s, enough Ukrainians settled in Bristol, Levittown, Langhorn, and surrounding communities to establish a new parish. Protection of the Blessed Virgin Mary UCC was organized in 1954, and the church was erected in 1963.

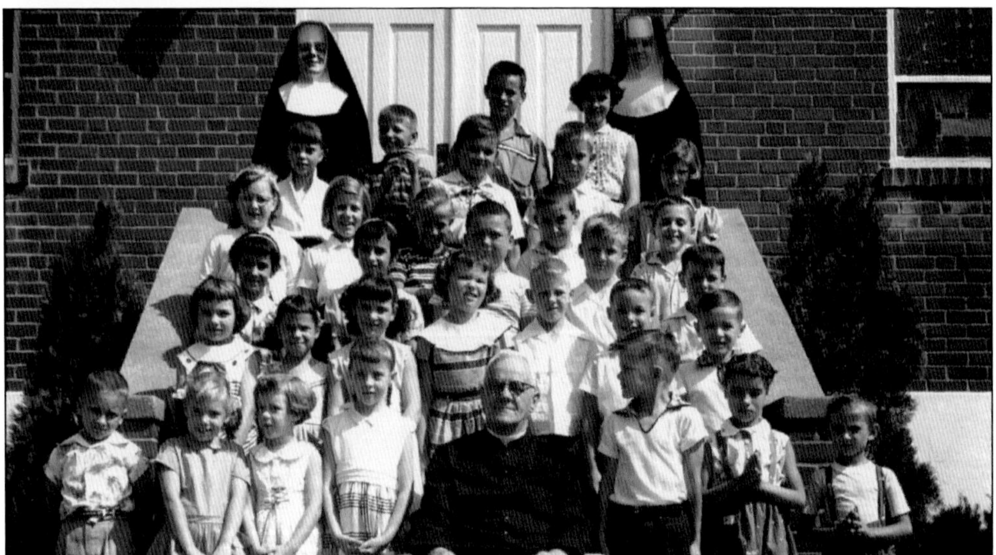

Rev. Nicholas Baranetsky, during his long pastorate at St. Michael's UCC in Pottstown, dedicated himself to religious education of the young. Even in his older years, he taught classes on Saturdays and at summer camps. With the coming of more refugees, he asked Sisters Servants of Mary Immaculate for much-needed help. The attendees at the 1965 summer camp are photographed with the pastor and their teachers.

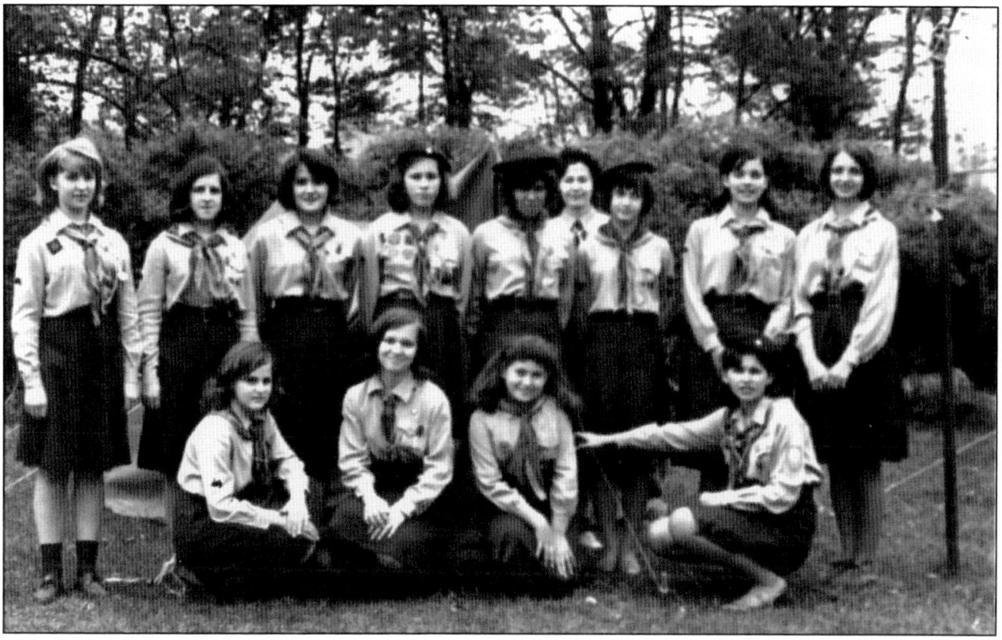

Plast Ukrainian Youth Organization of America in Chester was organized in 1950. In 1965 at Karpaty, Bohdan Maleckyj's Picnic and Dancing Grove in Chelsea, Pennsylvania, the young ladies camped for the weekend. From left to right are (first row) Olga Komandanczuk, Mary Makowska, Anna Maria Hawrylak, and Lubov Lesyk; (second row) Mary Chichanowska, Luba Wizniak, Joanne Kiczula, Oksana Lesyk, Olga Tarnowska, Irene Solczanyk, Mary Bagan, Christine Kyj, and Katherine Wenchak.

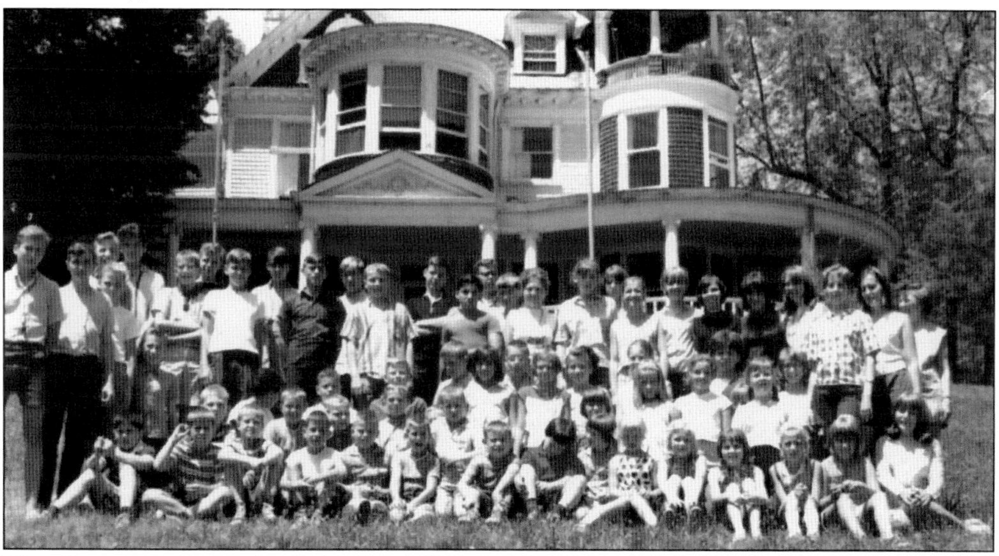

The Organization for the Rebirth of Ukraine (ODWU), a nationalistic organization, was established in 1931. The group had chapters throughout the Delaware Valley and is affiliated with the Ukrainian Gold Cross. In 1957, near Lehighton, Pennsylvania, they established Ukrainian Homestead, a multipurpose resort. Picnics, student conferences, dances, and summer camps for children run by the Ukrainian Gold Cross are just a few of the uses. Summer camp participants in 1962 are pictured above.

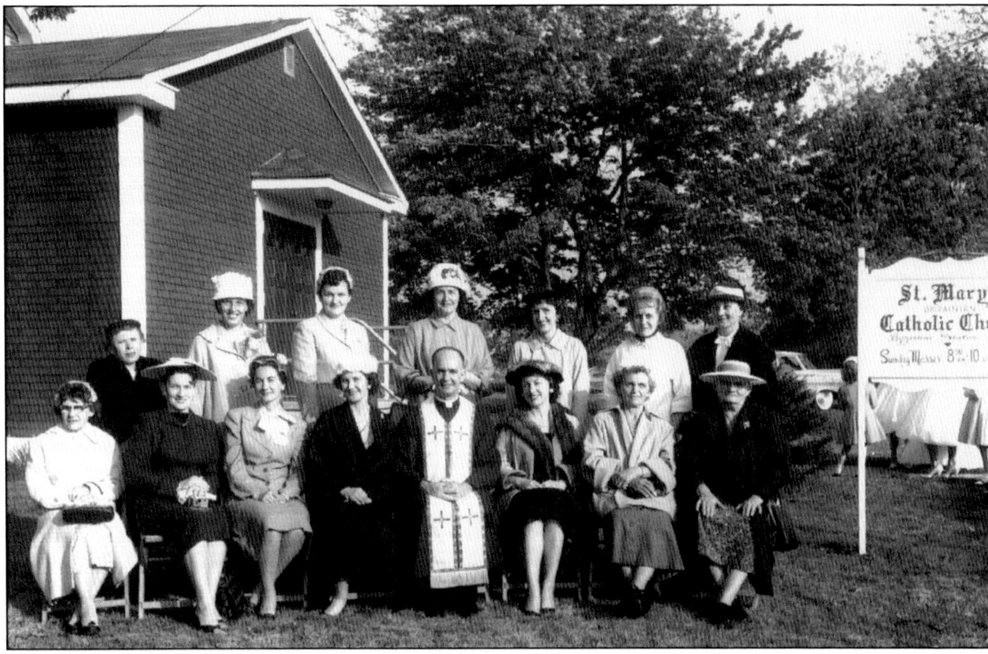

League of the Sacred Heart was the sisterhood that worked for the benefit of Protection UCC of Bristol. The members in 1960 are in front of the chapel. From left to right are (first row) Helen Rosetta, Rose Nottage, Verna Krysak, Stella Kravchak, Rev. Michael Fedorowich, Elizabeth Souchak, Agnes Triczchuk, and Ann Kitsock; (second row) Anna Sidorska, Henrietta Rutkowska, Helen McCarra, Irene Wargo, Helen Romanko, Helen Cedar, and Helen Chrin.

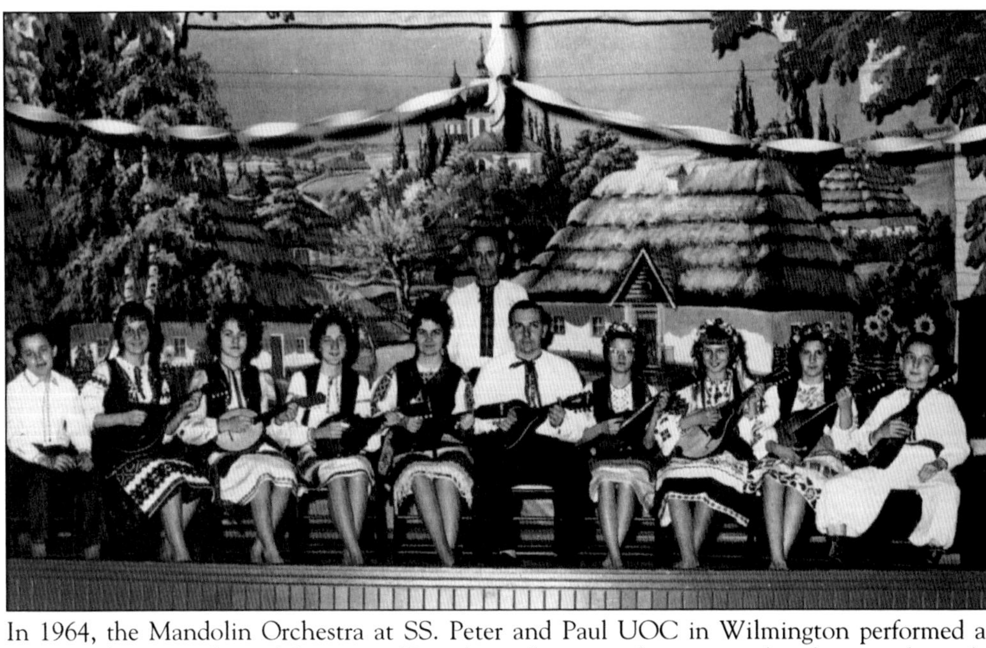

In 1964, the Mandolin Orchestra at SS. Peter and Paul UOC in Wilmington performed at various religious and social functions. Here the orchestra is playing at a church spring festival.

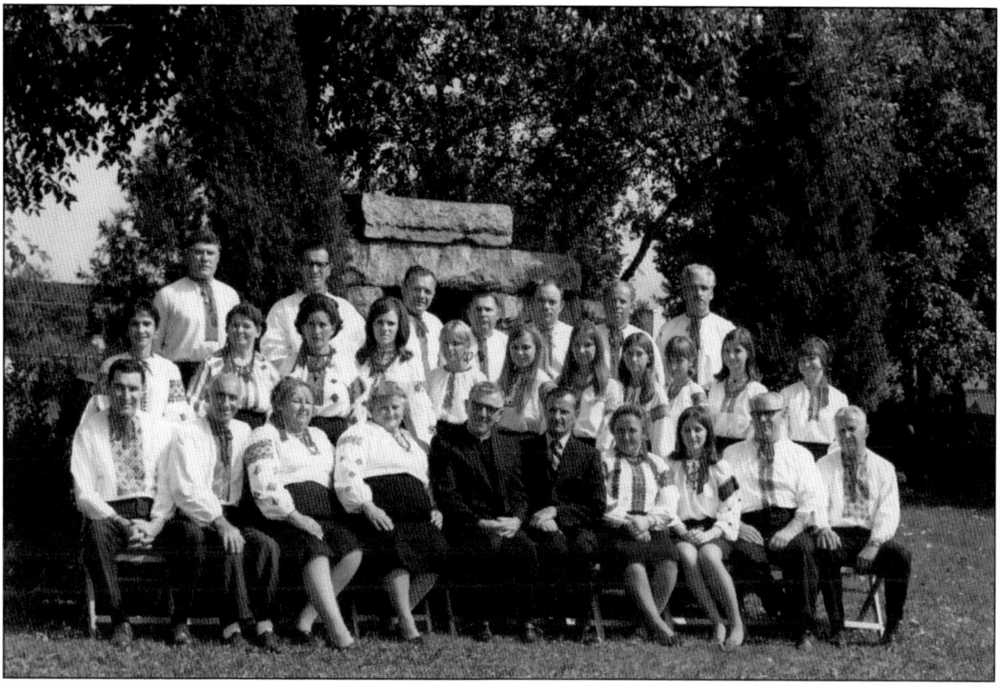

The Ukrainian community of Phoenixville marked the transfer of Rev. Isidore Nahayewsky with a concert. SS. Peter and Paul UCC Choir after presenting its program marked this occasion with a photograph. Reverend Nahayewsky is fifth from left, and to his left is choir director Stephen Zguta.

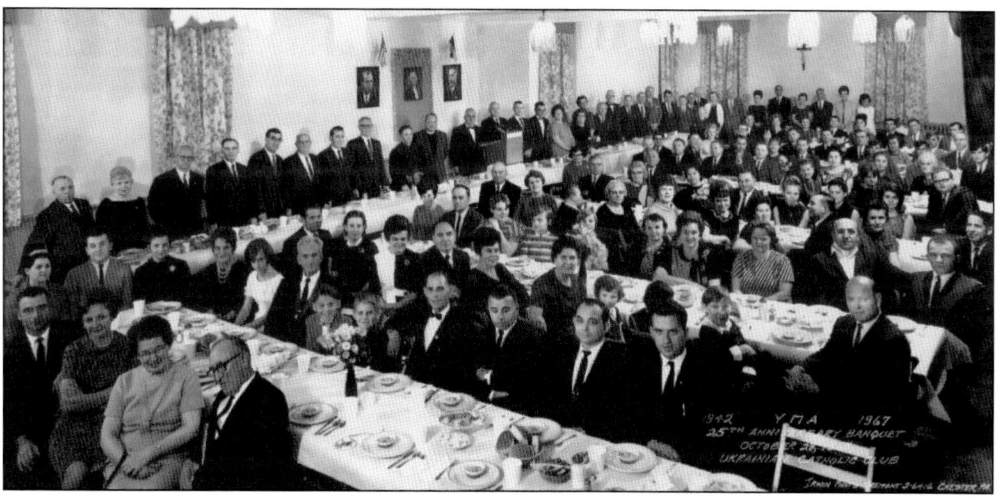

During World War II, Ukrainians fighting both the Germans and the Russians organized an insurgent army with the goal of gaining independence for Ukraine. In 1967, the Ukrainian Congress Committee of America, Chester Branch, honored them with a 25th-anniversary banquet held at the Ukrainian Catholic American Club in Chester. At the podium is Wolodymyr Korchynsky, president of the branch.

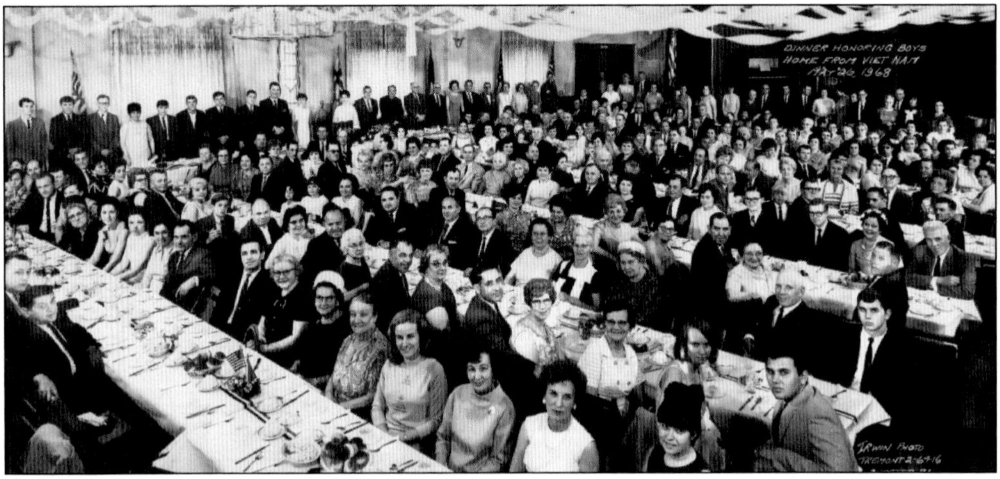

Communists overtook Ukrainian lands by 1922. Since then, Ukrainians everywhere fought this atheistic ideology. When the opportunity arose to fight communism as the enemy of the United States, Ukrainians wholeheartedly supported the war. The boys who came home from Vietnam in 1968 were honored at the UNH in Chester.

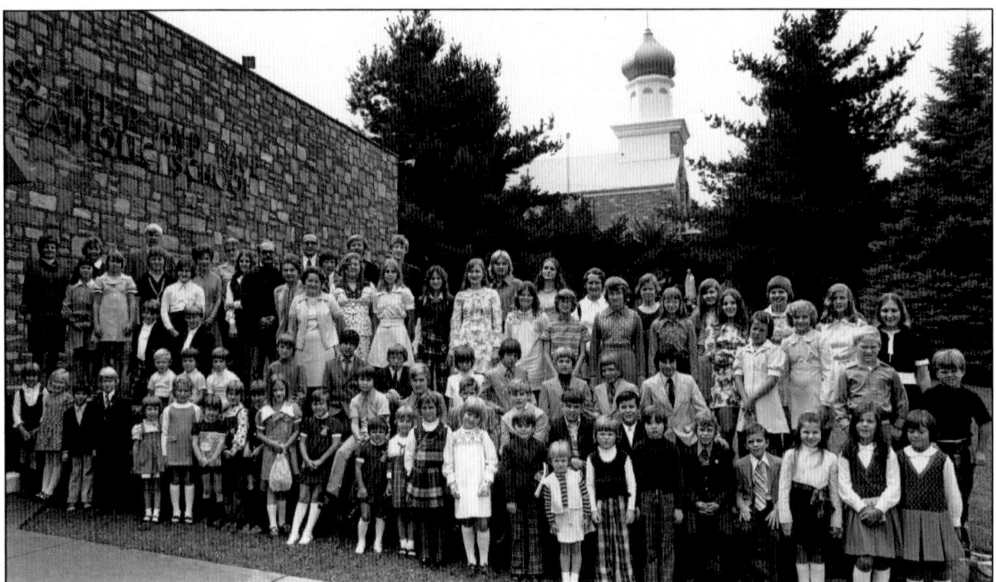

Even though a school building was built to host an elementary school, there were never enough pupils in Bridgeport for a full-time school. Instead the building was used on Saturdays or Sundays to teach religion and Ukrainian culture. In this 1973 photograph are the schoolchildren of SS. Peter and Paul UCC with the principals Walter Luciw and Michael Maslayak standing in the back row on the left.

Four

INTERTWINING CULTURES

We are honor bound to learn, create, and live to replace those who taught us how.
—Christine Kulchyckyj, Cinnaminson

As a result of great sacrifices and strict work ethics of Ukrainian immigrants after World War II, the Ukrainian American society, formerly composed of the working class with a faint sprinkling of intellectuals, now assumed a more balanced composition including laborers, artisans, businessmen, and other professional and educational classes. Gradually Ukrainian Americans began to assume occupations in the Delaware Valley benefitting an inherently cultural and talented people and, in the 1970s and 1980s, distinctly changing their immigrant image.

Moreover, these decades were also times of Ukrainian mobility within the United States. Partly as a result of the 1970s recession and the inflation of the 1980s, many first-, second-, and even third-generation Ukrainians moved south from northern Pennsylvania's almost defunct coal-mining regions. Attraction of big cities spearheaded the mass exodus of college-bound immigrants from the boroughs of the Delaware Valley, resulting in a distinct mixture of different generations of Ukrainians.

This migration and transformation created many cultural changes in the valley's Ukrainian American society. For example, when schools of Ukrainian studies were closed, and choirs, bands, dances, and other cultural activities curtailed, younger Ukrainian Americans easily transferred these activities to the newly centralized Ukrainian Cultural Center in Philadelphia (Jenkintown); Tryzub, a Philadelphia sports center for many years, relocated to Horsham, Pennsylvania. Catholic, Orthodox, and Baptist churches were constructed in new Ukrainian communities.

For the post–World War II immigrants, the first priority was to purchase a car and a house, not forgetting their main objective: instilling patriotism into the next generation and the desire for a free Ukraine. They adjusted to the needs of the young and their newly acquired forms of recreation, via the car, by establishing a series of resorts, first in proximity throughout the Delaware Valley, then expanding to the Jersey seashore and to the Pocono and Catskill Mountains. Young adults were given the opportunity to meet Ukrainians from other cities, and many met future spouses there, returning in later years to the resorts with children. These resorts were founded by Ukrainian fraternal or political organizations and catered to all Ukrainian Americans. Various youth groups also established Ukrainian educational summer camps for the children of new immigrants. Social and cultural goals were, to a degree, met by children attending these camps, young adults spending leisurely weekends at the resorts, and adults participating in a variety of cultural activities, picnics, and outings at the shore.

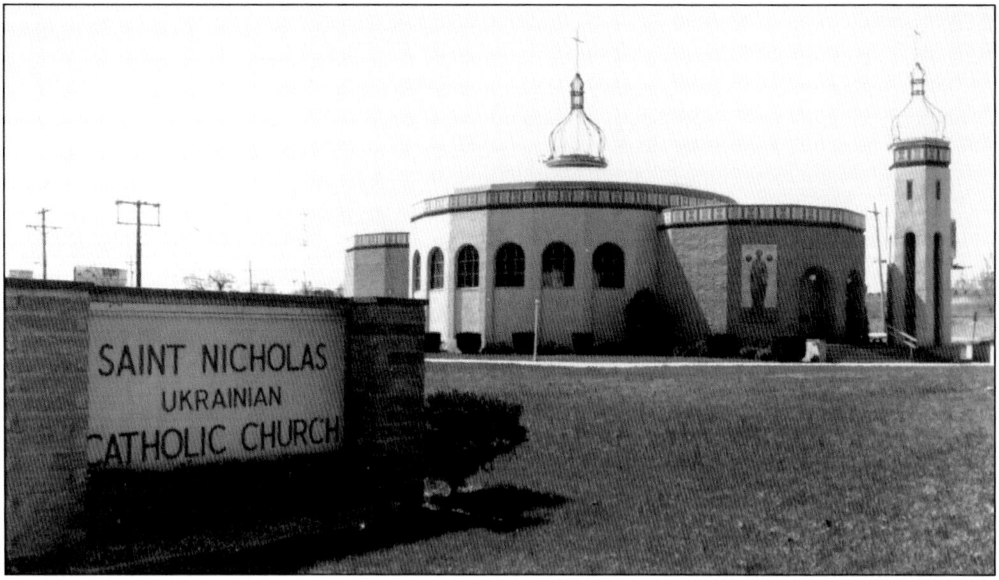

With the influx of new immigrants after World War II, St. Nicholas UCC in Wilmington became too small, so Rev. Stephen Hotra, then pastor and native son of Chesapeake City, decided to build a larger and more modern church. In 1964, a lot was purchased, and in 1969, the doors were opened to this Eastern-style church.

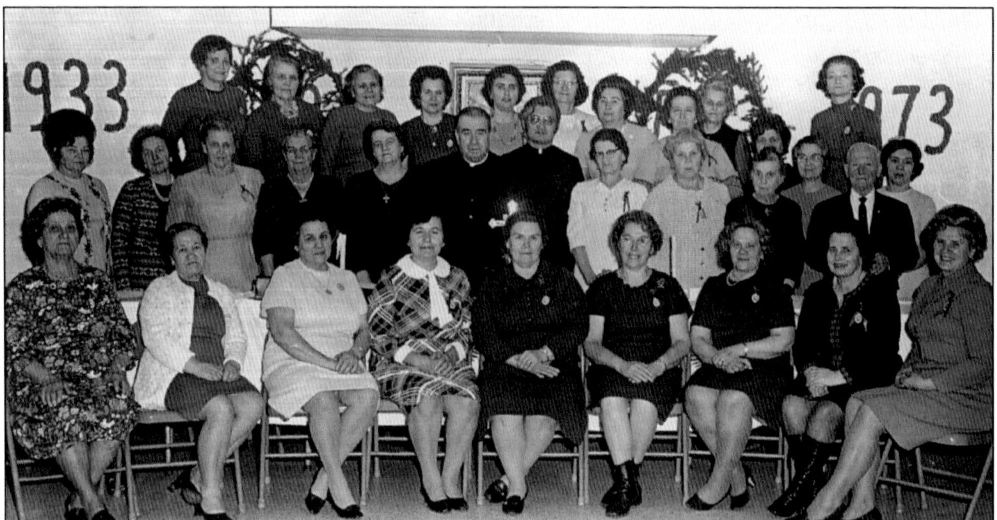

Celebrating the 40th Jubilee of the Apostleship of Prayer in Wilmington's St. Nicholas UCC are the women who work and pray to maintain the parish. From left to right are (first row) Anna Cycyk, Katherine Petesz, Olga Wozny, Wasylyna Koreniwsky, Anastasia Karacz, Pawlina Dziubak, Katherine Kostyshyn, Sophia Cybak, and Mary Kucaba; (second row) Katherine Husak, Anastasia Stecko, Justyna Szczerba, Maria Poczynok, Anna Pyrih, Rev. Michael Pyrih, Rev. Roman Dubitsky, Maria Lenio, Anna Bakomenko, Olena Sluzar, Stephania Hrycushko, Nicholas Chalus, and Mary Demko; (third row) Olha Paranczak, Kataryna Hlyniansky, Maria Woloszyn, Anna Ginsiorsky, Irene Serba, Eva Brown, Mary Bilecky, Olena Pukatsch, Vera Harwanko, Maria Maybroda, and Ivanna Dycio.

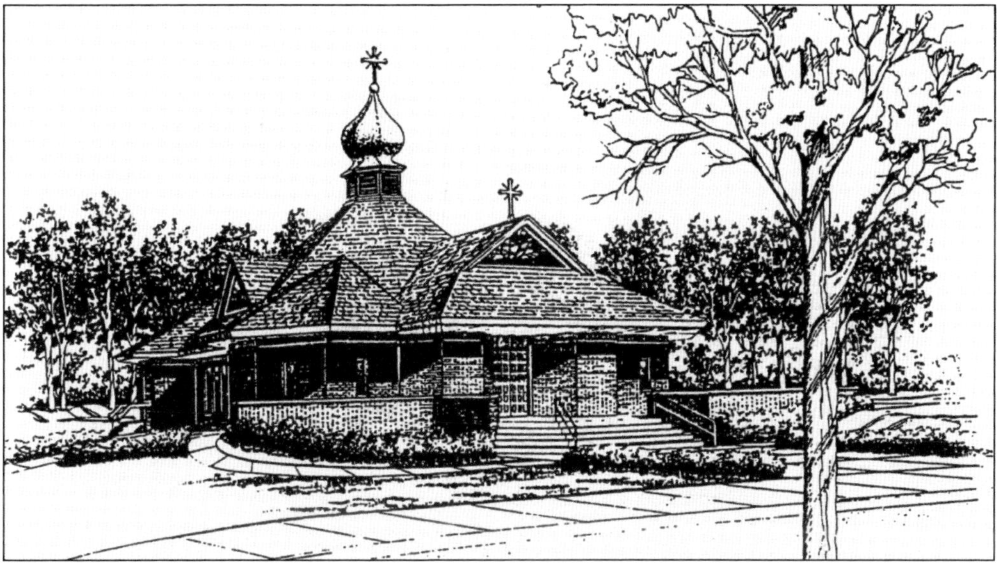

In the early 1900s, Ukrainians who lived on farms around the Lansdale area were too scattered to form a community. By the 1920s, they had a chapel, and for two years, priests were visiting them. In the 1950s, the Rusins were unsuccessful in forming a parish. With the influx of the DPs in the 1960s, Ukrainians formed the Presentation of Our Lord mission chapel in 1969. Finally in 1979, they built their own church not only for Ukrainians but also for Rusins and Slovaks.

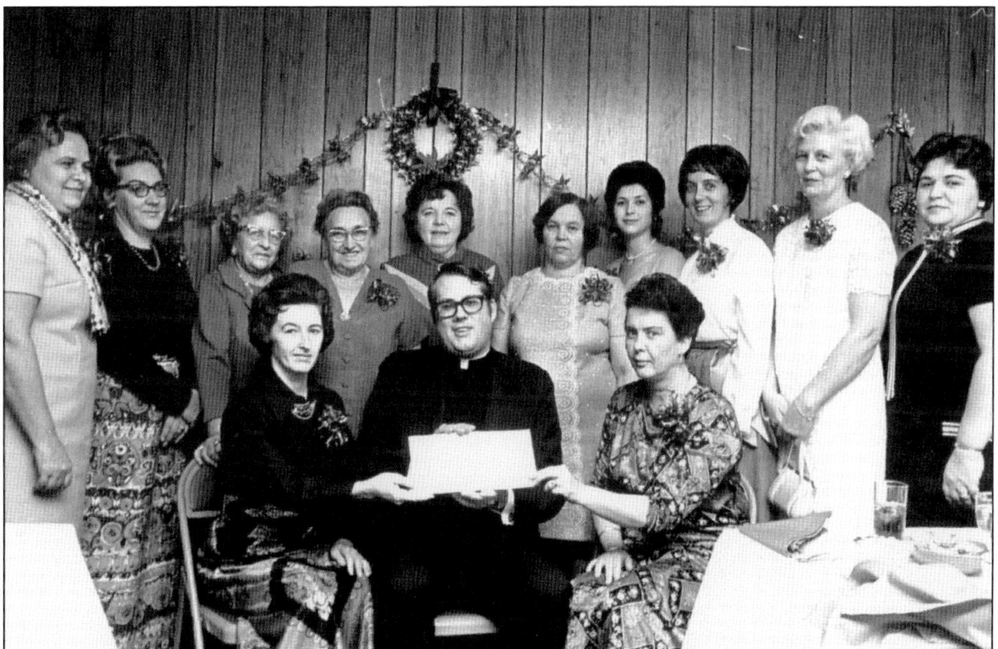

Our Lady of Lourdes Guild was the most active church organization at Presentation of Our Lord UCC in Lansdale. They work tirelessly preparing bake sales, Christmas bazaars, picnics, dances, dinners, and parties for children to help with church needs. In 1972, they presented a check for the building fund. Seated are, from left to right, Teresa Ksenics, Rev. Richard Seminak, and Clara Timtishin. Standing are other guild members.

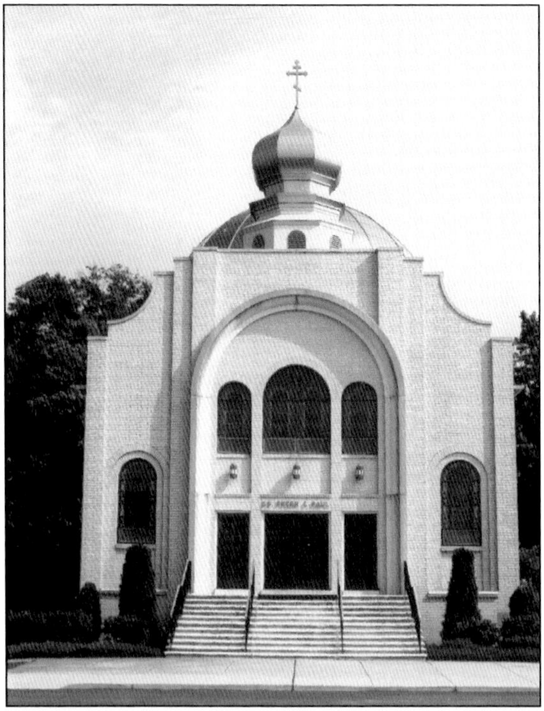

SS. Peter and Paul UOC in Wilmington began in 1928 when the Ukrainian Catholic Diocese insisted on having church property signed over to them. The four-year court battle ended in 1932 when the Orthodox built their own church. A UNH was built in 1933, and by 1938, the church was completed with the aid of the founders who supplied labor and money. In the 1960s, parishioners moved into the suburbs. A new complex was completed in suburban Wilmington in 1968.

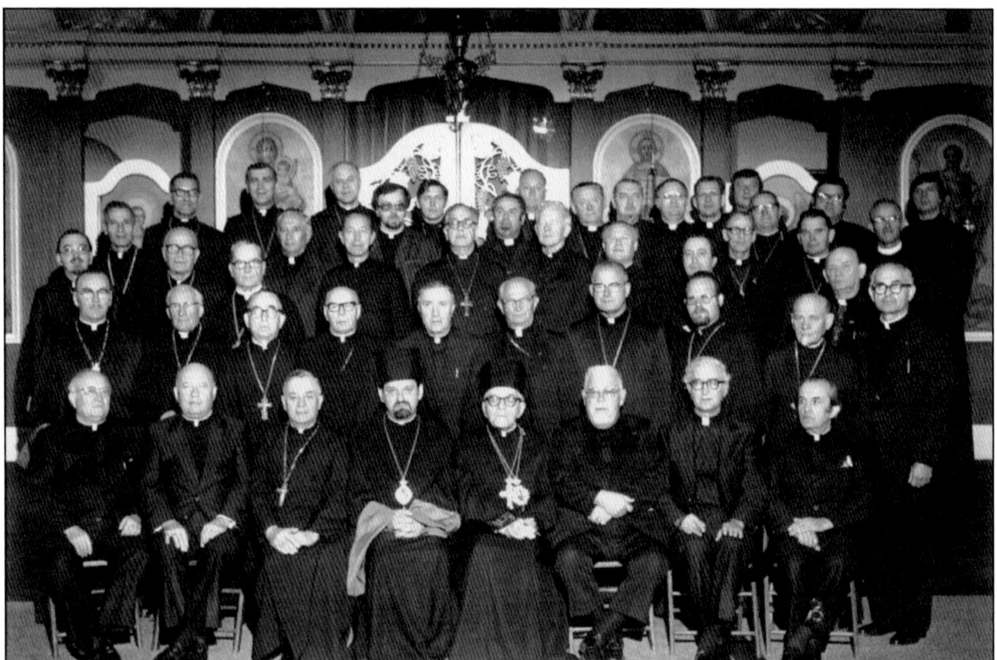

In the 1950s, SS. Peter and Paul UOC in Wilmington was the largest and most active Orthodox parish. The Conference of all Ukrainian Orthodox Priests in America was held in Wilmington in 1976. In the front row, fourth from left, is Bishop Constantine, and next to him is Archbishop Mark.

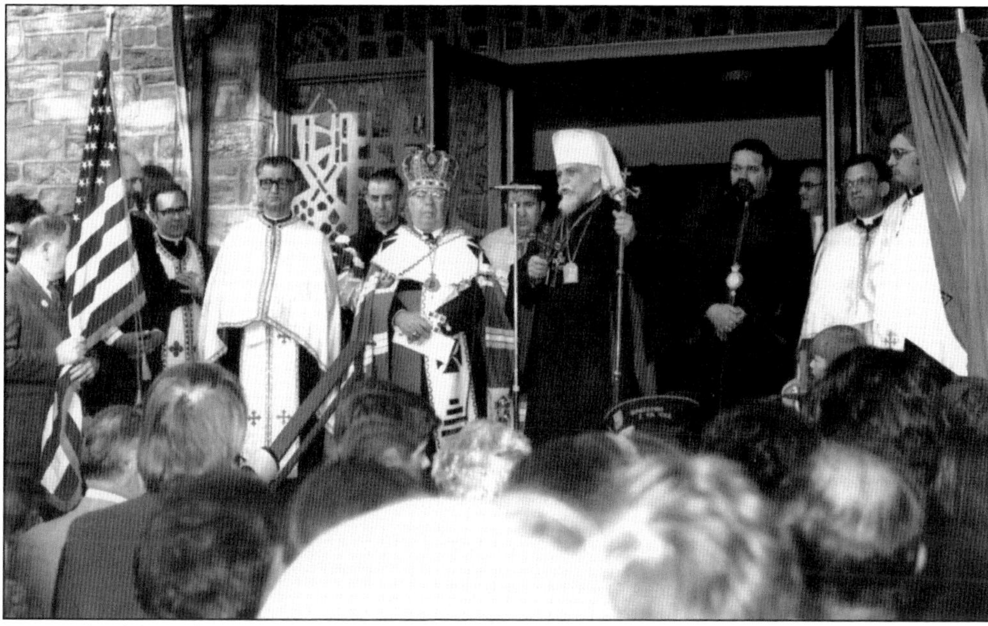

Patriarch of the Ukrainian Catholic Church Joseph Slipyj, during his visit to the United States in 1973, blessed the cornerstone of Annunciation UCC, the new parish in Melrose Park. By the flag are, from left to right, Revs. Robert Moskal (pastor), Myroslav Charyna, Paul Burak (founding pastor), Metropolitan Ambrose (Senyshyn), Myron Kozmosky, Patriarch Slipyj, Bishop Basil (Losten), Walter Paska, and James Melnic.

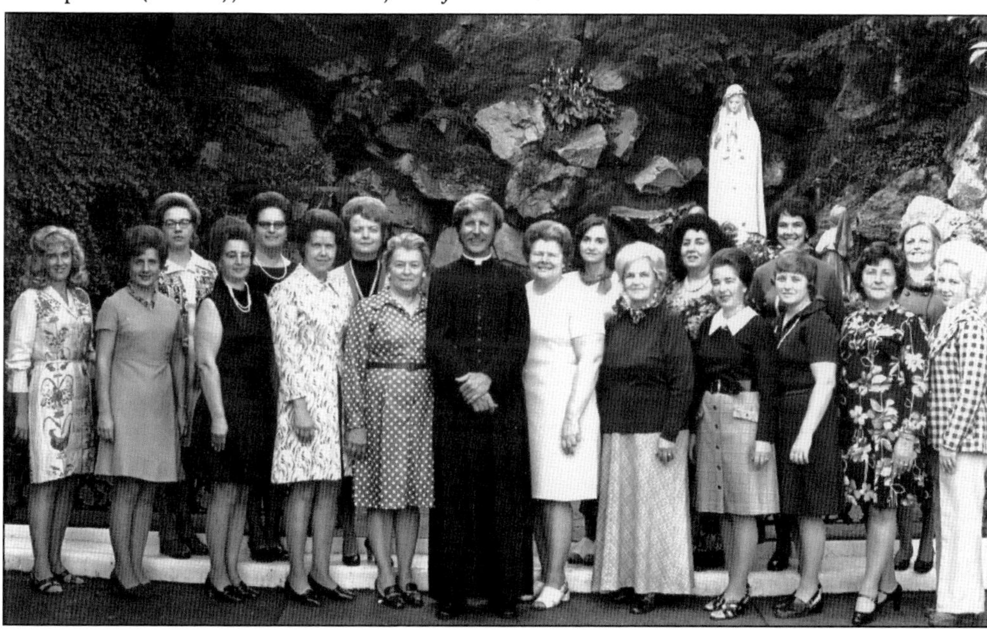

The 1974 Ladies Auxiliary of SS. Peter and Paul UCC in Bridgeport includes, from left to right, (first row) Mary Luciw, Mary Ann Erdek, Mary Martyniuk, Jeanne Berkezchuk, Mary Todor, Rev. Ronald Popivchak, Pauline Makowiak, Ann Smisko, Anna Iwanytska, Amy Bortnichak, Vera Moser, and Bobbi Smisko; (second row) Marie Lapotsky, Theresa Martyniuk, Sophie Tomchick, Lydia Dychdala, Betty Betz, Jean Berkezchuk, and Kathryn Solkshinitz.

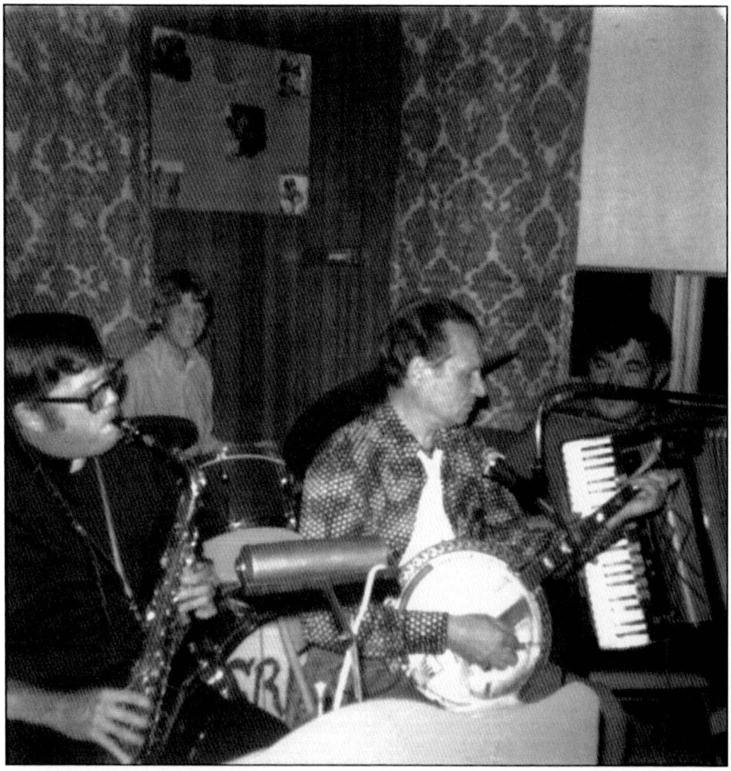

St. Anne's UCC in Warrington is exceptional in that several of the pastors were musicians. Rev. Robert Moskal, who also pioneered the church in Lansdale, has a fine voice. Parishioners claim that when he sings it is like "hearing angels sing." Rev. Richard Seminak played saxophone with the parish band. In a 1974 performance are, from left to right, (front) Reverend Seminak, Richard Chern, and Steve Chern; (back) Al Demusz.

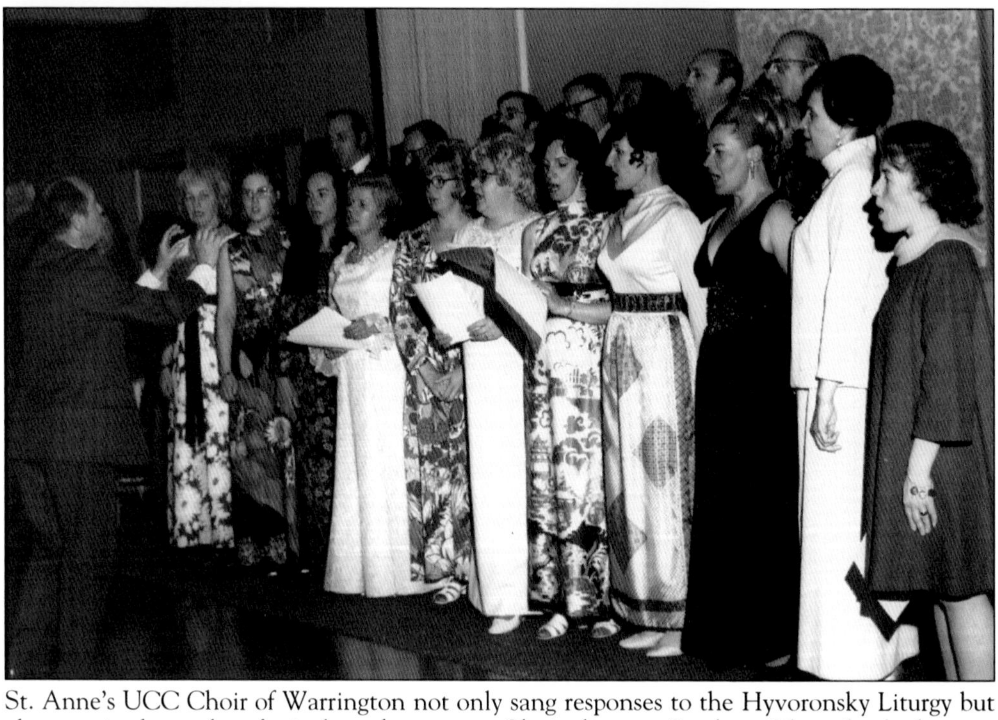

St. Anne's UCC Choir of Warrington not only sang responses to the Hyvoronsky Liturgy but also was in demand at festivals and concerts. Choir director Stephen Sikora leads them in singing Ukrainian melodies at a church hall concert in 1978.

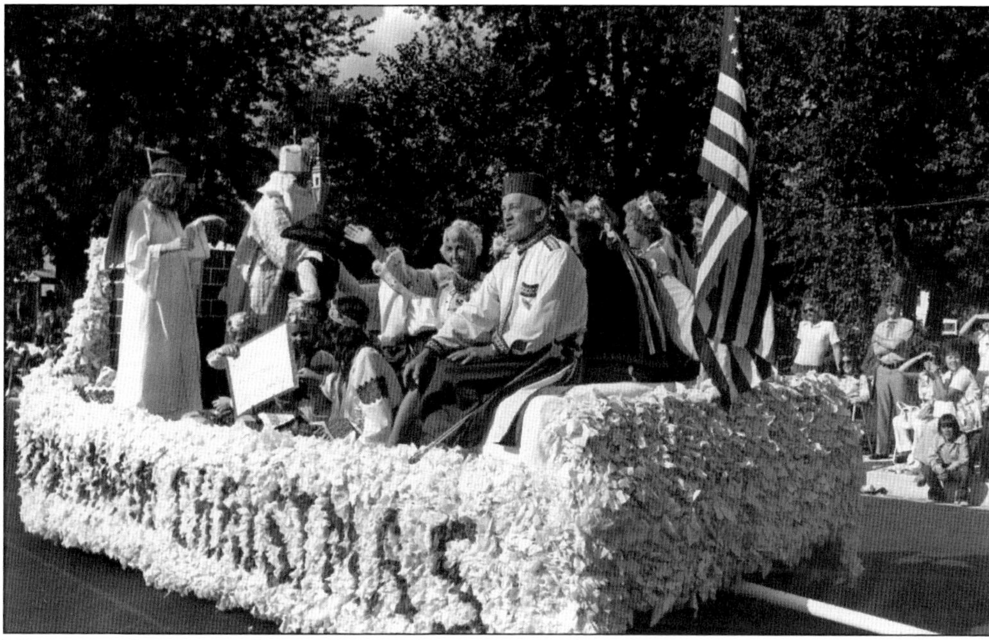

Ukrainian Americans from Chesapeake City contributed to Cecil County's tercentennial celebration in 1974 with a float portraying an old-fashioned Ukrainian Christmas. Participating in this celebration are, from left to right, Valeria Hotra, the angel; Michael Wasylczuk as St. Nicholas; three unidentified children; Dorothy Chicosky; Joseph Piri; Catherine Piri; Mary Terpeluk; and Helen Eder.

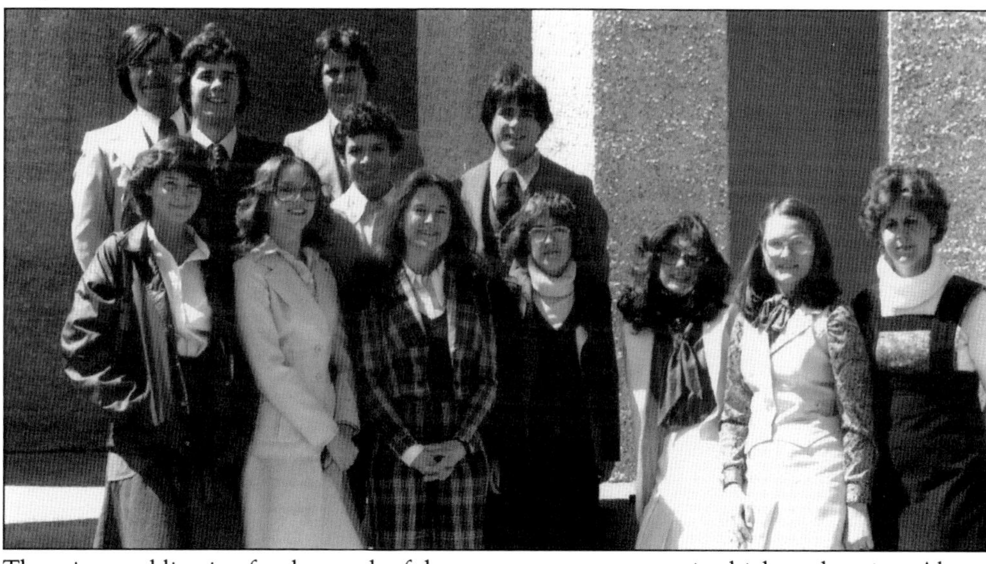

The primary obligation for the youth of the newcomers was to receive higher education. Almost all young adults enrolled in neighboring universities. The Ukrainian Students' Club at the University of Delaware sponsored cultural events, symposia, and dances. The 1978 club includes, from left to right, (first row) Ellen Rudavska, Irene Knehnetska, Patricia Kostyshyn, Doris Korzeniwska, Christine Morowana, Martha Matwijkiw, and Ulana Harwanko; (second row) Mark Morowany, Andrew Rudavsky, and Lew Korzeniwsky; (third row) Myron Korzeniwsky and John Kostyshyn.

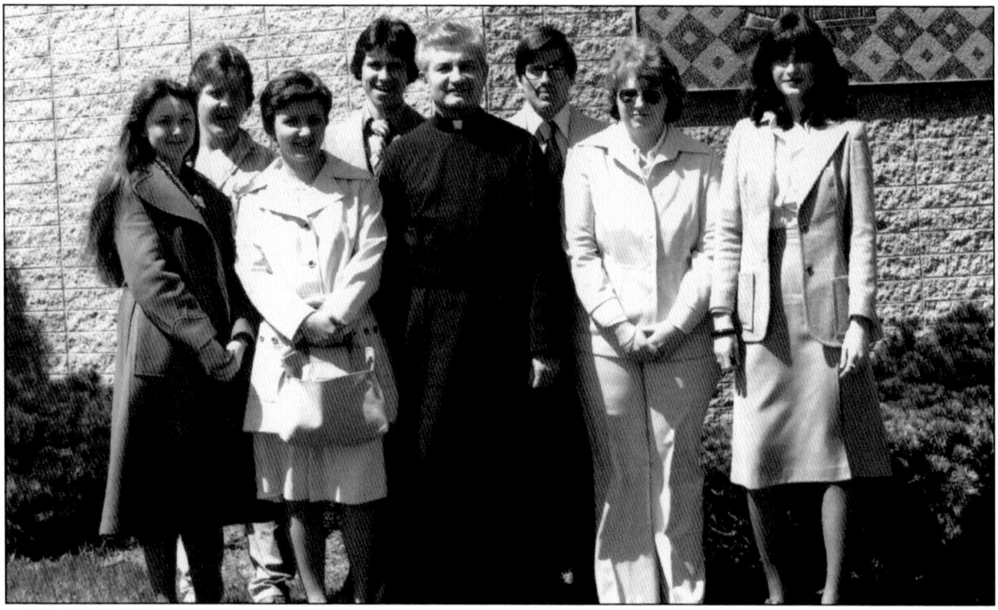

The League of Ukrainian Catholic Youth (LUCY) was founded in Chicago in 1933. It fosters Catholic principles and Ukrainian Eastern Rite heritage. This 1978 LUCY group at St. Nicholas UCC in Wilmington participated in and/or organized dances, hayrides, picnics, Ukrainian exhibits, and Christmas caroling, as well as spiritual activities. From left to right are Katherine Pastock, Elliot Zatwarnytsky, Karen Brown, John Kostyshyn, Rev. Roman Dubitsky, Charles Sevier, Sandra Dzwonshyk, and Donna Dycio.

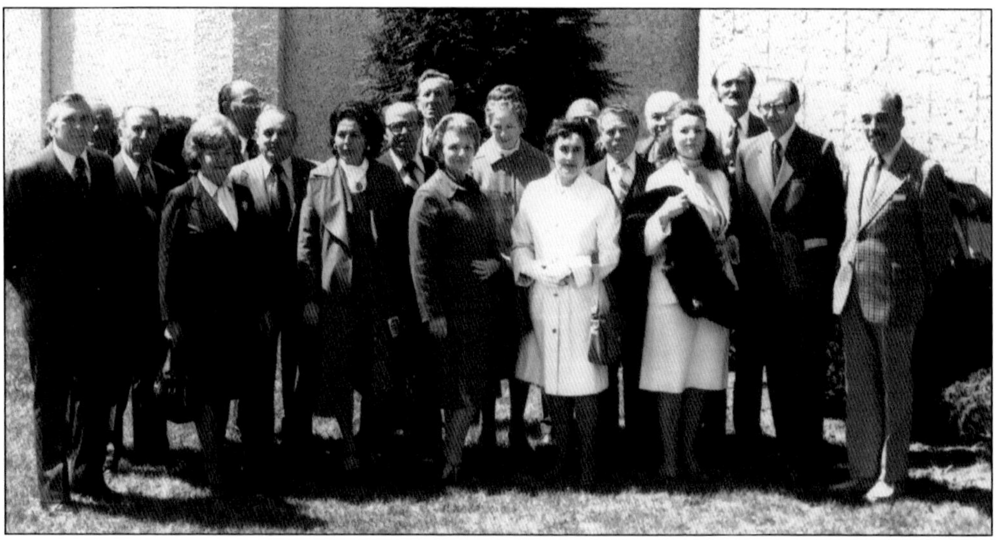

Ukrainian Congress Committee of America is an umbrella organization of all organizations in a given community. Members work to promulgate knowledge of Ukraine, its lack of independence, and its culture. The Wilmington Branch in 1982 includes, from left to right, (first row) Peter Serba, Ivan Wozny, Stanley Husak, Katherine Husak, Stephen Matwijkiw, Lidia Harwanko, Stephen Yatzus, Alla Rudavska, Olena Szatynska, Irene Serba, Peter Zarycky, Maria Morowana, Oleh Sluzar, and Theofil Kunyckyj; (second row) Yaroslaw Korzeniwsky, Eugene Romaniuk, John Balanchuk, Joseph Baczynsky, and Ivan Knehnetsky.

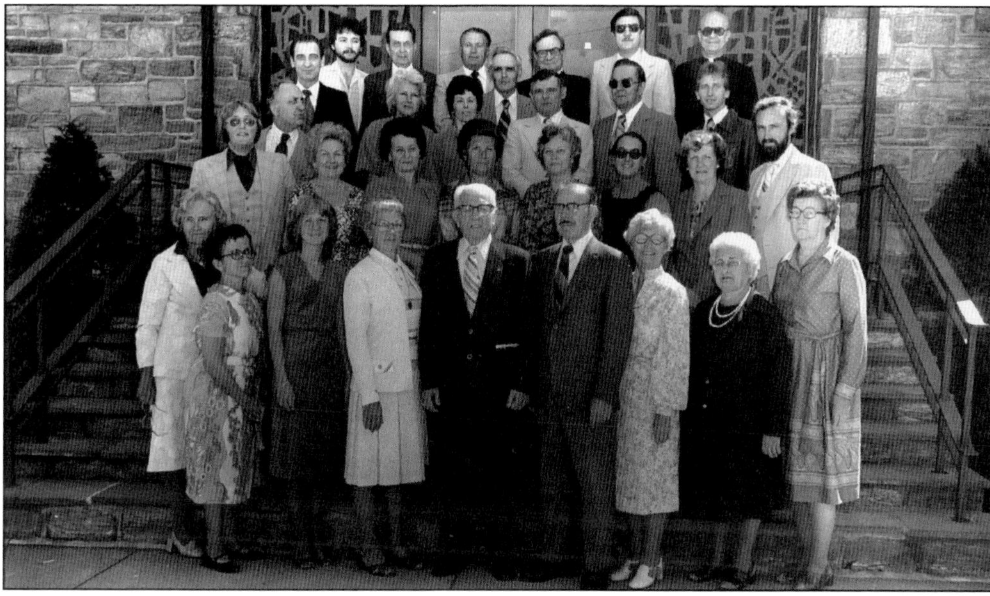

Annunciation BVM UCC's Choir became famous during the 1970s. This group from Melrose Park not only sang weekly during liturgy but also performed at the Disabled American Veterans Concert and at the Eastern Rite Mass during the 1976 Eucharistic Congress. Record albums were made of their singing, and their voices were beamed by radio to Ukraine. The 1979 choir is seen with director John Onuskonich (in the center).

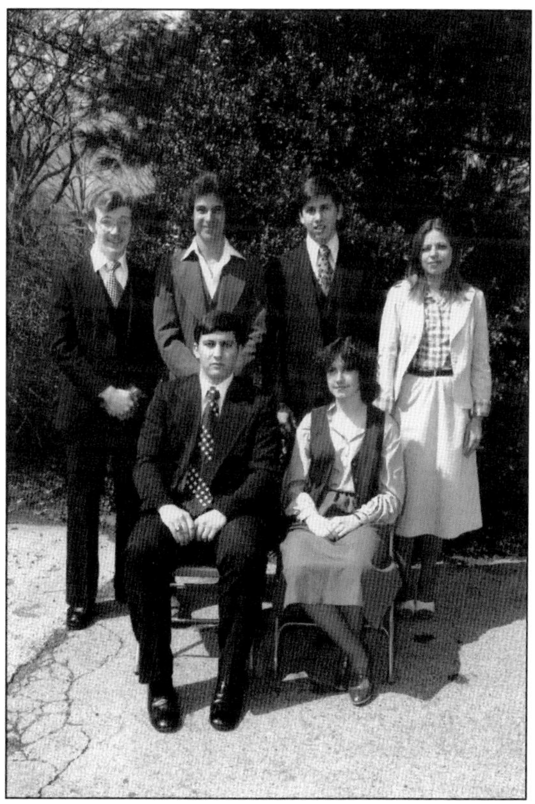

St. Michael the Archangel UCC, Jenkintown, became the center for two factions of Ukrainians in the Delaware Valley: those who arrived after World War II and were committed to establish a Ukrainian Catholic patriarchate and those who came after 1991 to renew religious beliefs that had been suppressed for decades. Officials of the youth guild Brotherhood of St. John the Beloved in 1979 are, from left to right, (first row) Roman Dubenko and Olena Lewycka; (second row) Danylo Zacharczuk, Michael Korchak, Zorian Dubenko, and Martha Lubynska.

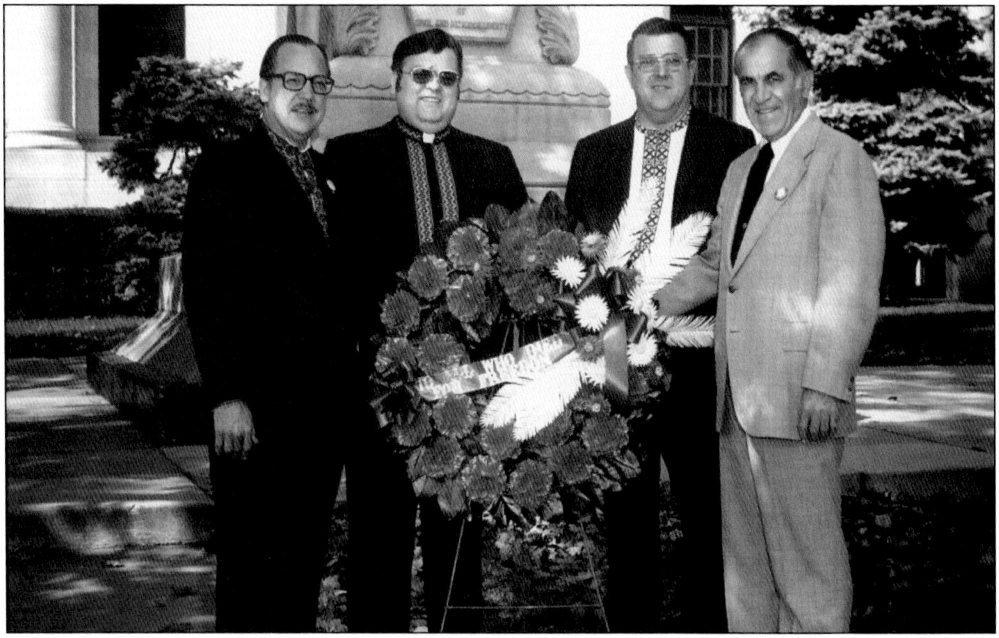

For all Ukrainians living in the United States, commemorating those who died defending their freedom is an annual event. In 1975, the foremost leaders of the Chester Ukrainian community presented a memorial wreath outside Delaware County Court House in Media. From left to right are William Pastuszek, a lifetime benefactor of the UOC; Rev. Joseph Kopchak, pastor of St. Mary's UCC; Joseph Kurman, president of the U.S. Bicentennial Committee; and Judge Charles Catania.

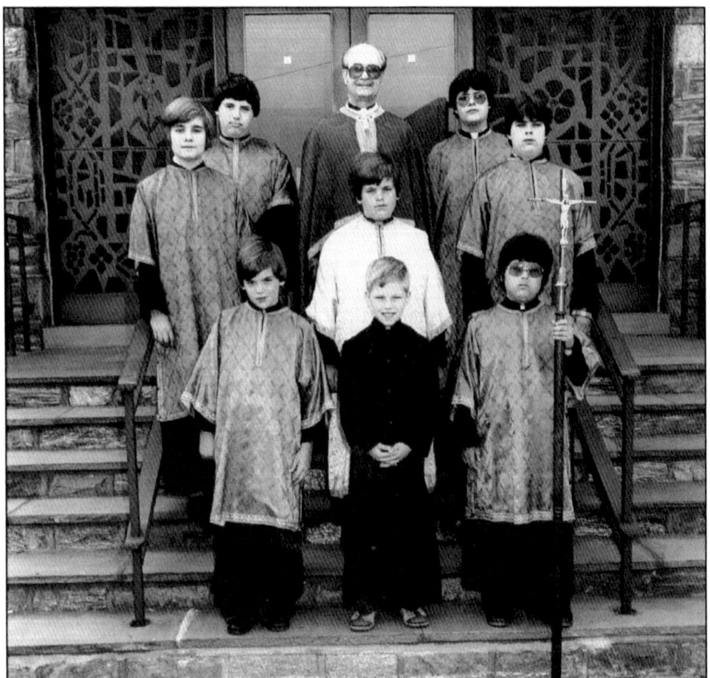

Altar boys have always played an important role in the history of Ukrainian churches. The Annunciation UCC in Melrose Park altar boys in 1979 are, from left to right, (first row) John Bartch, Andrij Szul, and William Wytish; (second row) Lonhyn Jasinskyj, James Bartch, and Joseph Borowyk; (third row) John Michalczuk, Rev. Michael Fedorowich, pastor, and Michael Wytish.

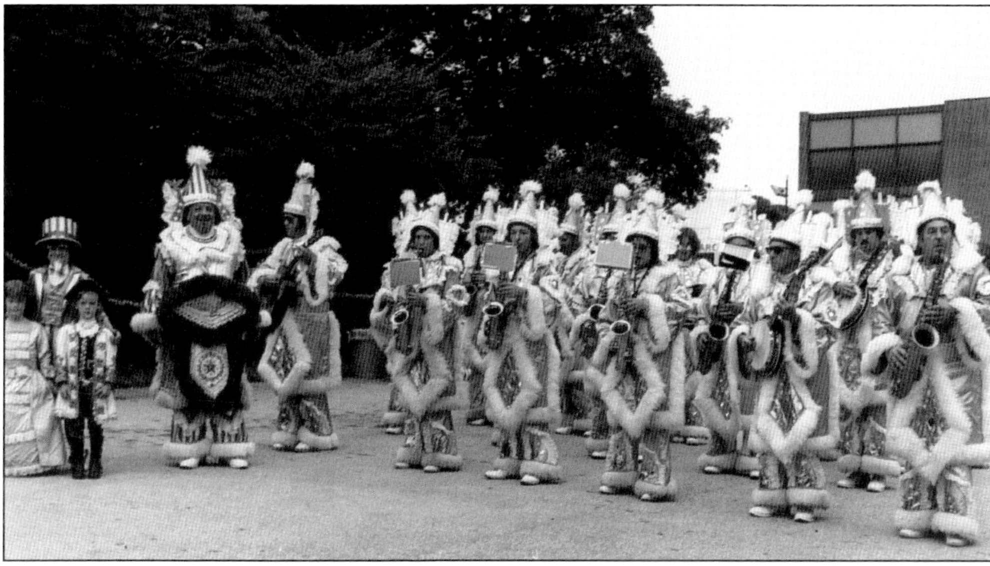

Annunciation UCC in Melrose Park during the 1970s and 1980s was famous for its picnics that were held on its property. Besides the usual picnic programs, dignitaries and famous personalities were invited. In 1976, the Ukrainian American String Band was asked to play.

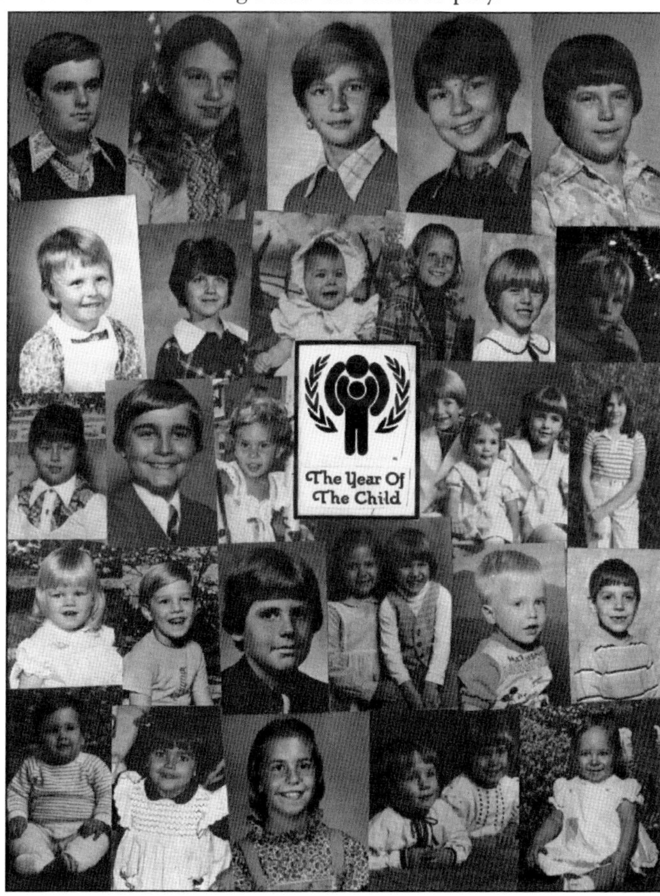

Annunciation UCC in Melrose Park took advantage that 1979 was declared the Year of the Child and dedicated the entire year to its youth. In that year especially, it celebrated the young by having special programs scattered throughout the year benefiting the church. As a result, the mortgage was paid off and ceremoniously burned.

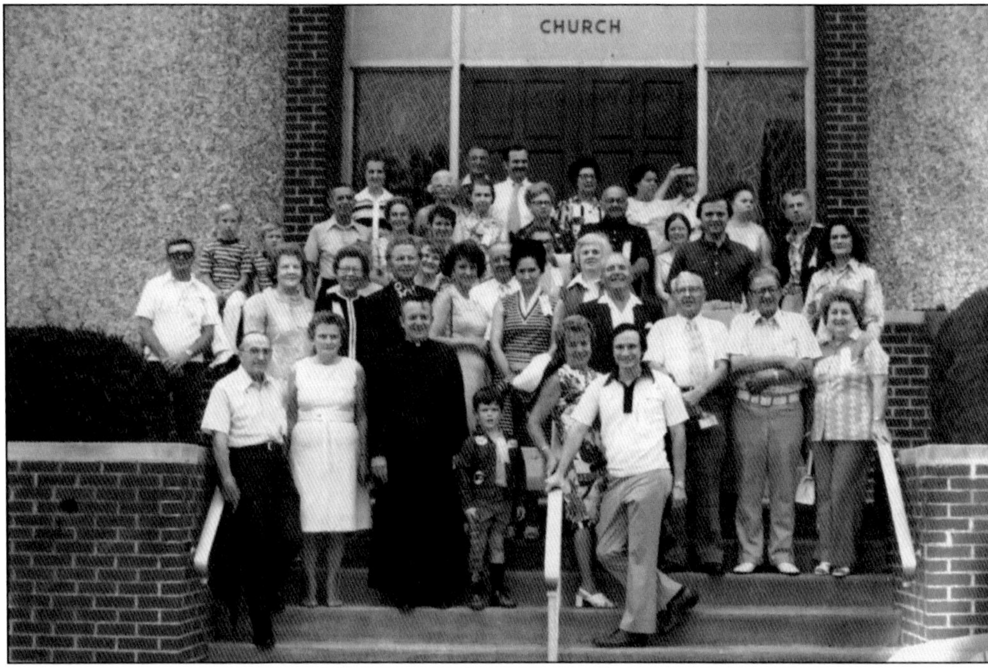

Since 1916 priests from neighboring parishes were called to serve on a part-time basis at SS. Peter and Paul UCC in Clifton Heights. A new church was built in 1967. Members were photographed as they were on their way to the Eucharistic Congress in 1979 with the pastor, Rev. Paul Harchison, third from left in front.

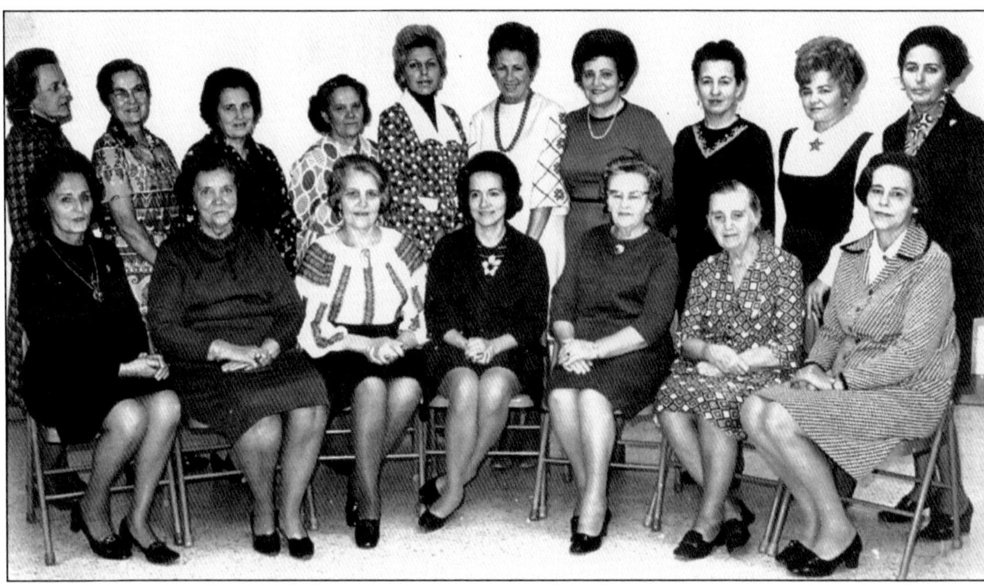

Soyuz Ukrainok Branch 54 in Wilmington was founded in 1958, choosing the name 500 Heroines in memory of 500 women who were run over by Soviet tanks. In this 1980 photograph are, from left to right, (first row) Maria Matwijkiw, Maria Ritz, Kateryna Hlynianska, Maria Korzeniwska, Olha Harwanko, Olena Sluzar, and Irene Kunycky; (second row) Lada Husar, Stephania Hrycushko, Sophia Cybak, Katherine Kostyshyn, Martha Trofimenko, Olena Szatynska, Olha Paranczak, Anna Zarycka, Katherina Husak, and Lidia Harwanko.

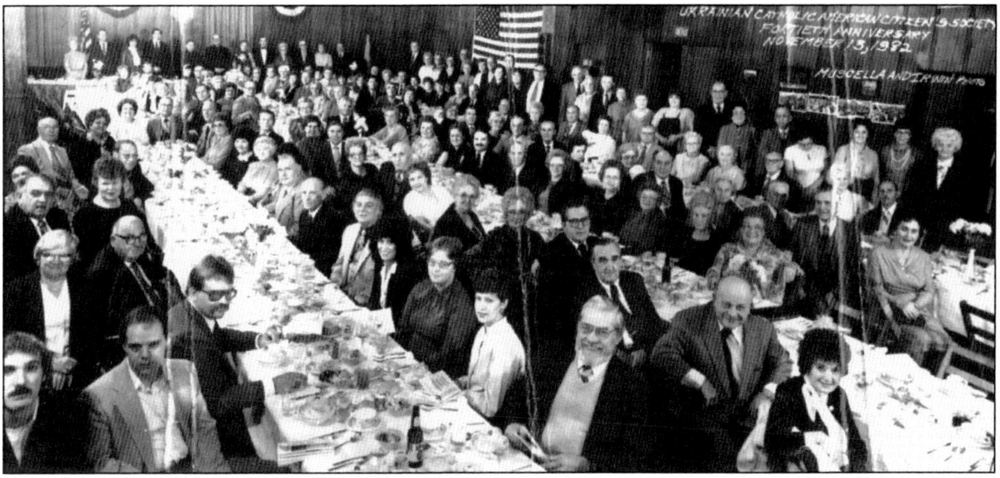

The Ukrainian Catholic American Citizen's Society (UCACS) was founded in 1942 in the west end of Chester. It acquired a building. The hall was on the upper floor, and the club was downstairs. Smaller rooms were used for classes for children, as well as for UCACS events. The profit from this organization went to Holy Ghost UCC. Its 40th anniversary was celebrated in 1982.

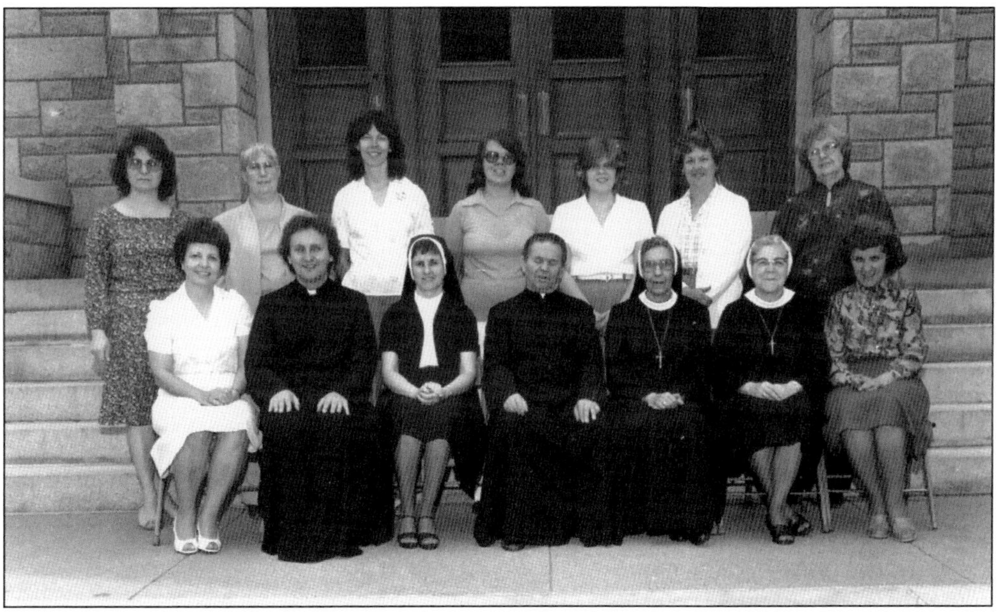

The faculty and staff at Holy Ghost UCC in Chester, during the 1982–1983 school year, are, from left to right, (first row) Olga Pastuszek, Rev. Paul Luniv, Sister Martin OSBM (principal), Rev. Peter Lypyn, pastor, Sister Dorothy OSBM, Sister Vincent OSBM, and Anna Steciw; (second row) Mary Lushnycky, Myrtle Bychkowski, Patricia Donnelly, Monica Kartesevich, Frances Garvine, Joan Kurych, and Margaret Wollner.

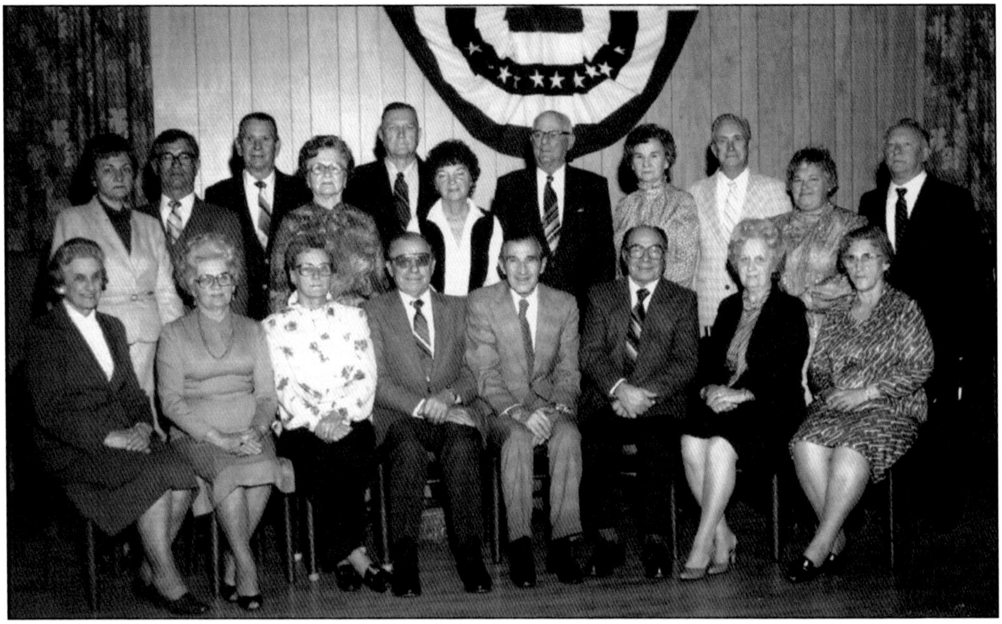

The UCACS of Chester Board of Directors for 1983–1984 includes, from left to right, (first row) Rose Maruschak, unidentified, Martha Salo, Teophil Pawluk, Michael Kowalchuk, Danylo Pankiw, Anna Fedgchin, and Catherine Kowalchuk; (second row) Maria Wenchak, Oleksa Wenchak, Benjamin Fedgin, Dorothy Lebischak, Michael Maruschak, Laura Brochet, John Lebischak, Rose Kartachak, Thomas Kartachak, Stella Matyszczak, and Stephen Matyszczak.

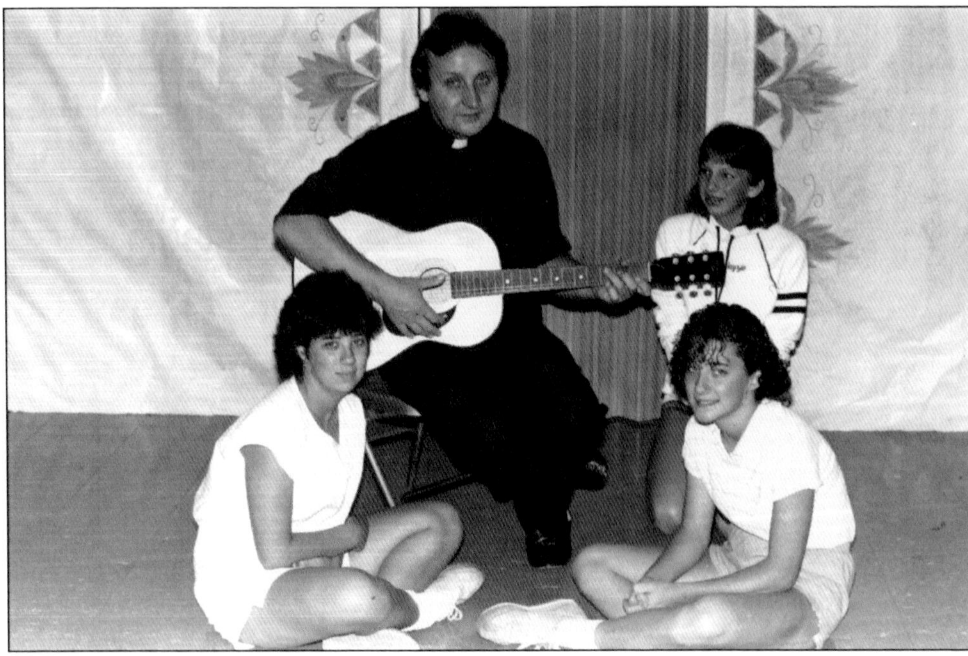

Rev. Paul Luniv was another gifted musician pastor of St. Anne's UCC in Warrington. He taught young people to sing Ukrainian folk songs at various parish affairs. From left to right are (first row) Karen Jubinski and Susan Jubinski; (second row) Reverend Luniv and Patricia Chern. They are preparing for a parish festival in 1986.

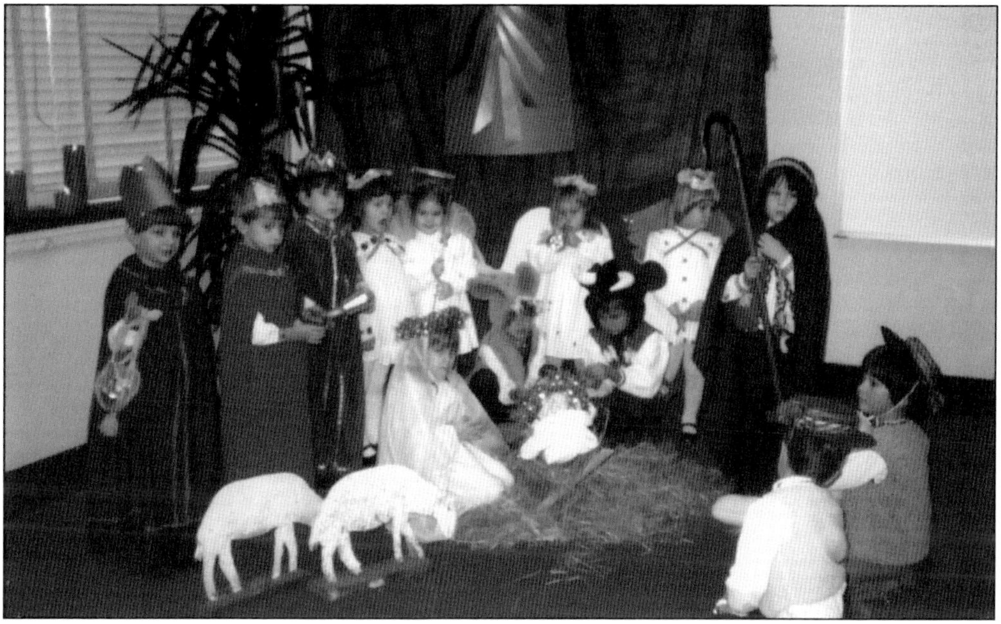

Nativity scenes played an important role in Ukrainian life. Throughout churches, the Christmas scene was venerated. In Ukrainian schools, this was played out, and in adulthood, it took the part of a theatrical production called *Vertep*. In the photograph preschoolers at Ukrainian Educational and Cultural Center in Jenkintown are reenacting the Christmas story in 1984.

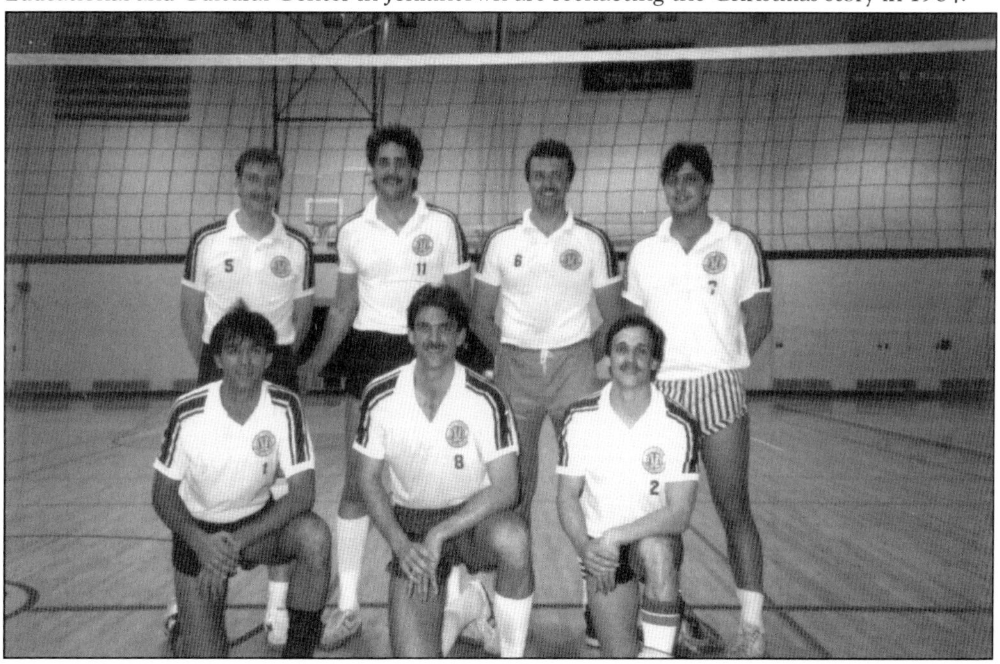

Tryzubiwka at Horsham, Pennsylvania, is home for Ukrainian athletes and sports enthusiasts. In 1986, Ukrainian Volley Ball Championship of North America was held in Detroit. The winner was the Ukrainian Nationals of Tryzubiwka. The champions are, from left to right, (first row) Ihor Kostecky, coach Bohdan Zawadowycz, and Leonid Hayduchok; (second row) Alherd Kazyra, Andrij Siryj, Bohdan Nowakiwsky, and Andrij Fedun.

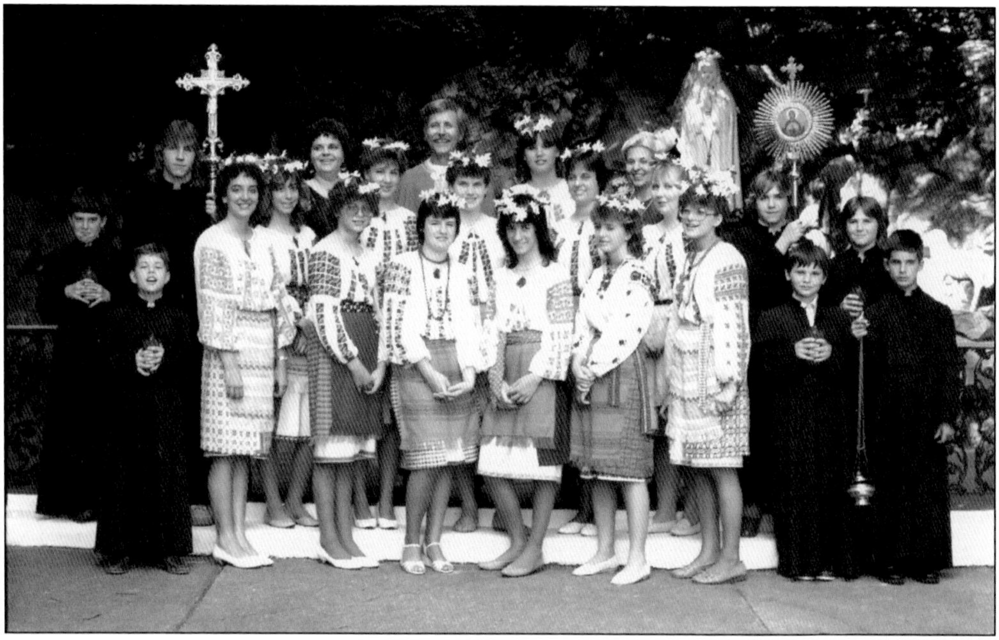

The most important youth organizations in UCCs are Sodality of the BVM and the altar boys. In 1985, members of both organizations at SS. Peter and Paul UCC in Bridgeport participated in the May Day Marian rites at the grotto on church grounds with the pastor, Rev. Ronald Popivchak, in back in center.

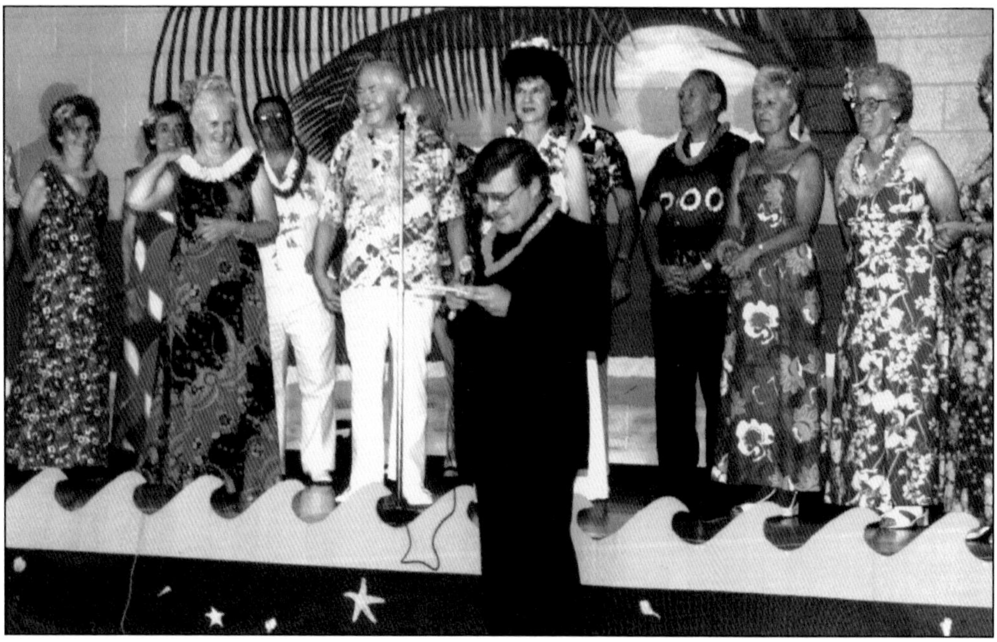

The Senior Citizens Club of Annunciation UCC in Melrose Park was organized in 1977 and was enrolled in District 7 based in Glenside, Pennsylvania. Programs such as police protection, changes in legal and health services, and communications are of interest to the membership. For recreation, they take one-day cultural trips. Rev. James Melnic (in the center) is presiding over a Hawaiian luau in 1986.

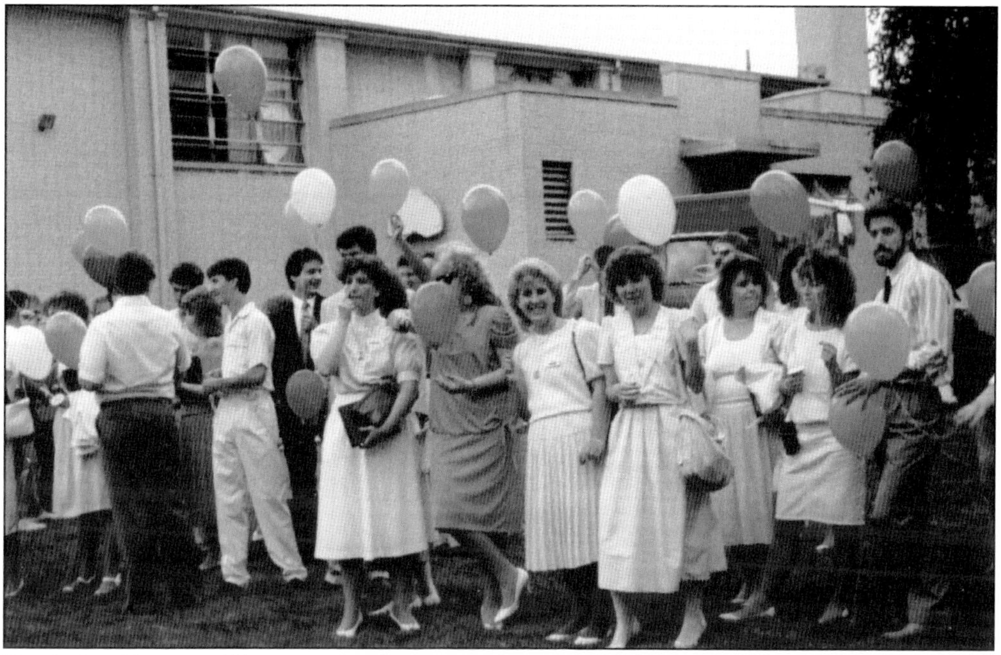

Youth for Christ, a Ukrainian Catholic organization, held its regional convention 1987 in Philadelphia, bringing together youth from the Delaware Valley. At the conclusion, the Chester Branch released balloons symbolizing prayers sent to the Lord.

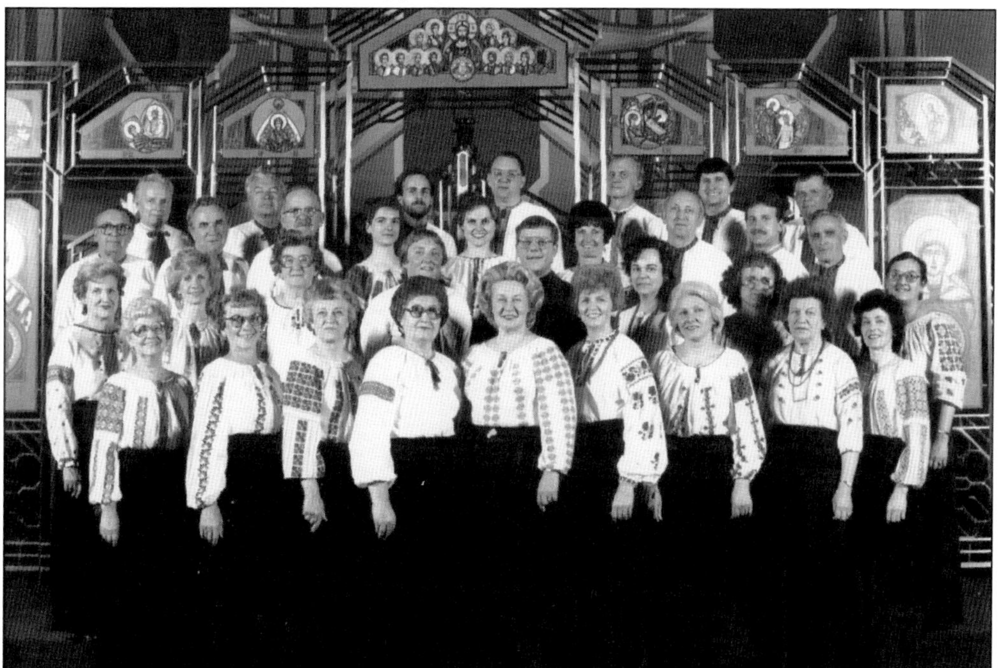

The Annunciation UCC Choir of Melrose Park was reorganized in 1985, under the direction of Ihor Kusznir, and its first professional recording of Christmas music was released. The iconostas seen in the background is the work of iconographer Andrij Maday. Rev. James Melnic is in the middle, and to his right is Ihor Kusznir.

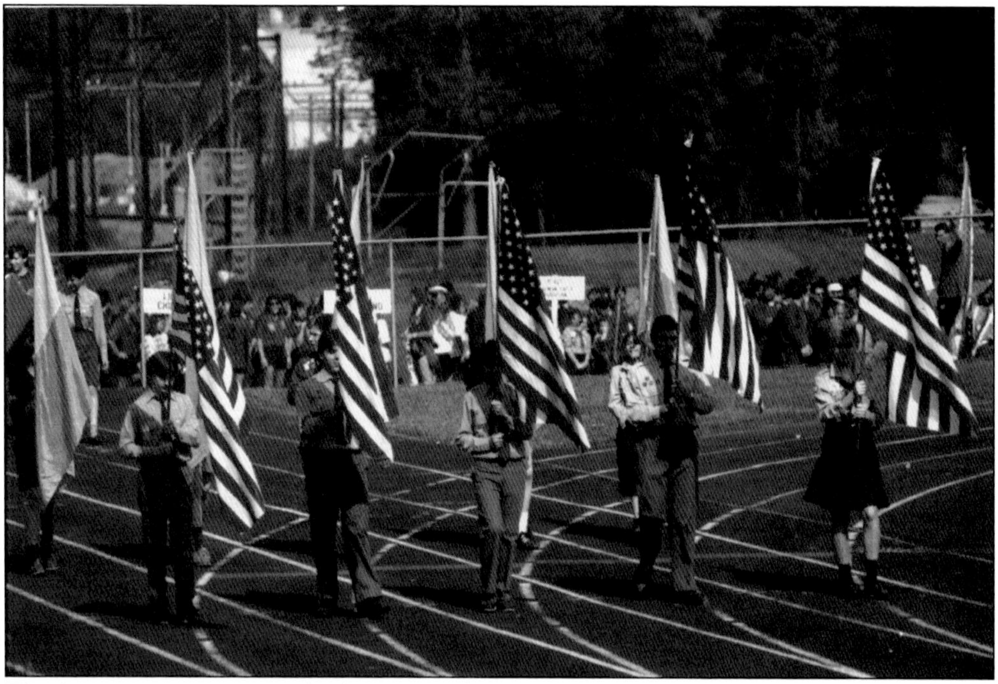

The biggest event at Tryzubiwka in Horsham is the Ukrainian Diaspora Olympiad. The first Olympiad marked the Millennium of Ukrainian Christianity in 1988 with Ukrainian Americans and Ukrainian Canadians competing. The opening ceremonies of the three-day event are shown.

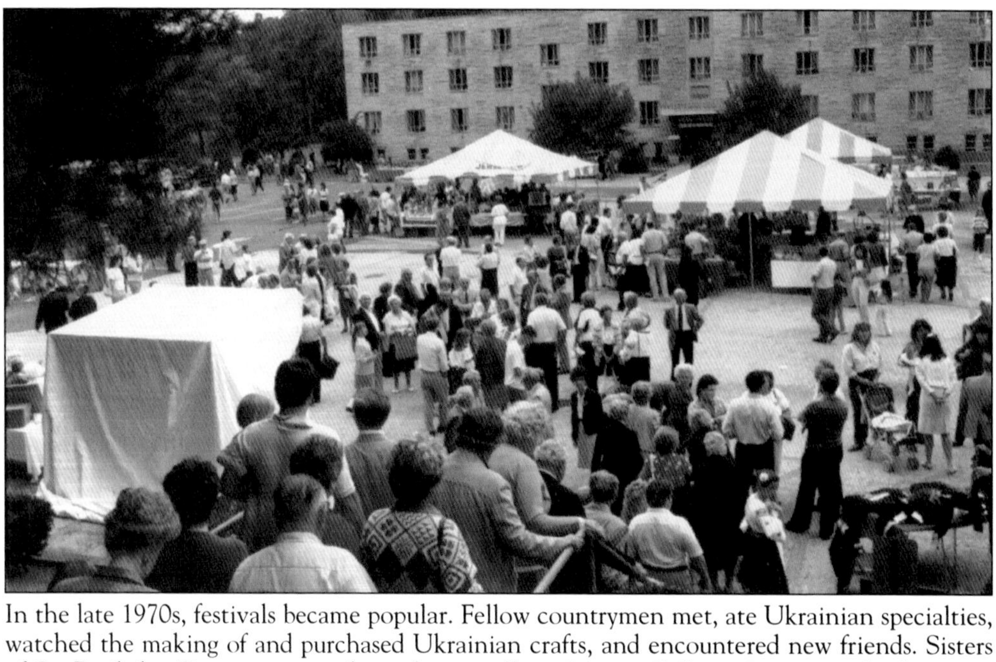

In the late 1970s, festivals became popular. Fellow countrymen met, ate Ukrainian specialties, watched the making of and purchased Ukrainian crafts, and encountered new friends. Sisters of St. Basil the Great organizes festivals annually at Manor College Campus in Jenkintown. Helicopter rides, horseback riding, and other interesting amusements for young and old are available.

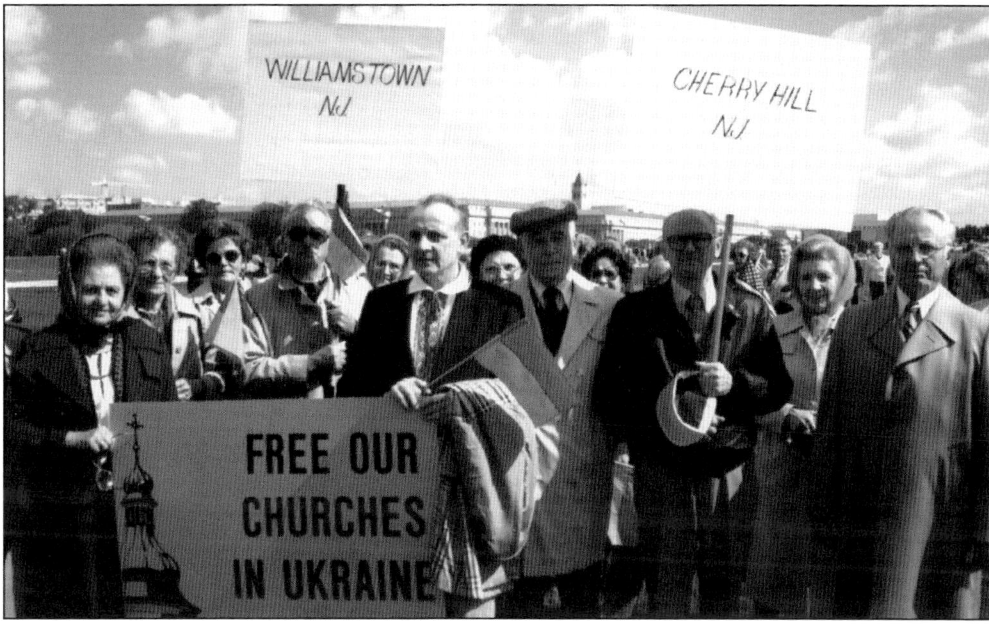

Parishioners from St. Michael's UCC in Cherry Hill and SS. Peter and Paul UCC of Williamstown participated in a 1988 protest march in Washington, D.C., commemorating the Millennium of Christianity in Ukraine and the lack of religious freedom under communism. From left to right are, in the front Halyna Stachnew, Nadia Lapowska, Valeria Kril, Andrij Stachnew, Lonhin Switenko, Nicholas Romach, Michael Romach, Marie Kuziw, and John Andrusiw.

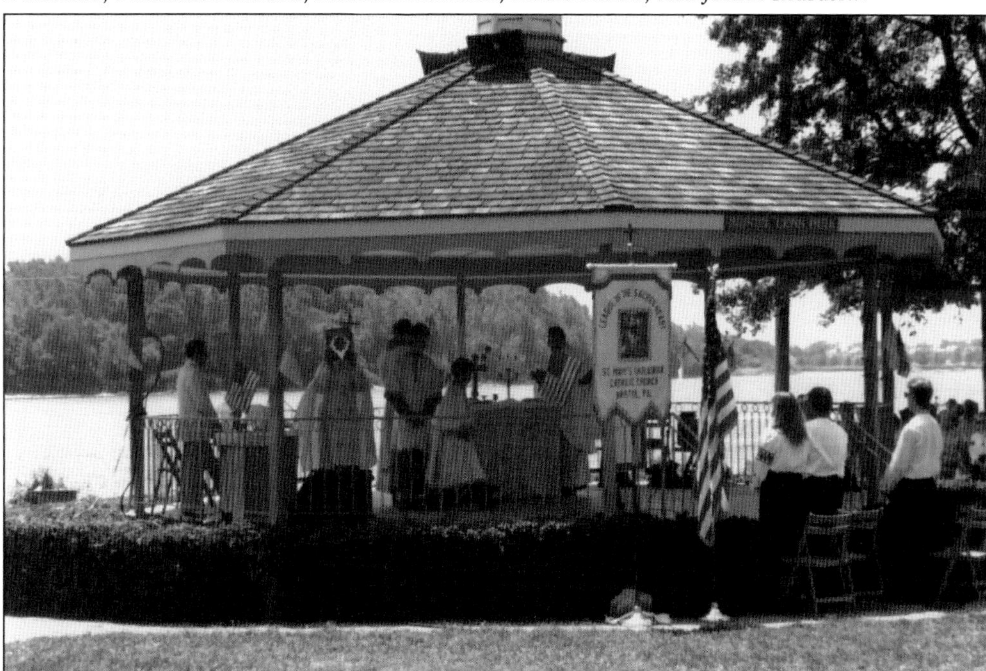
In 1988, the Bristol Ukrainian Community celebrated the Millennium of Christianity in Ukraine at Bristol Lions Park along the Delaware River. The celebration began with Holy Liturgy, then a display of Ukrainian crafts, and of course, the consumption of Ukrainian foods.

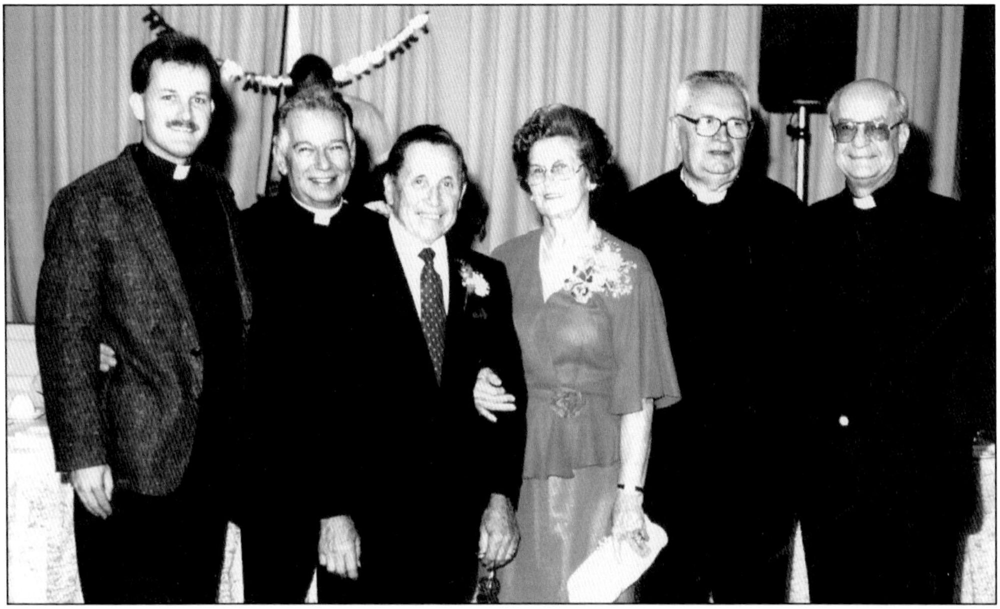

For the 50th wedding anniversary of Michael and Stefania Kravchak Sr. in 1989, all four former pastors of St. Mary's UCC came to celebrate with them. Hailing from Bristol, Pennsylvania, the two were parish pioneers. Michael Kravchak was the longtime cantor and choir director. From left to right are Revs. Joseph Korinchock and Raymond Revak, the happy couple, and Revs. Leo Tynkiw and Michael Fedorowich.

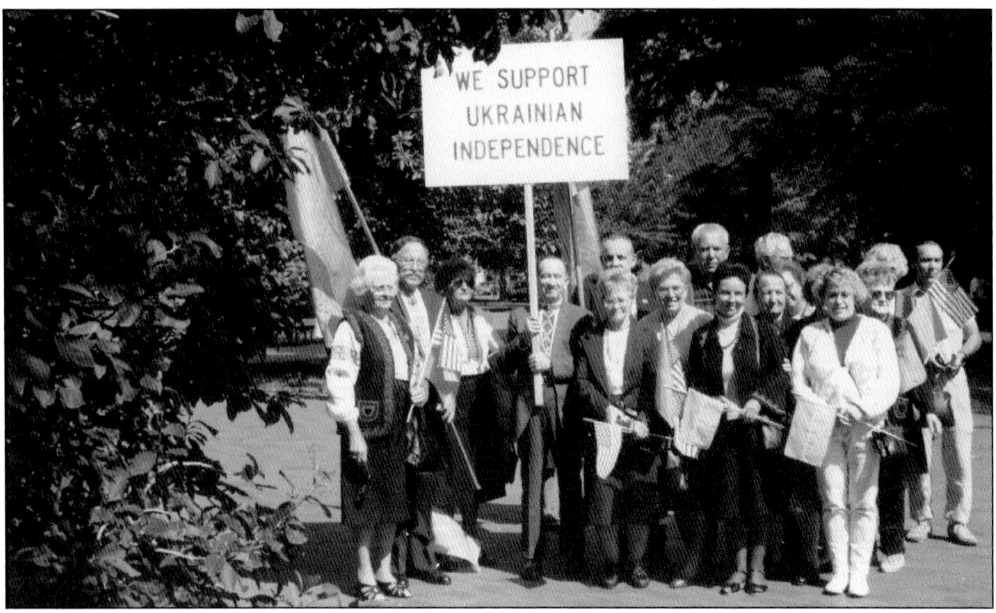

Alexander Kobasa, an agribusinessman, was the moving force behind the formation of the Organization for the Defense of the Four Freedoms of Ukrainian in 1963, Ukrainian National Aid Association in 1966, and Ukrainian Citizens Committee of South Jersey in 1986 for the Williamstown area. He organized the representatives of local Ukrainian associations to welcome the announcement of Ukrainian independence in 1991 in Washington, D.C. Kobasa is holding the placard.

Five

Enjoying America and a Free Ukraine

What a beautiful sight, to see our flags dancing in the breeze!
—Alexander Kobasa, Williamstown

Ukraine's independence in 1991 was a dream come true for all Ukrainian Americans. However, it did little to change Ukraine's economy, and almost immediately, economic refugees from Ukraine inundated large cities in the United States, where Ukrainian Americans welcomed them, and a new air of fraternity and congeniality emerged. Unfortunately, this euphoria did not last long. Through no fault of their own, these immigrants were not fully compatible with the established Ukrainian community, as they were the product of three generations of Soviet communist regimes, many were seen as not possessing the Ukrainian "soul" that the Ukrainian diasporas held so dear. Nevertheless they spoke the language and were expert in Ukrainian culture and traditions, even cognizant of the established churches, whether Catholic, Orthodox, or Baptist, and some came seeking further religious or political freedom.

In general, they settled in the major cities of the United States and only nominally assimilated into institutions established by previous immigrations, the Ukrainian Saturday school being one of these. In the Delaware Valley, the assimilation was even more minimal. Lack of well-paying jobs, inability to purchase homes, and no easy means of transportation have forced these new immigrants to settle mostly in the northeast suburbs of Philadelphia, with the exception of the areas of Crum Lynn, Chester, and Fox Chase. New communities exist in Coatesville and Brookhaven, Pennsylvania, which show signs of becoming vibrant and distinct Ukrainian cultural centers consisting mostly of semiprofessionals seeking full employment. However, if for any reason their goals cannot be met, they would prefer to return to Ukraine.

Their influence on Ukrainian American society can be illustrated by their participation in the congregation of the Ukrainian Catholic Church in Wilmington, which consists of the founding member families of the original Ukrainian community; of middle-age working families, born either in Ukraine, Germany, or the United States; and whose children come from eastern and western Europe, Pennsylvania, and Delaware. Intermixed are also a fair number of people from other faiths, rites, and nationalities through a combination of marriage or proximity to the church. These groups are not only seen in most of the Delaware Valley Ukrainian American centers but are also found participating at cultural activities of Ukrainian American communities.

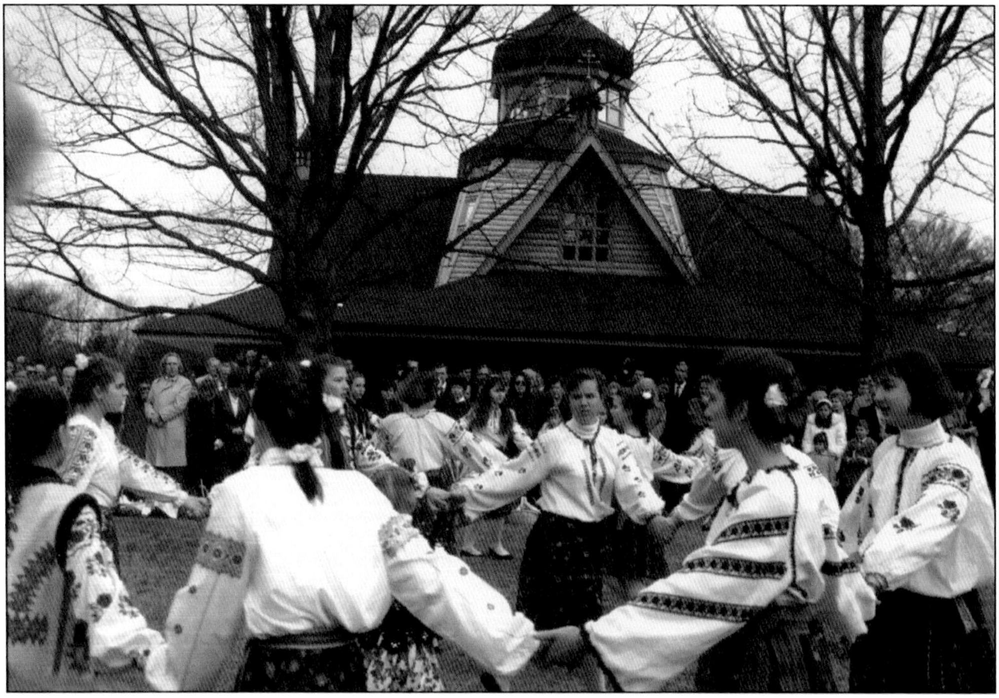

Ukrainian traditions at Easter time include singing *vesnyanky* and dancing *hahilky*. Ukrainians feel great joy and express this by creating songs, dances, and games imitating and celebrating nature. In 1992, youthful parishioners of St. Michael the Archangel UCC, in Jenkintown, participated in this ritual after Easter services.

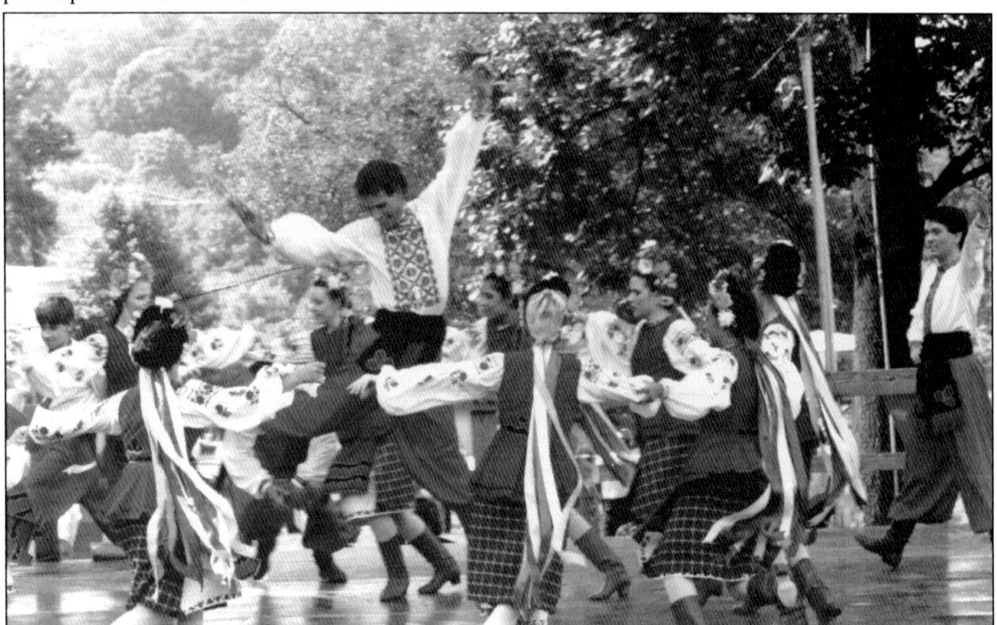

Voloshky Ukraine Dance Ensemble of Jenkintown traveled around the world performing Ukrainian folk dances. Here they are seen dancing at the St. Anne UCC festival in Warrington in 1986.

Holodomor, the genocide that occurred in Ukraine in the 1930s due to the man-made famine, has been memorialized since the 1980s. It was in that decade that the Soviet regime punished the Ukrainian nationalistic peasants by mass starvation. When the inhabitants of Ukrainian villages perished the areas were resettled with Russian peasants. Soyuz Ukrainok, Chester Chapter 13, annually venerates the casualties of Holodomor with a special display at the side altar in Holy Ghost UCC. The photograph shows the 1998 tribute.

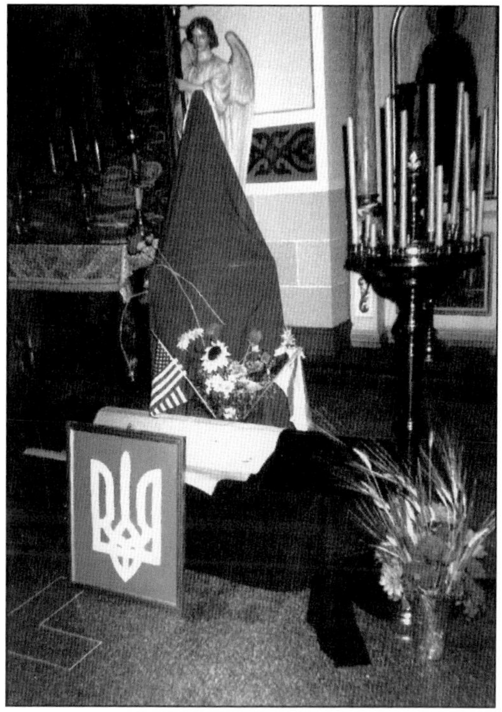

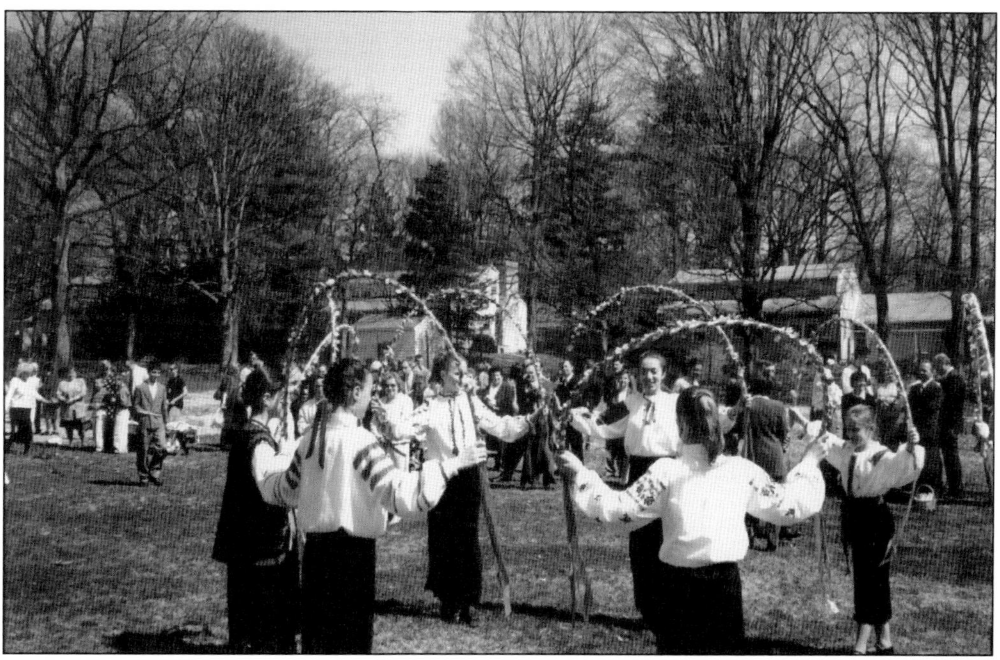

Communities in the Delaware Valley commemorate the 1986 disaster at Chernobyl in various ways. Students of Ukrainian Heritage School, in Jenkintown, memorialized this event on the 10th anniversary with this somber presentation. The young ladies wove flowered arches, and their movements reflected tragedy. "Lord have mercy" was sung in the background.

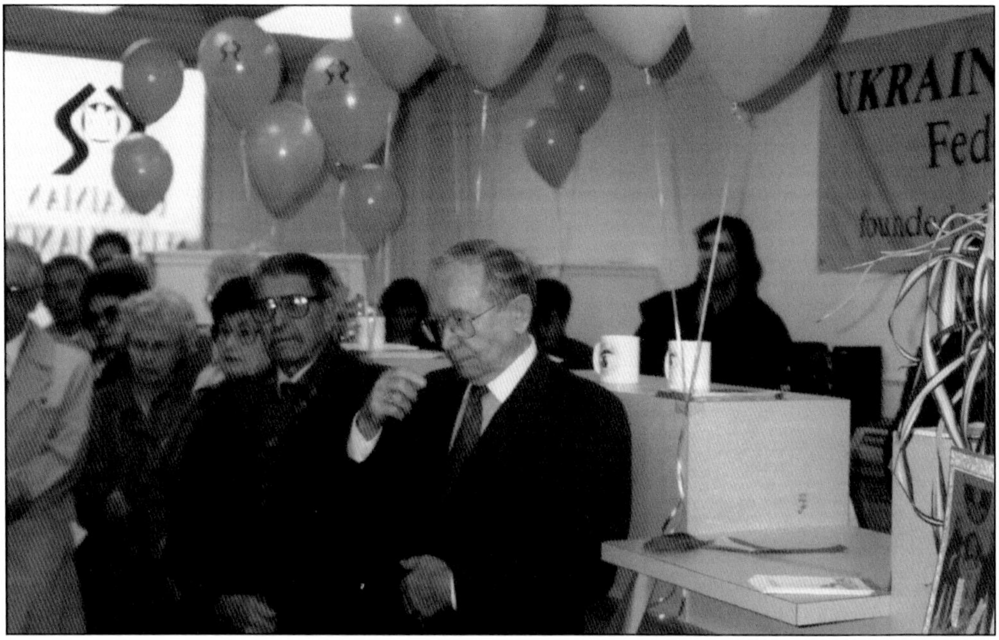

Ukrainian Selfreliance Federal Credit Union helps the community not only by lending money for mortgages but also contributes toward charitable needs. At the opening ceremonies of the new branch in Huntington Valley, Pennsylvania, in 1998, the pioneers of this organization are in the front; in the middle is Ivan Skalchuk, and to his left is Ilarij Mazepa.

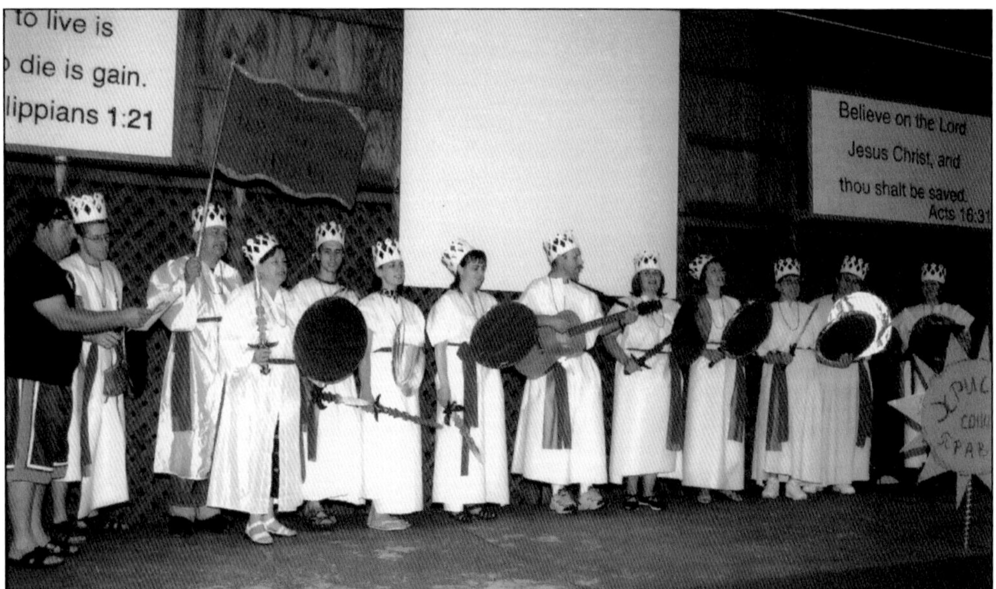

Historical Preservation Youth Chapter of Ukrainian Missionary Baptist Society, at the newly acquired campsite in Lancaster, Pennsylvania, presented a play based on Ukrainian history. The campsite is used for promulgating their mission by conducting cultural and recreational activities. The theme of this 2007 performance was the permanence of Ukrainian traditions through the ages. The flag signifies love.

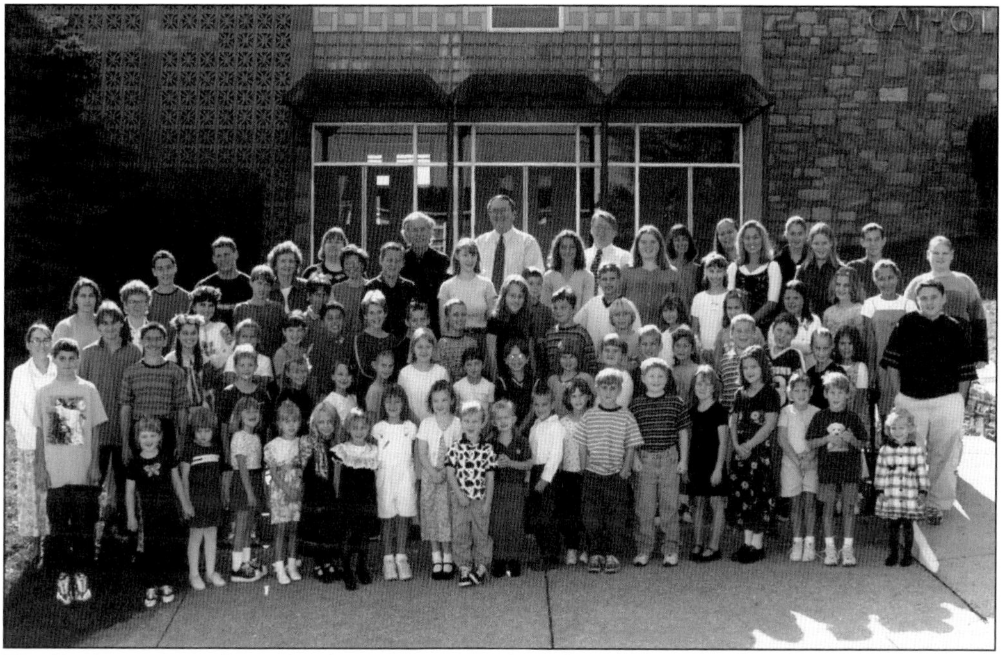

The Bridgeport Sunday School at SS. Peter and Paul UCC taught youth Ukrainian Rite and culture. Simultaneously the adults participated in a series of religious encounters with their pastor. Standing in the last row in the middle are, from left to right, Rev. Ronald Popivchak, pastor, and principal George Maxin, with the 1999 staff.

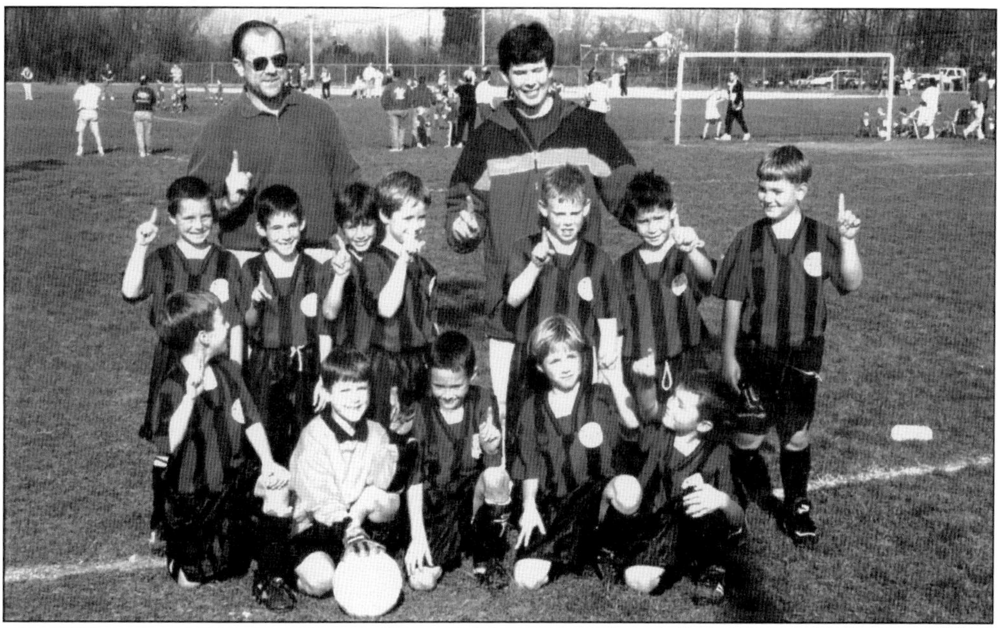

Non-Ukrainian professional teams also use the facilities at Tryzubiwka. United Junior Soccer League champions of 1997 are seen here on their home turf in Tryzubiwka. They competed with 40 teams for the title. The Under Eight Division of the Ukrainian American Nationals is shown with Orest Lesiuk, head coach, on the left in the back and his assistant Matthew Williams on the right.

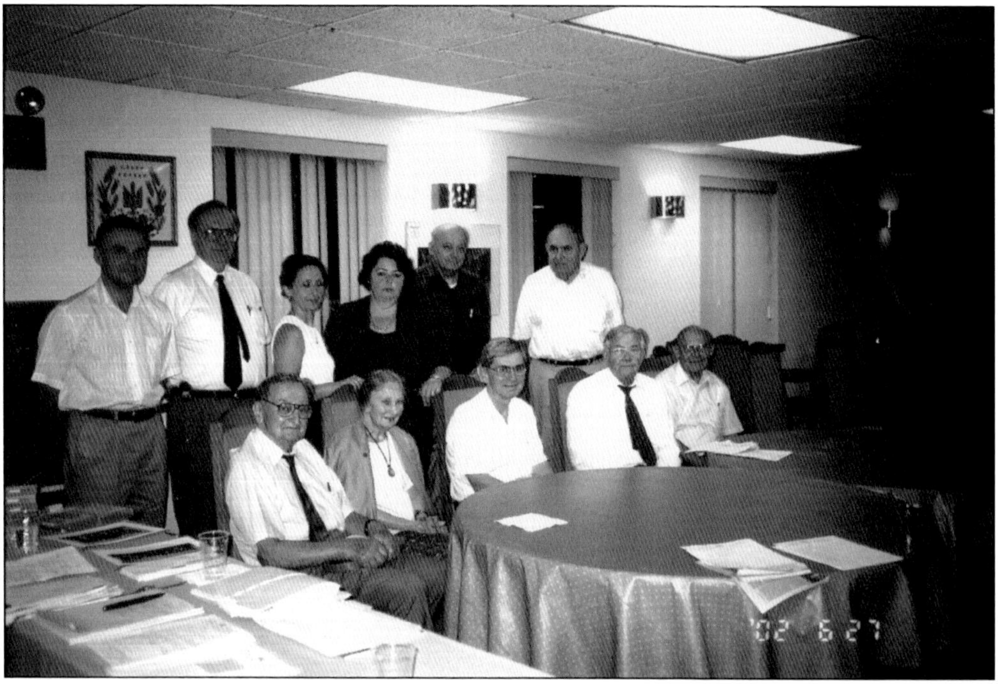

Ukrainian American physicians practicing in the Delaware Valley belong to the American Ukrainian Medical Society of North America. Their regional headquarters has been at the Ukrainian Educational and Cultural Center in Jenkintown since 1980. The photograph is from the annual meeting in 2002. From left to right are (first row) George Bereznycky, Stephania Bereznycka, Bohdan Doberczak, Wasyl Salak, and Jaroslaw Jarymowycz; (second row) ? Balycki, George Isajiw, Lesya Petrik, Oksana Baltarovitch, Orest Hawryluk, and Taras Nowosiwsky.

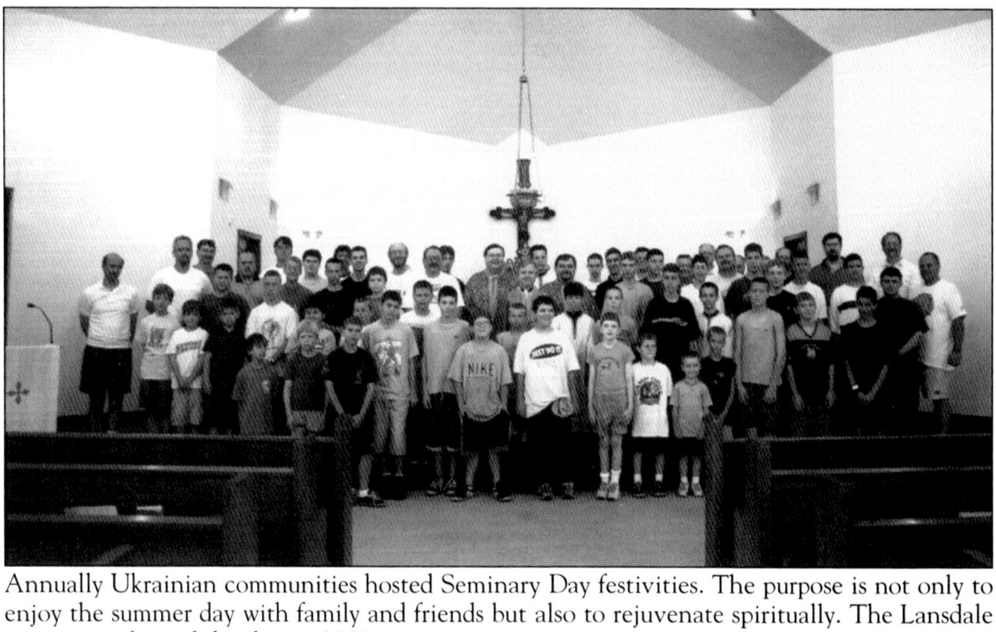

Annually Ukrainian communities hosted Seminary Day festivities. The purpose is not only to enjoy the summer day with family and friends but also to rejuvenate spiritually. The Lansdale community hosted this fete in 2000.

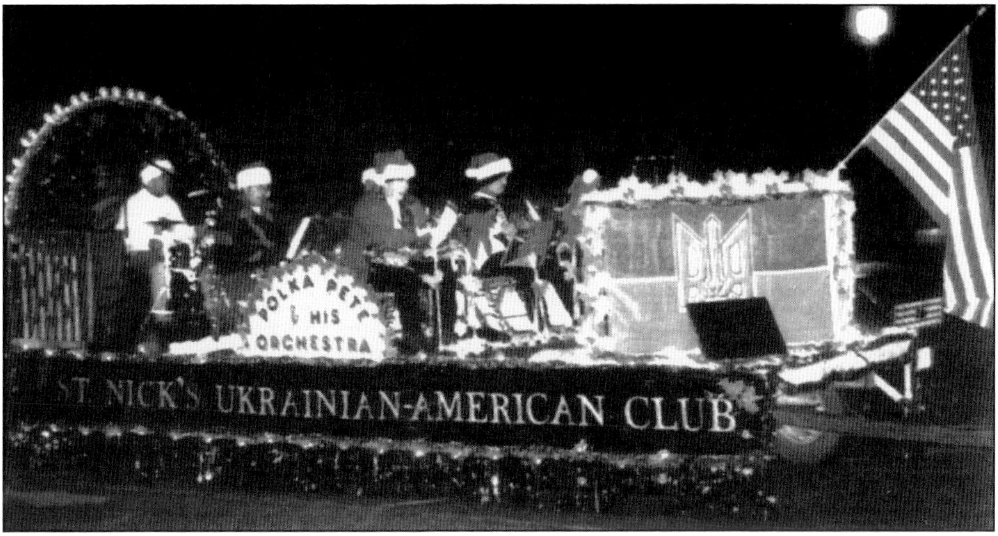

St. Nicholas Ukrainian American Club of Millville entered this float during the annual Christmas parade in 2002. The club celebrated 50 years of continuous activity and had been organized by Rev. Nicholas Staruch. The float featured live music by Polka Pete Commander and his orchestra.

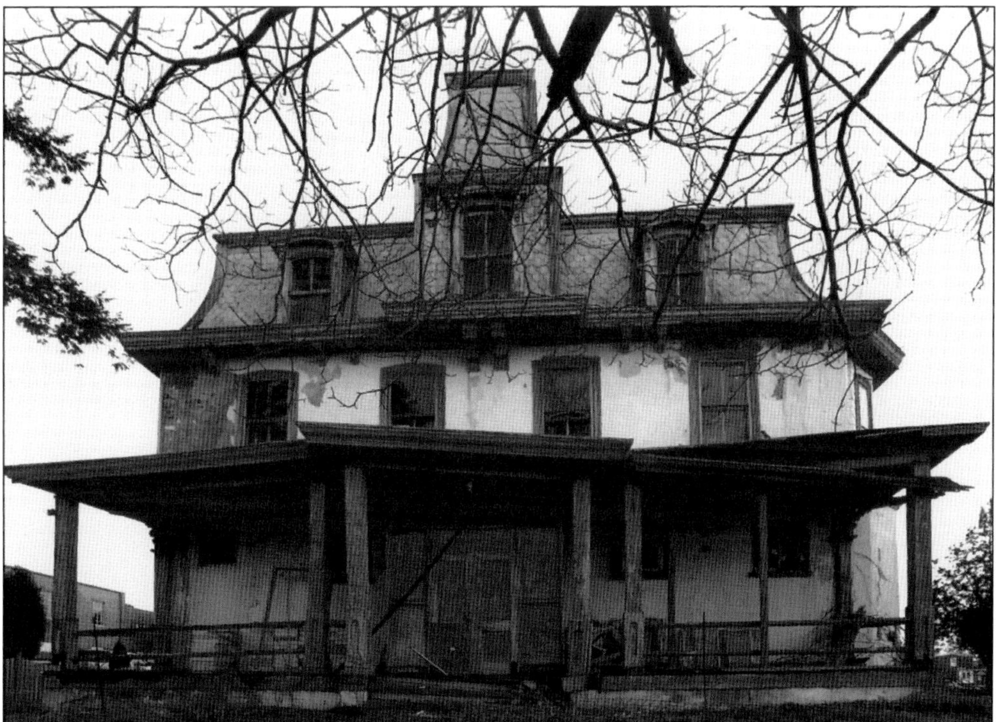

Not far from Phoenixville Bridge and Phoenix Steel, the main employer of the area, was the Ukrainian American Citizens' Club of Phoenixville. It was the centerpiece of community activity when purchased in 1945. When the industries left the area, so did the people, and the seemingly haunted house fell into disrepair and was finally sold in 2004.

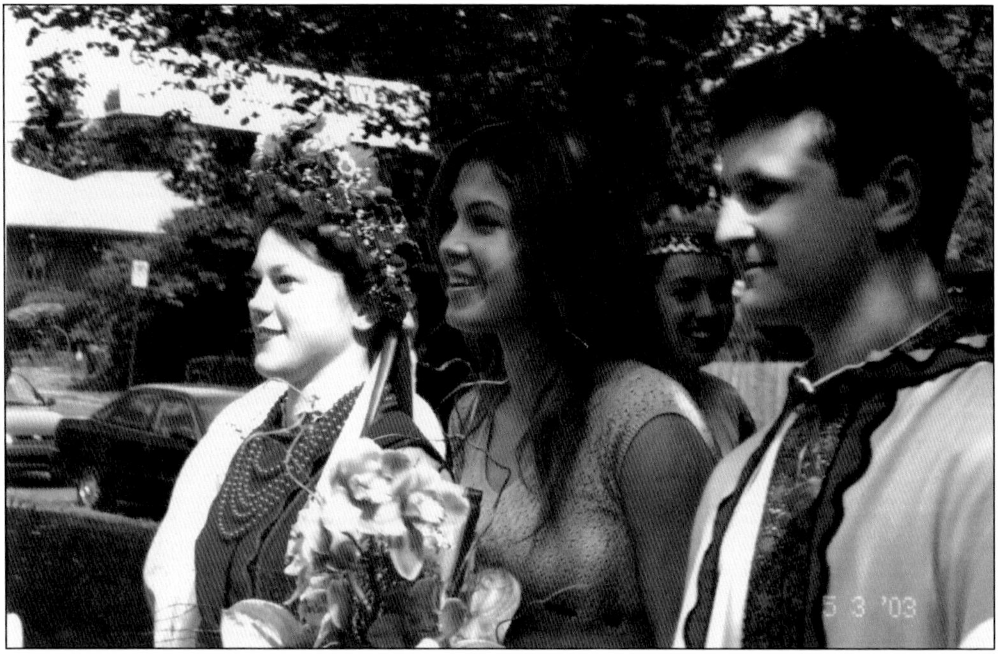

One service provided by Ukrainian Educational and Cultural Center in Jenkintown is to introduce various cultural and educational events to the community. Miss Universe 2003 Justina Pasek of Ukraine (center) was escorted by Natalia Antoniak (left) and Erik Risanow (right) when she visited Ukrainian Educational and Cultural Center.

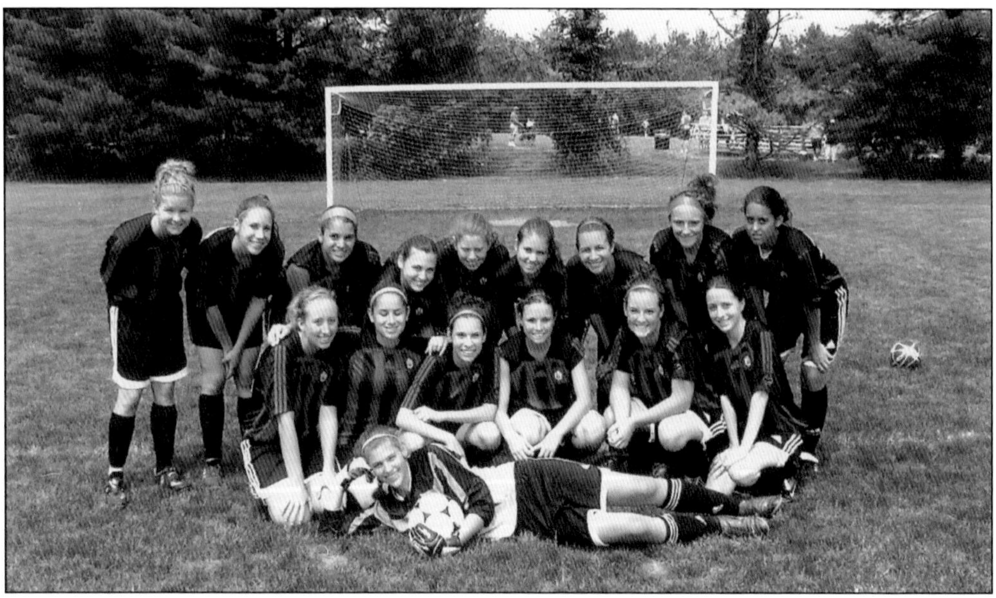

To illustrate the importance of Tryzubiwka to the American communities, 29 soccer teams train on the 40 acres of Tryzubiwka. Other sports teams also train there. Girls' soccer was organized in 1982 and is still gaining popularity. The 2005 team won the United States Swan Cup championship in Minneapolis.

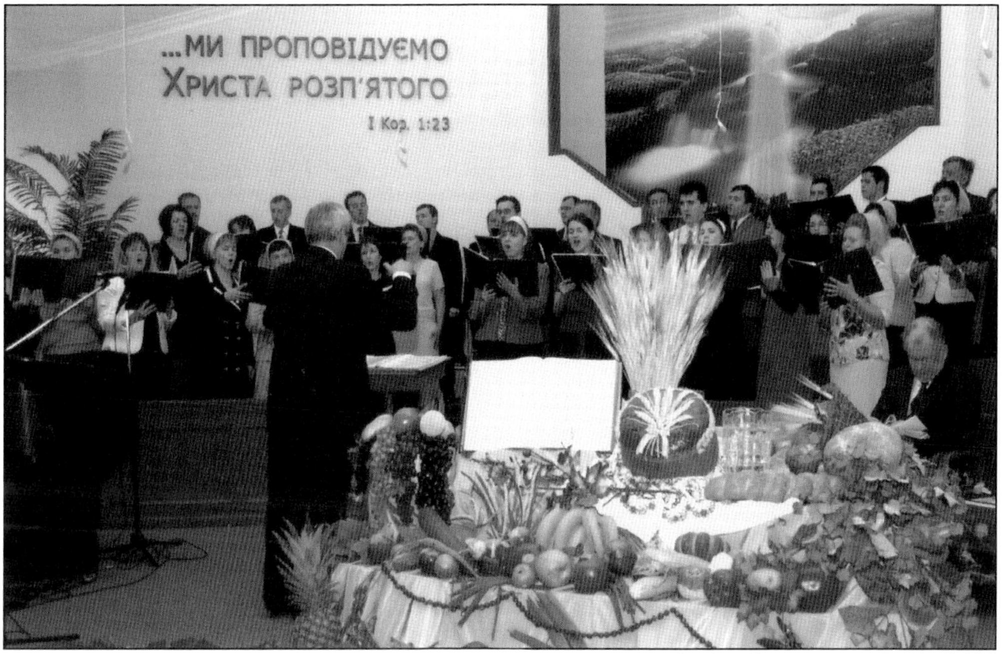

Annually Ukrainian Baptist Missionary Society of Crum Lynn celebrates the Feast of the Harvest around Thanksgiving time. The 2005 celebration was held in the House of Prayer. Through their beliefs, they have strong ties with nature.

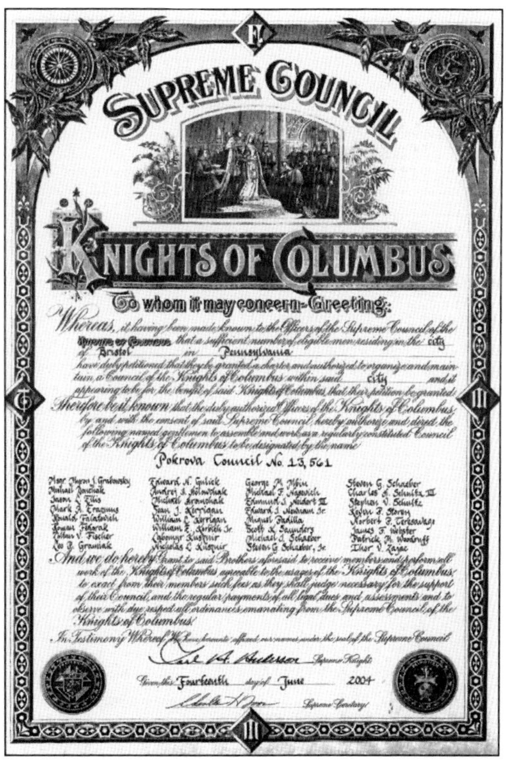

The Knights of Columbus is a fraternal beneficial society of men promoting Catholic values. Since 1924, the organization has been asked to participate in ceremonies, acting as honor guards for Ukrainian Catholic dignitaries at various functions. Pokrova UCC Council 13,561 of Bristol was founded in 2004 and is the first Ukrainian Council of the Knights of Columbus in the Delaware Valley.

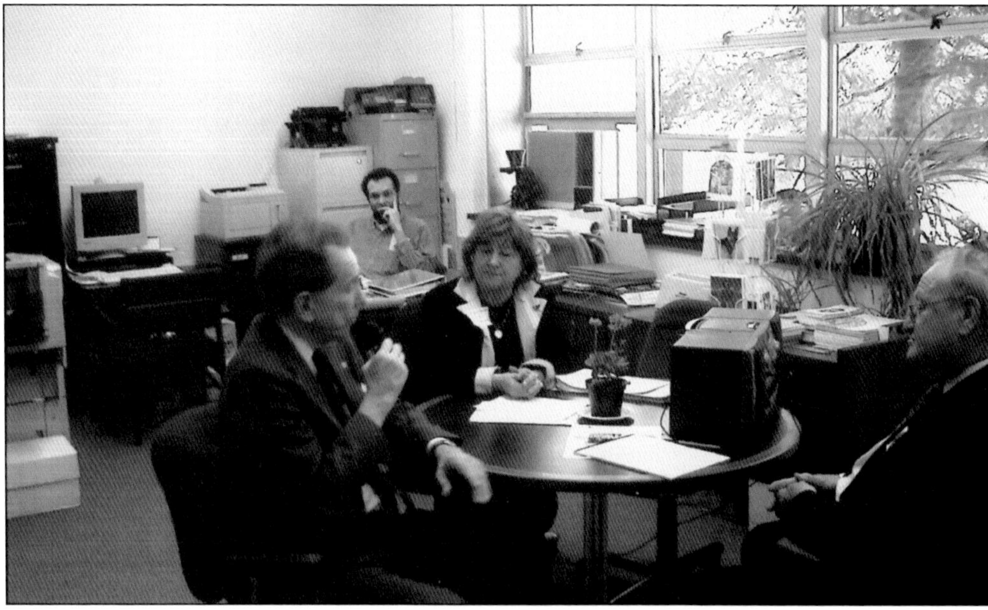

Radio played a major role for Ukrainians. In the Delaware Valley, they listened, since the 1930s, to Ukrainian radio programs beamed from Philadelphia. From time to time, some participated as guest. In 2004, Pennsylvania's Sen. Arlene Spector was a guest on the Ukrainian Education and Cultural Center's hour on station WNWR. Recording the question-and-answer session are, from left to right, Senator Spector, Orysia Hewka, and Boris Zacharczuk; in back is Boris Kortiak.

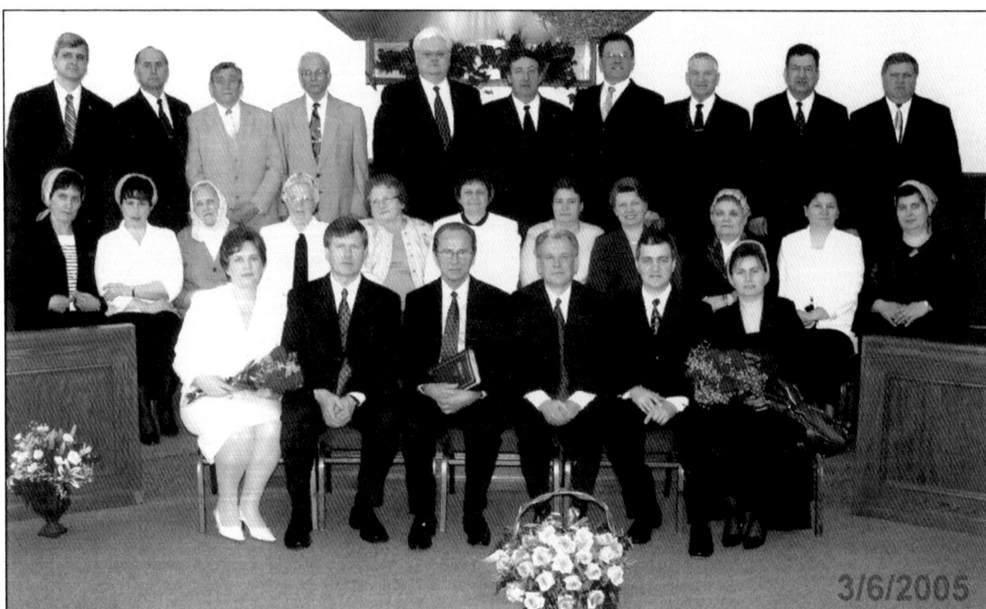

Periodically special recognition is given to pillars of the congregation at Ukrainian Mission and Bible Society (UMBS) of Crum Lynn. In 2005, they were honored along with their wives. Pastor Vasiliy Kravchuk is seated behind the basket of flowers.

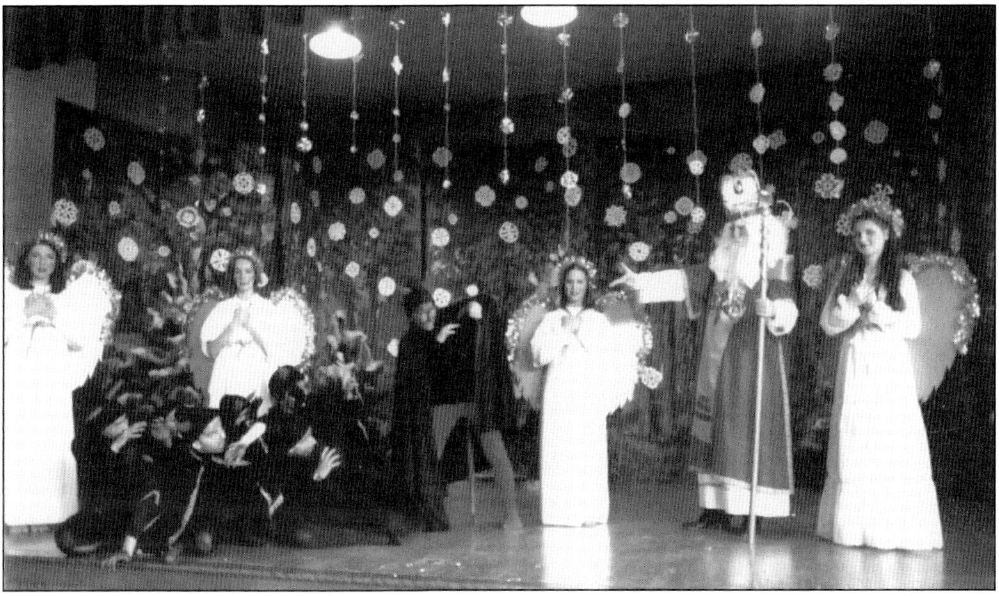

A visit from St. Nicholas brings joy to the good and trepidation to others. The traditional Ukrainian St. Nicholas event included angels and devils. In this scene, St. Nicholas is surrounded by his angels and is expelling the devils that tempt humanity to evil. The program is presented by and for St. Michael's UCC in Jenkintown. After the banishment, gifts are handed out to the deserving. This photograph is from 2000.

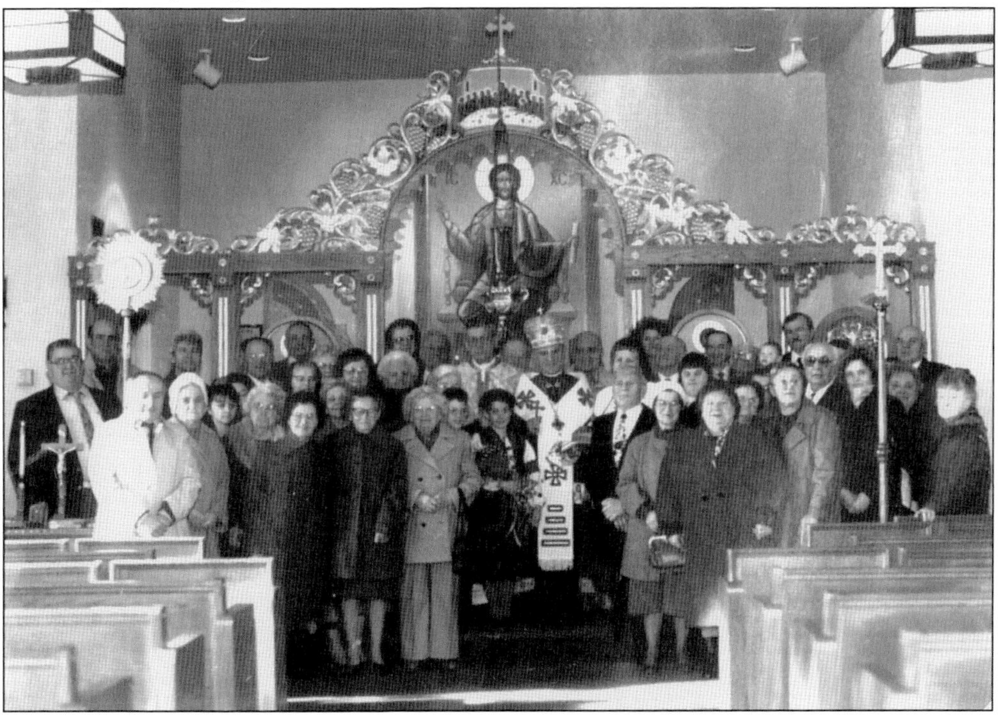

Pontifical visitations were always an important affair in the Ukrainian community. Metropolitan Stephen (Sulyk) visited SS. Peter and Paul UCC, in Williamstown, in 1995. He is surrounded by parishioners, and Rev. Joseph Martyniuk, the pastor, is on his right.

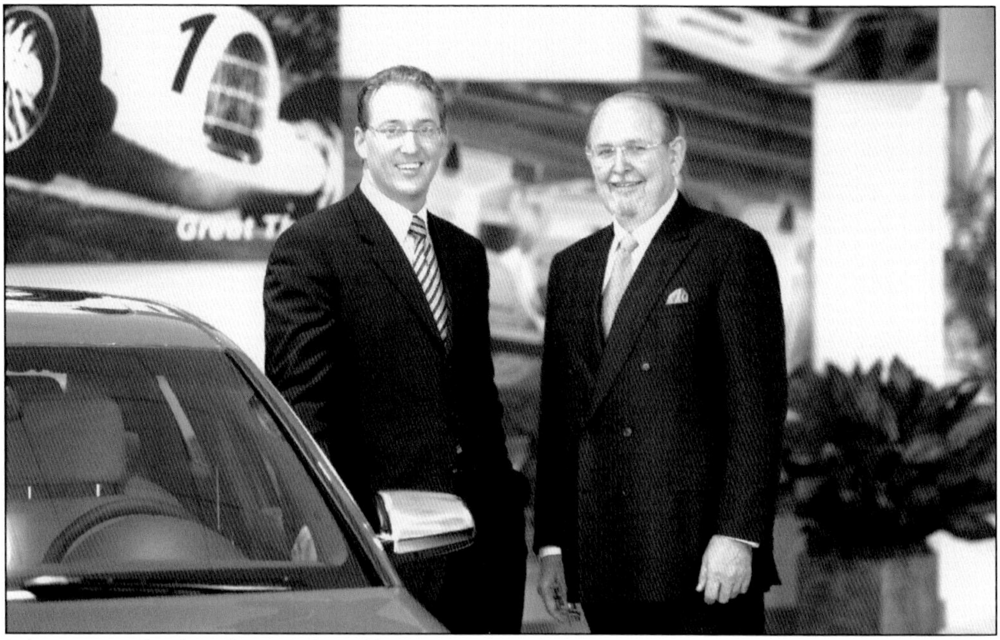

John Hynansky (on the right) and his son Michael (on the left) are in one of the showrooms of Winner in Wilmington. John Hynansky began as a used car salesman and worked his way to become the owner of Winner Automotive Group in the United States and Ukraine. The first dealership was opened in 1976. Throughout the years, he was a benefactor to the Ukrainian community in the Delaware Valley.

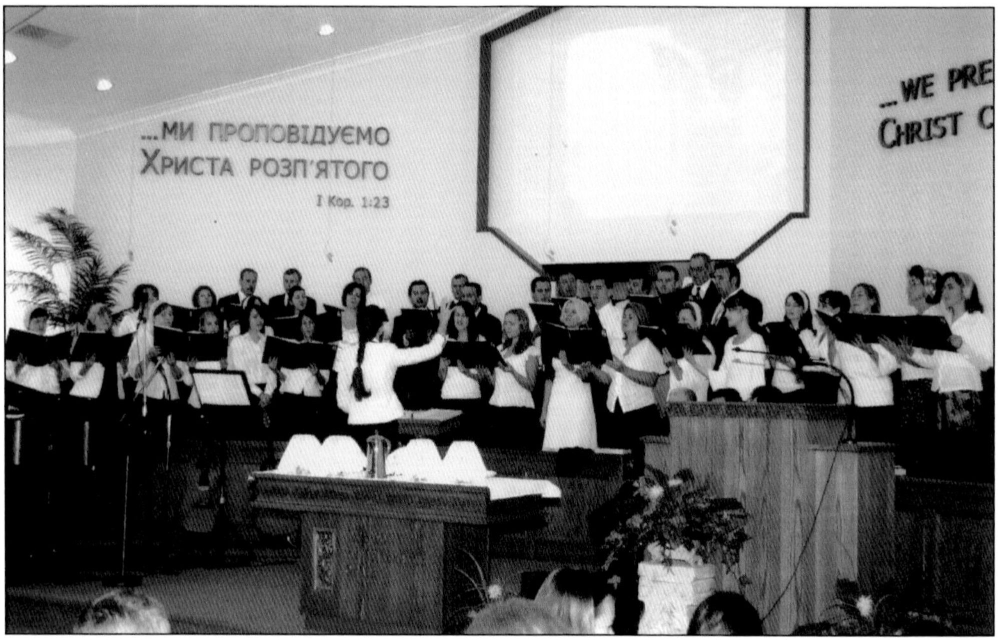

The Ukrainian Mission of Bible Studies Choir of Crum Lynn in 2007 is composed mainly of young adults who emigrated from Ukraine during the last 15 years. In their House of Prayer, as the choir sings, the large screen above them illuminates the theme of the hymn and simultaneously translates the words into English.

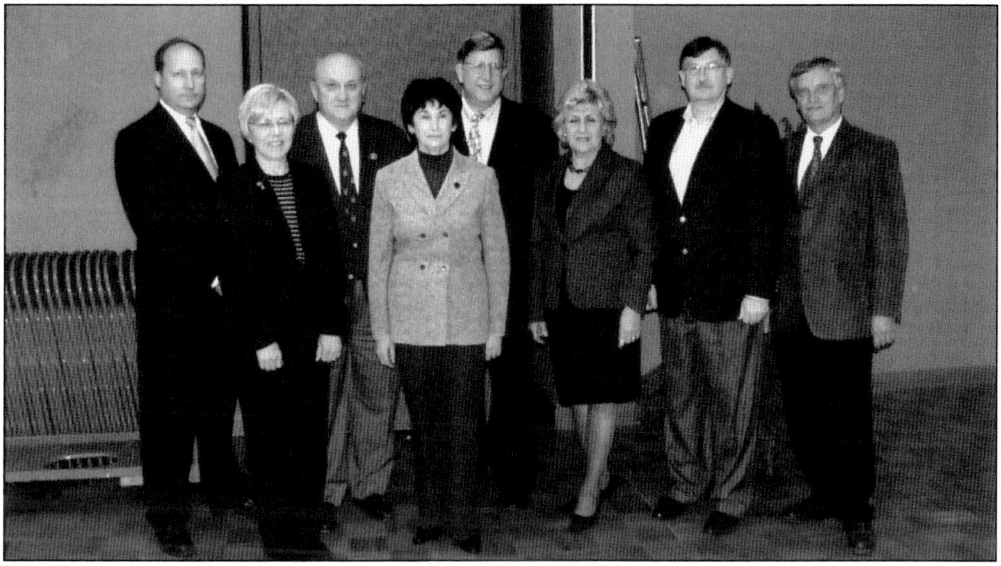

Ukrainian Federation of America, organized in 1991 and headquartered in Elkins Park, Pennsylvania, is a humanitarian organization. The board of directors and staff were presenting their 2007 Appreciation Awards to two former congressmen, founders, and chair of the Congressional Ukrainian Caucus. From left to right are Andrij Horbowy, Daria Lissy, Charles Dougherty, Zenia Chernyk, John Fox, Vera Andryczyk, Walter Marushchak, and Roman Cyhan.

For Ukrainians, January 22 was the most memorable date. On that date in 1918, Eastern Ukraine became free. A year later on the same date Western Ukraine united with Eastern Ukraine. Ukrainians and Americans annually commemorated this short-lived independence. In Chester, Ukrainian schoolchildren observe this Independence Day with a performance in 1939 at the old Holy Ghost UCC hall.

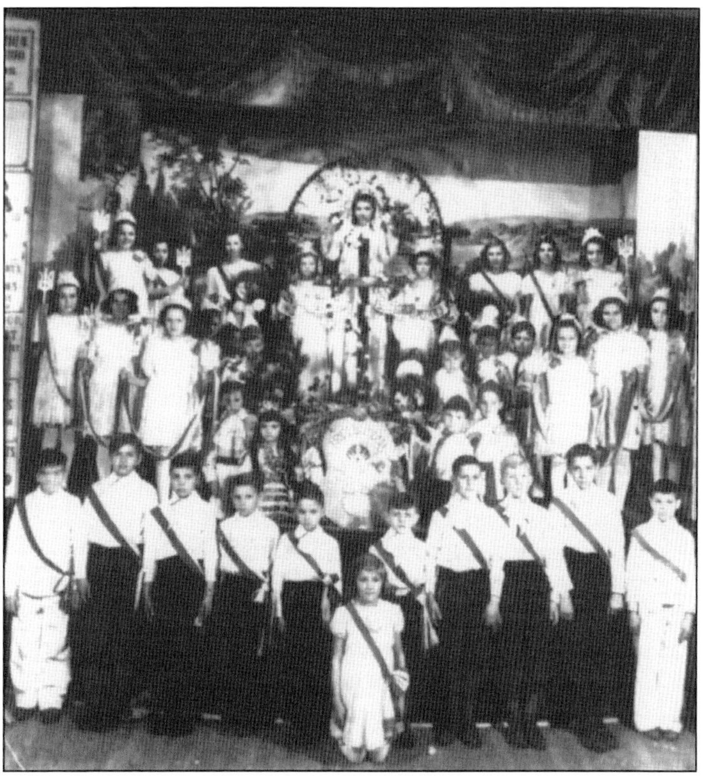

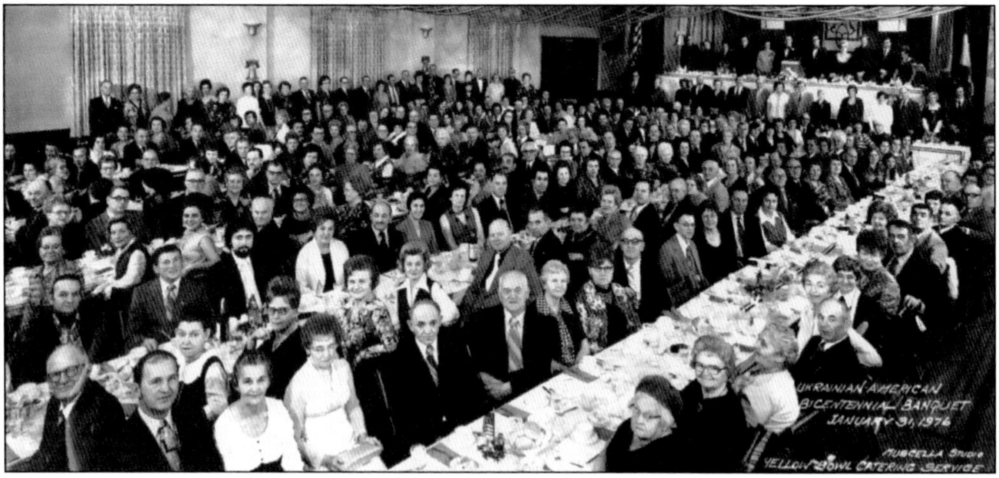

Throughout their 110-year history in the Delaware Valley, Ukrainians did not forget the open arms with which this great country welcomed them. Every time the Americans celebrated a special event Ukrainians gave them their full support, thanking them for the great freedoms that the United States gave them. The American bicentennial was celebrated in Chester at Ukrainian Catholic American Club (UCAC). It was one of the largest gala affairs with full support of all Ukrainian organizations.

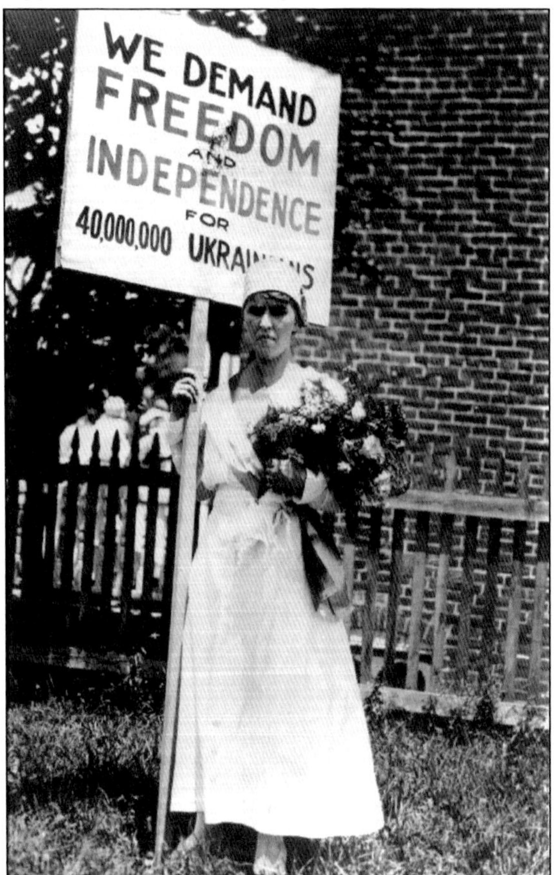

Throughout their 110-year history in the Delaware Valley, Ukrainians never forgot their enslaved homeland. They protested and initiated parades, rallies, and boycotts. They published pamphlets and books informing of conditions in Ukraine and seeking help from the United States. Tatianna Kressa from Wilmington, seen here at one such rally in 1924, is demanding freedom for Ukraine.

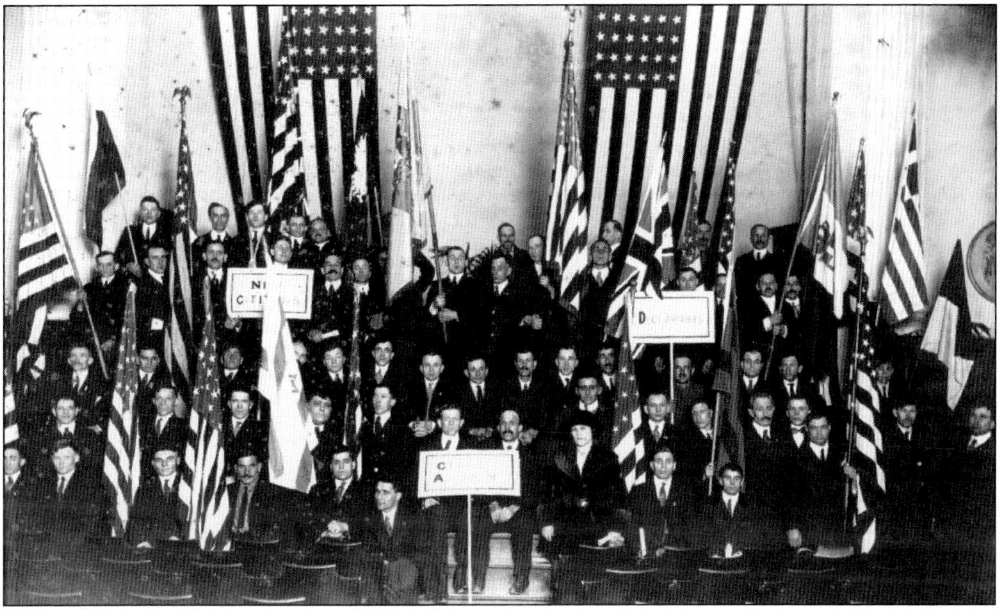

Throughout their 100-plus-year stay in the Delaware Valley, Ukrainians yearned for freedom in Ukraine. The freedom of choice they found in the United States was indispensable for their countrymen back home. Those who remained took English-language classes to become citizens as soon as possible. They were aware that as citizens they could help their country more. Around 1916, one such multinational group, including Ukrainians, was photographed in Wilmington after taking the oath of allegiance, thereby becoming naturalized citizens.

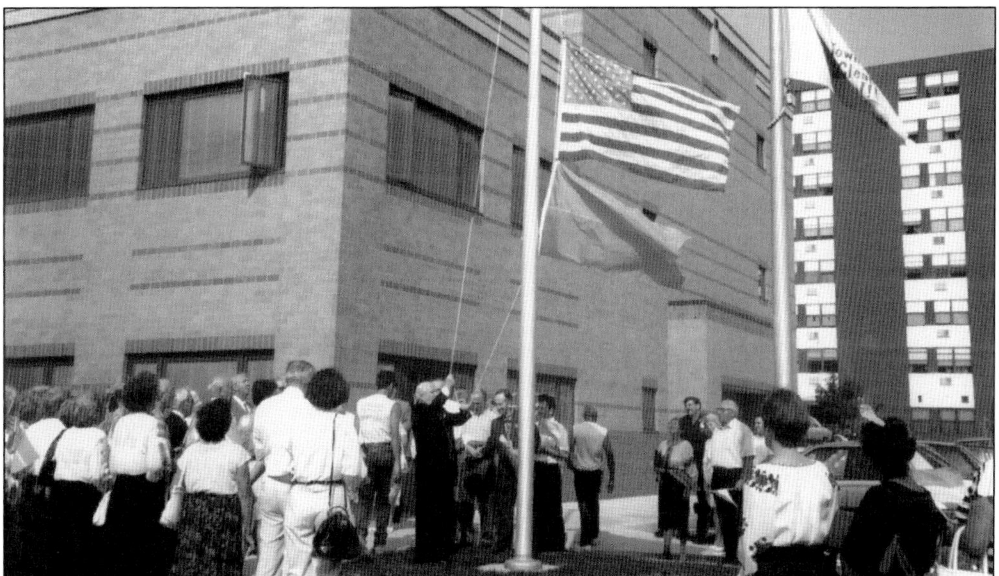

Throughout the history of Ukrainians in the Delaware Valley, Americans have always supported them in their struggle for freedom and human rights for Ukraine. The local governments, either by declaration, flag raising, or both, support these Ukrainian goals. Mayor Carmen Dinovi of Williamstown in 1999 is raising the American and Ukrainian flags at city hall to commemorate Ukrainian 1991 independence. Facing him is the initiator of these events, Alexander Kobasa.

Consistent with our mission to preserve history on a local level, this book was printed in South Carolina on American-made paper and manufactured entirely in the United States. Products carrying the accredited Forest Stewardship Council (FSC) label are printed on 100 percent FSC-certified paper.